# WORKING
## for Yourself

# WORKING
## for Yourself

## An entrepreneur's guide to the basics

**26th edition**

**Jonathan Reuvid**

**KoganPage**

LONDON   PHILADELPHIA   NEW DELHI

**Publisher's note**

Every possible effort has been made to ensure that the information contained in this book is accurate at the time of going to press, and the publishers and authors cannot accept responsibility for any errors or omissions, however caused. No responsibility for loss or damage occasioned to any person acting, or refraining from action, as a result of the material in this publication can be accepted by the editor, the publisher or any of the authors.

First published in 1975
Twenty-sixth edition 2009
Reprinted 2010

| 120 Pentonville Road | 525 South 4th Street, #241 | 4737/23 Ansari Road |
| London N1 9JN | Philadelphia PA 19147 | Daryaganj |
| United Kingdom | USA | New Delhi 110002 |
| www.koganpage.com | | India |

© Kogan Page Limited and individual contributors, 1995, 1997, 1998, 1999, 2000, 2002, 2003, 2004, 2006, 2007

© Kogan Page Limited, Jonathan Reuvid and individual contributors 2008, 2009

ISBN   978 0 7494 5590 3

**British Library Cataloguing in Publication Data**

A CIP record for this book is available from the British Library.

**Library of Congress Cataloging-in-Publication Data**

Reuvid, Jonathan.
    Working for yourself : an entrepreneur's guide to the basics / Jonathan Reuvid. -- 26th ed.
        p. cm.
    Includes index.
    ISBN 978-0-7494-5590-3
    1. Self-employed--Great Britain. 2. Entrepreneurship--Great Britain. 3. New business enterprises--Great Britain. I. Title.
    HD8037.G7R48 2009
    658'.041--dc22
                            2009009596

Typeset by Jean Cussons Typesetting, Diss, Norfolk
Printed and bound in India by Replika Press Pvt Ltd

# Contents

**Part Four: Necessary Administration**

**Appendices**

# Acknowledgements

We are grateful to the experts who have provided information for past editions of this book that has been retained and updated for the present edition. Thanks in particular to Nathan Donaldson of KSB Law who wrote Chapter 16, 'Employing People' for the 23rd edition (now abridged), and to Paul Waite of Aspen Waite who updated the information on revised tax rates, thresholds and allowances introduced or updated for the 2008 Budget.

Finally, our appreciation to Barclays Bank for permitting us the use of their survey data and some information from their *Efficient Business Guides*.

We continue to be grateful for readers' comments and suggestions. There are as many ways of running a small business and working for yourself as there are proprietors, and any advice on methods other than those we have indicated will be considered for inclusion in future editions of the book.

Comments or suggestions should be sent c/o the publishers.

# Do you need free legal advice on starting up or running a small business?

The Law Society

Legal pitfalls have been the downfall of many promising businesses. Through the *Lawyers For Your Business* scheme The Law Society offers you:

- access to business-related legal advice
- a free half-hour initial consultation with a solicitor in your area

Call a *Lawyers For Your Business* member for advice on a range of legal issues, including:

- Finance
- Taxes
- Insurance
- Cash flow
- Company structure

- Franchising
- Employment
- Business premises
- Contracts
- Health & safety

For a list of solicitors in your area who are members of *Lawyers For Your Business*

call: 020 7405 9075
e-mail: lfyb@lawsociety.org.uk
www.lawsociety.org.uk/lfyb

The Law Society

# Lawyers For Your Business

Setting up in business should be an exciting process, but without the right advice it can also be a minefield, particularly where legal issues are concerned.

Often businesses do not consult with a solicitor for fear of large legal bills, by which time any remedy still available is likely to be expensive. Early consultation is advisable if there is legislation to be complied with or important legal documents, such as contracts, to be signed.

Lawyers For Your Business is a network of 1,000 solicitor firms in England and Wales offering specialist advice to small and medium-sized businesses.*

To help firms access business-related legal advice, Lawyers For Your Business offers a free half-hour initial consultation with a solicitor in your area who is a member of the scheme. Advice could be sought on a range of legal issues including finance, taxes, employment law, contracts, company structure and health & safety.

The initial Lawyers For Your Business consultation is free, however, it is important that you clarify estimated costs at the outset before you decide to proceed. You should ask for a forecast of how costs will change in various eventualities, for example, if a matter goes to court.

For a list of solicitors in your area who are members of Lawyers For Your Business.

**call: 020 7405 9075**
**e-mail: lfyb@lawsociety.org.uk**
**www.lawsociety.org.uk/lfyb**

*Lawyers For Your Business members pay the Law Society an annual fee of £95.00

# Introduction

## THE FACTS OF LIFE

The vast changes in the labour market that have taken place over the last 34 years since the first edition of *'Working for Yourself'* was published have swelled the ranks of those who work for themselves. In recent years, the number of newcomers to self-employment either as sole traders, in partnerships or through limited liability companies which they have formed employing themselves, and perhaps others, has been consistently at the level of 400,000 annually.

Even before the present recession there were no signs that preferences for self-employment would slacken. Indeed, there are at least six permanent changes in the UK work environment that make it highly likely that the numbers of men and women who opt to work for themselves will rise:

■ Job security is a thing of the past. Everyone who is in employment and is nearing the age of 35 is advised to develop a 'Plan B' for self-employment to be revisited regularly.

■ Employers hesitate to take on new employees when reliable outsourcing alternatives are available. Our compensation culture means that making mistakes in recruitment that lead to dismissal are more expensive.

■ Working from home has become respectable; it no longer carries the suspicion of being out of work or unemployable. (The IT revolution has helped to make home-working a normal work alternative).

❚ Changes in the pension rights of long-serving employees, as companies have switched from final salary to money purchase schemes, mean that less favourable pension terms are offered for the remaining period of an individual's employment.

❚ More women seek to fulfil family commitments and work independently, often after having children, rather than returning to their previous job or taking on part-time work.

❚ Of the new jobs that have been created in the last few years, primarily in the services sectors, statistics show that the majority are being taken up by recent immigrants from the EU member countries that joined in May 2004 and more recently.

For those leaving university or school the job prospects in 2009, and probably 2010, are particularly bleak. However well-qualified you expect to be, you may have to consider self-employment as the only way to earn a living. It may be a good idea to take vacation jobs, however ill-paid, with someone you know who has started up their own business in a field that interests you and is happy to take on temporary help. Such work experience, albeit limited, will give you a taste of what it is like to operate in a small business environment. Equally, if you were planning a gap year without work experience in exotic climes you might choose to think again, unless you intend to explore emigration possibilities.

## YOUR PLACE IN THE UK ECONOMY

It is not widely appreciated that 95 per cent of the nearly 4.3 million small businesses registered in the United Kingdom are either sole traders, partnerships, single-director companies or self-employed owner-managers employing fewer than five people. These statistics do not include those in employment who also run a small business in their spare time, perhaps as a first step in taking the plunge of leaving their jobs It may encourage you that if you do decide to work for yourself, for whatever reason, you will be in good company.

## Successes and failures

Whether you succeed or not in whatever line of business you select will largely depend on your own efforts and skills. However, it is useful to know what is the success and failure experience across the board. In general, those that do best are either service businesses with low overheads, those that have spotted a genuine gap in the marketplace (but have the imagination and flexibility to exploit other opportunities when they sense that their original business sub-sector is going off the boil) or those that manage to plug into a sustainable, recession-proof niche.

However, such business sectors are highly diverse and not all will flourish equally or consistently. Even before the downturn which began in 2008, the published statistics suggested that one in three business start-ups fail within the first three years. The types of service business with low overheads (at least while they remain small) include:

■ skilled crafts and trades including those related to the construction industry (especially those that require multi-skills);
■ catering;
■ home maintenance, repairs and cleaning;
■ tourism and travel;
■ sales and distribution;
■ IT services;
■ franchises;
■ specialist consultancy;
■ the professions.

Not surprisingly, the sectors where business start-ups have declined include the retail and wholesale trades, agriculture and manufacturing. A sub-sector where existing businesses became vulnerable in 2007 is that of the small retail post office, particularly in rural areas, where the government announced closures the previous December. The new sub-sector of Home Improvement Pack (HIP) assessment, which seemed an attractive business opportunity for the self-employed before legislation came into effect, is no longer promising since the residential property market went into free fall.

# GETTING THE MOST OUT OF THIS BOOK

## Part One – Making Your Decision

Part One of the book advises on the decision-making process that you should put yourself through before committing to working for yourself full time, and then focuses on the numerous start-up issues and how to address them. These include how you should structure your business at the outset to give yourself the best chance of success.

The key considerations are listed below:

■ Have you got what it takes?
  – understand your strengths and weaknesses;
  – examine your motives;
  – consider the advantages and disadvantages;
  – be realistic about the risks you are taking;
  – are you committed totally to the project?
■ Do your homework
  – research your market;
  – talk with others who have chosen to work for themselves.
■ Business planning
  – take objective opinions on your plan;
  – make sure your family and friends are behind you.
■ Structuring your business
  – take advice;
  – self-employed sole trader, business partnership or limited company?
■ Funding your business
  – savings, investment from family or friends, or bank finance.
■ Choosing your advisers
  – not just accountants and lawyers but people like yourself who have started up on their own.
■ Making your case for raising capital.
■ Take a last look at the employment alternatives before starting a business.

## Part Two – Preparation

So, you've survived the self-examination process, convinced your family and friends that you haven't taken leave of your senses, taken advice and have the funding in place to start your business. You are now into the practical preparation phase.

You are eager to get started, but there are some things that you should attend to first before you become immersed in marketing and sales and servicing your first customers. Part Two deals with the organization issues that are better addressed upfront to ensure that you appear businesslike and that your business functions smoothly from day one.

- Making the most of your bank accounts.
- Budgeting and cash-flow forecasts.
- Legal basics.
- Choosing premises.
- Simple accounting systems.
- Invoicing and credit control.
- Costing, pricing and estimating.

## Part Three – Building Your Business

Now you are ready to start trading and to concentrate on selling your services, gaining and servicing customers. Part Three discusses the building bricks for developing and maintaining your business.

- Effective marketing.
- Using IT to build and run your office.
- Is foreign trade fun?
- Planning for growth.

## Part Four – Necessary Administration

Your satisfaction will increase as your business grows, but growth brings new pressures as well as opportunities and administration will demand more of your time. These are the range of issues on which Part Four aims to provide advice:

- VAT.
- Employing people.
- Other taxation.
- Pensions and health insurance.

No guide of this kind can hope to be comprehensive but I hope that we have covered the range of topics that are essential to working for yourself in sufficient detail to be useful without being confusing. Parts One to Three include boxed notes in each chapter to help you pick out information on particular points that you wish to study. Part Four chapters are more complex, involving detailed legal obligations and you will need to absorb their complete content rather than focus on a few points.

*Working for Yourself* is written for two kinds of reader: those who turn to self-employment after some period of working as an employee for an organization or other people; and those leaving school or completing advanced education who are drawn to working for themselves immediately. For the latter, the book aims to provide an essential grounding.

I hope that '*Working for Yourself*' works for you.

*Author's note:*

The text was correct at the time of going to press. It incorporates the 2008 Budget and requirements for self-employed tax returns to HM Revenue & Customs for the 2008/09 tax years, but readers should note the Government's tendency to bring in further fiscal measures between Finance Acts.

For the latest information on tax matters, visit: www.hmrc.gov.uk

# Part One

# Making Your Decision

# 1

# Have You Got What It Takes?

Working for yourself is personally demanding in ways quite different from those of employment – however great the employment pressures. Nor is there any certainty as to how successful you will be or what level of regular net income you will be able to generate. Therefore, you need to be sure before you commit yourself that you have the temperament and outlook on life that suit going it alone.

> Be sure that you have the temperament and outlook on life that suit going it alone.

Self-analysis is not easy and you may need 'a little help from your friends' – those who are close to you, or business colleagues if you are in employment – to assess your strengths and weaknesses. The questions that you need to ask yourself vary depending on your personal circumstances and we'll look at some of those later in this chapter. First, however, are the key considerations for everyone who considers working independently.

# KEY CONSIDERATIONS

- motivation;
- persistence (sticking with the job);
- resilience (coping with the unexpected);
- being competitive;
- human relations skills;
- being decisive;
- sound business judgement;
- lifestyle implications;
- knowing when to ask for advice or help.

Over the years there have been surveys of one-person businesses by Barclays Bank and others, asking respondents to rate the personal strengths that they consider most important in starting up and running a successful business. Invariably, the factors listed above are mentioned among the top ten, although not always in the same order. The first five factors always score a better than 80 per cent rating. It is worth looking at each in turn.

> The first five factors always score a better than 80 per cent rating.

## Motivation

There are positive and negative motivations to working for yourself. Most of the negative motivations relate to personal circumstances and are discussed in the sections that follow.

Positive motivations include:

- the urge to achieve success by building a business;
- preference for being self-sufficient;
- ambition to generate a good income;
- self-respect from independence.

If you are driven by these four motives you are a potential entrepreneur and you are probably an optimist in outlook.

There are several negative motivations that do not relate to any particular personal circumstances, and if these are your main drivers, you should probably think again: a belief that being your own boss means that you can work when and how you like or that it is a route for getting rich quick or that you do not have to pay attention to other people's problems or agendas. All of these motivations are misconceived and do not reflect the real world.

1. Your time will not be your own. You can order your priorities, but if you are serious about your business, the hours that you work will be determined by the demands of your customers or clients – and that means evenings, weekends and even planned holiday periods.
2. You may not be able to do the job as you would wish. The customers' wishes come first even if you don't like what they choose. Your only other option may be not to take the work.
3. Getting rich quick is an illusion. Your business is most unlikely to achieve instant lift-off. Prepare yourself for lean times in the early days, however hard you work.

**Self-employment is seldom, if ever, a soft option.**

> Overall, the one character strength that is essential to working for yourself is self-belief.

Overall, the one character strength that is essential to working for yourself is **self-belief**. This is very different from blind optimism. It means that you have taken into account all the difficulties, disadvantages and uncertainties that you can identify and still believe that you will succeed.

## Persistence

If your motivations are positive, persistence will come naturally to you. You will need it most in marketing and sales situations, not taking 'no' for an answer and following up on sales leads and proposals to unresponsive customers. Chapter 16 tells you much more on persistence in the sales techniques section.

## Resilience

Allied to persistence, you will need the courage and self-confidence to face setbacks and manage them swiftly, whether it's potential clients that turn you down or that 'cheque' in the post that a customer promised which doesn't arrive. More serious setbacks, such as an unexpected tax demand, are stressful and require an ability to bounce back and continue focusing on your main business activity while you sort it out. Pessimism, as opposed to realism, can be fatal in business adversity.

> Pessimism, as opposed to realism, can be fatal in business adversity.

Of course, the unexpected may take the form of opportunities and resilience is also required to address them positively, particularly if they involve major change or stretch your resources beyond present levels. Again, the realistic optimist is at an advantage.

> The realistic optimist is at an advantage.

## Being competitive

Competitive prices, products and services are essential tools for doing business, but competitiveness of outlook goes far beyond. Do not confuse a competitive attitude with aggressiveness either, although a touch of aggression is not out of place sometimes. Being competitive involves relishing the challenge of facing competitors, gaining the business from them and negotiating hard with customers and suppliers. Effective salesmen have this quality in abundance as well as self-belief. So do successful entrepreneurs. If you get up in the morning looking forward to the day's work ahead, however tough the challenge, you are probably competitive.

## Human relations skills

You will need to have communications skills: to be able to make yourself understood face to face and over the telephone whatever your business and also in writing, if you provide advisory or consultancy services. Beyond that, you will need listening skills, the ability to understand what is meant beyond the written or spoken word, to create a relationship with whoever you are talking to, and to put over your point of view. A little charm, if you have it, goes a long way too.

> You will need to have effective communications skills.

If you are awkward and uncomfortable with speaking to people and interacting with them, that is a serious handicap in working for yourself. Even if communications skills do not come naturally to you, you will have to school yourself in the basics. There will always be difficult calls that only you can make – cold calls to potential customers or late payers and calls from the bank or creditors pressing for payment. And talking of communications skills, you will need to be fluent in basic IT skills, if you engage in any kind of 'knowledge work'.

> There will always be difficult calls that only you can make.

## Being decisive

Snap decisions are often ill-advised, but dithering never inspires confidence. In particular, customers expect a prompt response on pricing and service queries even when the queries are uncomfortable for you.

At the least, answering all e-mails within 24 hours, preferably the same day, will help to maintain good business relationships.

> Dithering never inspires confidence.

It has been said that if you wait long enough problems may go away or become irrelevant. That may be true sometimes for large organizations. It is never true for young growing businesses, except in the sense that if you do nothing there may be no business left at the end of the day.

> If you do nothing there may be no business left at the end of the day.

## Sound business judgement

Good business judgement is important for sound decision-making in the conduct of day-to-day business. It is even more important in matters of strategy and tactics.

In strategy, sound judgement will help you to assess market opportunities for your products or services and where to position them in relation to identified markets (eg sectors of local or online markets). In tactics, sound judgement will guide you in selecting channels to market, how to sell your products or services effectively, how to generate customer satisfaction and loyalty and much more.

Good judgement is also needed in developing management and administration policies that will serve your business best. It will also help you to decide how to manage crises and problems as they arise and when to walk away from opportunities where the risks exceed the potential rewards.

## Lifestyle implications

Do not underestimate the fallout on your way of life of working for yourself. First and foremost, financial insecurity is a necessary consequence of working for yourself.

> Financial insecurity is a necessary consequence of working for yourself.

If you are accustomed to a regular wages packet or a salary payment to your bank account at the end of each month, you may find the absence unnerving. Your income and living standards are likely to fall, at least in the short term and maybe permanently, if your business does not take off as you had planned.

Long hours are inevitable.

Second, long hours are inevitable. Even if your business is in a trade providing services to customers at their business premises or homes and you try to maintain 'working hours', there will always be out of hours emergencies and administrative paperwork that occupies too many of your evenings.

Aside from your own ability to handle these pressures and whether or not your health can stand the demanding work regime, you have to consider how your family, if you have one, will react. Will your partner or spouse be prepared to pay the price for your independence and will he or she be willing to lend a hand? Barclays Bank in their surveys have found that although an increasing number of owner-managers try to draw the line at letting work eat into their weekends, they work on average 24 hours a week longer than the rest of the UK workforce.

Owner-managers work on average 24 hours a week longer than the rest of the UK workforce.

For those who run their business from home the separation of work from private life is surely impossible. Homilies that 'hard work is its own reward' are cold comfort for partners and family hoping for 'quality time'.

## Knowing when to ask for advice or help

Working for yourself can be a lonely business even if you are working from home. If you are used to an office where you could share problems with close colleagues and ask their advice, you will probably feel isolated for a time. There is a temptation to become introspective, taking all decisions on your own without input from others. If you starting out on your own with no business experience, you will find that a mentor with experience is invaluable.

## Be careful of becoming too blinkered

When you are uncertain in making major decisions or faced with a crisis, be humble and seek advice or help, however difficult that may be.

In financial matters you can consult your accountant, but in these days of computerized banking you will be lucky to find a bank manager who can give you objective advice beyond the head office online programmes to which he is bound. For most issues the best advice will come from others in similar lines of business to yourself, preferably more experienced and further down the road in their development. Try to build a network of such people locally with whom you can meet informally on a regular basis. You will be surprised how many of you encounter the same problems. This book seeks to cover many of the most common.

> You will be surprised how many of you encounter the same problems.

## PERSONAL CIRCUMSTANCES

### School leavers and graduates

Those who have never been in full-time employment and elect to work for themselves when they leave school or university are both advantaged and disadvantaged.

*Advantages*

- **No family baggage.** Shared ambition with your partner may be a help when starting up, but family responsibilities are a hindrance. He or she travels fastest who travels alone.
- **Low financial commitments.** You may have a student grant which has to be repaid over the next few years, but you won't have a mortgage to worry about and you may be able to continue living cheaply in your parents' home for a time.

▮ **Low short-term income expectations.** You won't have to adjust from a comfortable standard of living and tighten your belt.

▮ There are **Career Development Loans** available to those planning to acquire skills and a number of grants from funds that specialize in helping young innovatory businesses get started.

## Disadvantages

▮ **Little or no work experience.** You can mitigate your lack of knowledge to some extent by taking holiday employment while you are still a student in the kind of business that appeals to you and, if you are a university student, by taking a gap year and spending it wisely to gain work experience.

▮ **No business experience.** However many books you may read on operating a business, including this one, you can't hope to be fully prepared for the real-life experience of building your own business. Nor can those who have been employees, although they have at least worked in a business environment. If your work experience has been weak, in normal circumstances you might decide that it is wiser to take a job for a year or so while you are developing and refining your plans. In the recession climate of 2009, where most kinds of job opportunity are scarce, the government's recently announced 'intern' initiative with major companies could offer an alternative.

If you have self-belief and think that you can satisfy the criteria already discussed, the advantages probably outweigh the disadvantages.

## Those in early mid-career

If you are in a relatively safe job and moving steadily up the promotion ladder, your motives for resigning and setting up on your own may be positive or negative. Positive motives are:

▮ wanting to have a go at making more money than you earn now or are ever likely to be paid;

▮ wanting to work in another field of activity that really interests you.

Finding work from nine-to-five dull and repetitive or having no authority or status are rather negative, although they may be important drivers in your decision to quit. For most people deciding to leave employment, the motives are a combination of negative and positive.

## Those in later mid-career or nearing retirement

The positive motivations are the same, to which we can add the desire for a satisfying achievement to complete your career. There are some less positive motives that may come into play also:

■ **Job security.** If you can see that due to company restructuring or following merger or acquisition your job position is threatened, you may be prompted to plan now before the axe falls. By all means take your redundancy or early retirement benefit if you can but don't wait until the decision to work for yourself is forced upon you.

■ **Pension changes.** As mentioned in the Introduction, most companies have changed or are changing their pension schemes by cutting short plans under which you receive a proportion of your final salary, and replacing them with plans for the remainder of an employee's service where the amount of contributions is fixed but the pension receivable is uncertain (money purchase schemes). Almost certainly your pension will be less than it would have been.

If you calculate that the pension you will receive by hanging on is insufficient for you to live as you had expected, the closing of the old fixed-benefit scheme is good timing to make a break for it.

■ **Reduced financial commitments.** If you've paid off the mortgage and your children no longer need support, the financial risk of working for yourself is reduced. This may be the time to do what you have long wanted and secretly planned to do for the rest of your working life.

## Those facing unemployment

In today's harsh world, if you have been declared redundant you should face up to the strong possibility that you may not find another permanent job that will use your skills and capabilities. However reluctant you may be to become self-employed, that may be the only realistic alternative to going on the dole. There are a number of sub-alternatives within the self-employment field, many of which are discussed in Chapter 8.

Looking ahead, if your job was in manufacturing, in a production function, companies that are coming out of recession may well be restructuring their plants and need the management skills that they had discarded to carry out the task. They will be reluctant to take on new employees, but hiring self-employed experts with the necessary practical skills for a limited assignment will be more attractive than engaging expensive firms of management consultants. There may be opportunities for you in this scenario.

## Mitigating the risks

In normal economic times, it is often not necessary to jump in at the deep end and risk everything. Many businesses can be started on a part-time basis or, if they are IT-based, as online virtual businesses (see Chapter 17). Either way, you are giving yourself the opportunity to put a toe in the water and test whether your concept is likely to succeed and provide you with a satisfactory income.

> Many businesses can be started on a part-time basis.

# TAKING THE PLUNGE

If you have survived the self-analysis exercises of this chapter and are undeterred by the negative elements, you should have proved to yourself that you are a resourceful and enterprising person – an entrepreneur in the making. If you have been forced by circumstances into entering self-employment and can muster the confidence now to make the commitment to work for yourself, the rest of Part One will guide you through the planning process.

# 2

# Doing Your Homework

## BASIC MARKET RESEARCH

While you are still in the 'thinking about it' stage, you should set out to acquire as much information as you can about the kind of business that you are considering from:

- published sources (particularly the internet);
- others in the same line of business;
- agencies such as your local Business Link (Business Connect or Business Shop if you are based in Wales or Scotland);
- institutions.

> Acquire as much information as you can.

The major high street banks now publish extensive guides and pamphlets on the general issues relating to setting up your own business and they are well worth including in your reading list. Better still, they all have websites with detailed information on start-up and business bank account management. The online information provided by HSBC and Barclays is particularly helpful.

Depending on the nature of your request for help, Business Links should direct you to the appropriate body for advice on training, the availability of funding and consultancy services, premises and even business opportunities. For details of your local Business Link, ring 0845 600 9006.

## Desk research

The collation of available information and advice in written form, on the internet or by word of mouth is known as 'desk research' and is just the first step in the market research that you need to carry out. The research needed will depend on whether or not you are thinking of starting up on your own in a trade or business where you are working currently or have direct prior experience.

> Desk research is just the first step.

For example, if you are a stylist in a ladies' hairdressing salon and are thinking of opening your own salon in the same or another town, you already know a lot about hairdressing even if you don't know much about managing a business. The same would be true, in terms of product knowledge, if you are a jobbing gardener and

> Field research will help to evaluate the opportunity for your products and services.

would like to open your own garden centre. In either case, the most important research task is to evaluate what the opportunity is to sell your hairdressing services or garden products. This exercise involves local investigation known as 'field research' through which you try to develop estimates of the number of customers and the value of the business that you might reasonably expect to gain. The questions that you will need to address in both cases are much the same:

▌ What is the catchment area for my business? From how far afield can I expect to draw customers and what therefore is the total market?

- What is the value of the market? How often do customers visit the hairdresser's or a garden centre, and what is the average amount spent each time?
- How strong is the competition: how many hairdressing salons or garden centres/garden shops are there in my catchment area and how much business do they take? What are the market shares of the leading competitors?
- Are there any gaps in the services or products that competitors offer for which there is a market demand? For example, do any of the current hairdressing salons have a first-class colourist? Do any of the garden centres sell products for water features?
- How many new entrants in my kind of business have failed?
- What is the value of the business that I could take and is that enough for a profitable business?

## Carrying out field research for a local service business

There are also differences between the two examples. In the case of the hairdressing business, if you are now working for another salon in the catchment area there may be an opportunity to take customers with you who are satisfied with your personal services. (In some businesses staff are required to sign an employment contract that prevents them from approaching old customers when they leave for a period of time, but that is unlikely in hairdressing.) Since you will probably have to employ staff to work in your salon, it will be helpful that you already know the going rates for hiring staff and the tips that they are likely to earn. However, you will still have to survey what are the differences in the prices that other hairdressers charge locally as a part of your field research.

In the case of a new garden centre development, even if you are a jobbing gardener whose clients can tell you how much they spend at garden centres and on which kinds of products, you will need to carry out much more field research and desk research too. On the one hand, you will need to visit all the other garden centres that form the major competition to survey their product ranges and the brands of tools, fertilizer, garden seed, weedkiller, garden furniture and other products that they stock. On the other hand, you will want to contact suppliers to find out what prices and terms they offer and to match those against the retail prices that you have surveyed. As a part of your field research, you should also talk to the managers of existing garden centres, not necessarily in your area. You will be pleasantly surprised at how willing people are to talk about their own businesses.

## Research through experience

If you want to start a restaurant but have no previous experience, even if your partner is a superb gourmet cook, the depth of research required will be even greater. If you are an experienced business manager, you may be able to grasp the business essentials of the restaurant trade quite readily but that is not the same thing for either of you as actually having worked in a restaurant. The best way to gain first-hand practical experience may be to work in a restaurant part time for a few weeks behind the till or as an assistant manager or waiter.

# MARKET RESEARCH TECHNIQUES

If you intend your business to address more than a local market you will need to employ more sophisticated research techniques. As your business grows and you plan to extend your market or diversity, you will also need to undertake further detailed market research.

## Different types of research

As already noted, desk research normally precedes field research, and can be carried out from home by accessing published information and interrogating information sources by telephone, fax and, above all, via the internet. It will enable you to develop a profile of the market you are seeking to enter and the past history and product offerings of market leaders who serve it.

> Desk research precedes field research and can be carried out from home.

Formal field research, as its name implies, involves person-to-person research 'in the field', either by face-to-face or telephone interview or sometimes – usually less successfully – by fax or e-mail questionnaire. Field research on a regional, national or even global scale is conducted with potential customers and suppliers, or with product users in the case of research into new product design or packaging.

Of course, professional market research can be purchased from a market research agency, but this is expensive and it is unlikely that your funds will stretch to having the work done for you by experts. However, you can achieve much by carrying out the research yourself, provided that you follow the basic rules for researching objectively and thoroughly.

> Most people are happy to talk about their business.

One research avenue that you should not neglect is established competitors who are in the same line of business but operating in locations both within and outside the territory you have chosen. You will find that most people are happy to talk about how they have developed their businesses, current problems and opportunities, provided that you are not a direct competitor.

## Research objectives

The starting point is to construct your research brief, specifying the information that you need to evaluate your target market and the opportunity for you to gain entry: the same brief that you would give to a market research agency to develop its proposal.

The following are 10 key questions that you need to answer:

1. What is the value of the market you propose to enter?
2. Is the market growing or shrinking?
3. What and where is the main competition?

4. What are the market shares of your main competitors?
5. Are your competitors profitable?
6. What are consumers/customers looking for?
7. Where in the market should you position your product/service?
8. What is the profile of your average target customer and what market share could you capture?
9. How can you satisfy consumer/customer demand profitably?
10. How can you promote yourself economically to your target audience?

Depending on the nature of the business and its scope, there will be more or less information that you can gather by desk research before you begin to consider how to survey the target market yourself through field research.

## Carrying out desk research

Let us consider two completely different kinds of business, both service industries: one a specialized form of consumer retailing, the other a service to industrial and commercial clients.

_Business A_ is the operation of a local garden centre, for which you have no prior experience except as an enthusiastic amateur gardener.

_Business B_ is a consultancy to train telephone call centre customer-service staff. (Suppose that before deciding to work for yourself you were a supervisor in a call centre servicing national companies.)

For Business A, desk research will enable you to answer just a few of the 10 key questions on a national basis. You will be able to identify the overall value of consumer expenditure at garden centres and on horticultural products, and to confirm the rate of growth of the overall market. Local competition is readily identifiable, but not market share or profitability. There are a few listed companies engaged in garden centre operations that are obliged to file detailed accounts, and an inspection of these will provide some indications of how profitable these activities may be and whether their profitability is increasing or declining. However, in the context of planning a local business, desk research alone will not provide answers to the last seven questions.

For Business B, your prior work experience will help you to conduct desk research and to answer more of the 10 key questions. You should not rely on your experience alone to answer Question 6 (What are consumers/customers looking for?) or Question 7 (Where in the market should you position your product/service?), although it may provide strong pointers that you can test at the next stage.

> Do not rely on past experience alone to answer your questions.

Indeed, there are two possible markets for your proposed call centre training services: one is in staff training on a freelance basis in call centres that subcontract for clients; the other working directly with clients who prefer to set up their own telephone customer service operations in-house and need expert consultancy to train new or reallocated staff. Within the latter market, there are probably a number of niches in terms of the size of clients and the nature of their products or services. You will have to check out both markets by direct contact with each one in your field research.

The sources for desk research are wide-ranging. They include statistical reports, trade and specialist consumer journals, competitors' catalogues and, increasingly, competitors' and target customers'/clients' websites.

## Engaging in serious field research

The most important feature of useful field research is that it should be completely objective. There is a great temptation, particularly if you are enthusiastic about your business concept, to wander round putting a few questions to possible customers and suppliers, perhaps people who know you quite well, and to fool yourself that you have conducted a useful research exercise. Worse still, you may phrase your questions so that the response you are hoping for is clearly evident, and people who know you and want to encourage you are likely to give you the answers you are looking for.

> Discipline yourself to draw up a representative sample and a formal questionnaire.

The best way to avoid these traps is to discipline yourself to draw up a representative sample of the market you are researching and to prepare formal questionnaires, whether you will be interviewing face to face or by telephone. It also helps to condition yourself to conduct interviews as if you were a professional researcher carrying out the assignment for clients rather than on your own behalf.

## Sampling

A truly representative sample that accurately reflects the total market in terms of income and social groups, age groups, occupations and purchasing profiles is the ideal that researchers strive for when surveying consumer markets. But this is probably impossible to achieve. Instead, professional market research agencies often design 'quota' samples and instruct their researchers to interview fixed numbers of respondents, whose circumstances and buying habits conform to various templates. (The preliminary questions of each interview are used to establish into which quota definition the respondent falls.)

Alternatively, the research agency may decide to adopt 'random' sampling. For example, if a survey of 100 households was commissioned in a neighbourhood of 1,000 houses, interviewers would be instructed to call on every tenth house. A random sampling approach might be more appropriate for your own research in our Business B example, where you decide to interview potential clients for call centre training among a range of selected industries located within your local region. A simple way to pick your sample would be to refer to the telephone book _Yellow Pages_ or _Thomson Local_ directory and pick your interview targets according to the number of companies listed in each business category.

What size of sample should you pick? Statistically, you might think the bigger the sample the better. In practice, a sample of 100 is normally sufficient for consumer products or services if the sample is chosen carefully. For industrial products, as few as 30 interviews may suffice.

In the case of Business A, it should be possible to survey your local garden centre market and produce unambiguous findings from 100 interviews of customers leaving local garden centres, selected on a random basis. If there are two or three centres in serious competition, you should split interviewing between them.

For Business B, a quota of five or six extended telephone interviews in each of, say, six targeted industry sectors should give a clear picture of the market for your training services. If the findings are ambiguous, you may need to extend interviewing selectively.

## Questionnaire design

Most of us have been interviewed from time to time in the street, in shopping centres, or at railway or bus stations – often when we are short of time and do not want to be stopped; so we know what to expect when the lady with the clipboard approaches!

> Try to design your questionnaire in a similar way to conventional interview techniques.

Try to organize your questionnaire in a similar way to conventional interviewing techniques. Here are a few tips that may help you:

1. Use short introductory phrases for each question to 'lead in' your respondents, for example: 'I can see that you're a keen gardener; how often do you visit a garden centre?'
2. Arrange the topics for your questions in a logical order: proceed from the general to the particular. In the case of research for Business A:
   - frequency of garden centre visits;
   - weekend/weekday shopping;
   - with/without family or partner;
   - range of products purchased;

- seasonal variations in purchasing;
- opinion of this garden centre (product quality and range, price, service);
- other garden centres used;
- other sources for garden products (DIY centres, department stores, mail order and so on);
- customer spend per visit (range/average).

3. Always position questions about money towards the end of the interview (they may be 'turn-offs' and cause the respondent to terminate).

4. Try to ask questions in open-ended form first, so that they cannot be answered just 'Yes' or 'No', before offering structured alternatives, for example: 'How many other garden centres do you visit regularly?' before:
Which of these other local outlets for garden products do you visit?

|  | Regularly | Sometimes | Never |
|---|---|---|---|
| a. | | | |
| b. | | | |
| c. | | | |

5. Include a few personal questions at the end of the interview to establish the demographic identity of the respondent (eg age group, occupation, residential neighbourhood, size of garden).

## Surveys by fax or e-mail

Surveys by e-mail or by fax for business-to-business (B2B) products or surveys have become increasingly common. There is no problem in assembling a random sample of businesses in the industries and locations that are of interest to you, either through trade directories, internet searches or, more laboriously from the _Yellow Pages_ – although the latter involves multiple telephone calls to identify fax numbers and e-mail addresses.

However, there is a fundamental disadvantage to either method as an effective market research channel. The respondents who reply are a self-selected sample. You will have no idea of the opinions of those who choose not to reply, perhaps because they are too busy or bin all questionnaires on principle. And the non-respondents may be exactly those businesses to whom you would most like to market your products or services. For this reason, a selected sample of face-to-face or telephone interviews is always a more reliable barometer.

It is also easy to put up questionnaires on the internet on consumer websites if you want to research consumer reactions to your products or services; indeed some manufacturers and online retailers do that. You might persuade an online retailer to include your questionnaire if your product is one that has caught their fancy and that they would consider stocking. Nevertheless, the value of the responses that you receive is even more doubtful than the results of B2B fax or e-mail surveys – for much the same reason. The completed questionnaires will represent only a self-selected sample rather than a consumer profile.

## Other field research

Of course, you will want to carry out other fieldwork in addition to interviewing customers or prospective clients. For Business A, you will need to visit each competitor location, examine the layout, product range, quality and pricing, display, point of sale material and promotional offers, and observe store traffic. You will also need to approach potential suppliers to check the availability, lead times, prices and delivery terms that you could negotiate and the possibilities of growing your own stock from seed.

For Business B, you may want to sample the quality of the telephone customer service that potential clients offer currently in order to assess their training needs.

## Using your market research findings

The market research you carry out yourself will deepen your understanding of the business opportunity and provide much of the background data needed to support your business case. It may also throw up attractive niche market opportunities that you had not identified previously, or cause you to modify or extend your product or service offering.

Research may throw up attractive niche market opportunities or cause you to modify your product or service offering.

The Business B example differs from Business A in another important respect. Interviewing by telephone may establish your first list of actual business prospects among those who register a demand for the services that you intend to offer: in this case, call centre training. The same outcome is likely in the case of most business consultancy services that you may research. You will be able to follow up on the prospect list later when your plan is complete, funding is in place and you are ready to launch your business.

The final test of objectivity, if your market research findings are negative in any important respect, is to decide whether you should proceed with the business concept or abandon it. It is a good idea, in any case, to write up your research succinctly and to show the report to an adviser or friend who will give you an unbiased second opinion. If you are in any serious doubt, abandon the concept and go back to the drawing board. The research exercise has not been wasted. It will stand you in good stead next time.

If your research findings are negative, take an unbiased second opinion.

## QUALIFICATIONS

There are many skilled occupations where trade association training and membership or professional qualifications are essential for success as a sole trader or in establishing a business practice. For plumbers, heating engineers, electricians, carpenters, thatchers and many others, trade qualifications are really important in

Do you have the essential qualifications?

setting up their businesses. For one thing, it will be very difficult to secure third-party indemnity insurance unless you are qualified. Therefore, until you are qualified you will be well advised to continue working for your present employer and to complete your training. For training in any of the trades related to the construction industry, you should refer to the Construction Industry Training Board (tel: 01485 577577; website: www.citb.org.uk).

## Professional qualifications

The same considerations apply even more strongly to the professions, in some of which it is impossible to practise without qualification. You don't have to be a qualified solicitor to carry out conveyancing work for clients in house purchase or a qualified accountant to be a freelance bookkeeper to small companies or to complete clients' tax returns. However, if you want to represent clients in magistrates' and county courts you need to be a qualified solicitor; and if you want to audit companies' accounts you need to have an accountancy qualification. Estate agents don't need a formal qualification to open an office, but any surveys or valuations you make won't be accepted by banks, building societies, other mortgage providers or insurance companies unless you have a professional qualification, preferably from the Royal Institute of Chartered Surveyors (RICS).

## Consultancy and financial advisor qualifications

Business consultancy is a field where professional accreditation has become increasingly important. Unless you are registered as an independent financial adviser with the Financial Services Authority (FSA) you are at risk in offering financial advice and you should certainly acquire that qualification before starting to practise on your own. In the non-financial areas of management consultancy there is no legal requirement to be qualified, but you are unlikely to gain many corporate clients unless you have the appropriate specialist qualification or have, at least, become a member of the Institute of Management Consultancy (IMC) and preferably gained the qualification of Certified Management Consultant

(CMC) through examination. Incidentally you can become a CMC while still employed as a business manager through project management experience, which may qualify as internal management consultancy.

Market research and qualification are just two aspects of the preparation and planning that you will have to undertake before venturing too far in going it alone. **The first step in the process is to assess whether self-employment is right for you or, perhaps more accurately, whether you are right for self-employment.**

You are now ready to move on to the business planning process. Based on your research, you should start to consider how much capital you will need for start-up costs, including your living costs, until income starts to flow.

## Checklist: researching your market

1. Do not rely on your instinct or perception of an opportunity without carrying out the basic research to support the business case.

2. Define your research objectives first in terms of the key questions you need to answer.

3. Carry out desk research first from home by accessing published information and interrogating sources by telephone, fax and the internet.

4. Do not neglect others in the same line of business but operating in a different location. Unless you are competing directly, they will probably be informative.

5. Visit your competitors' locations and investigate product range, quality, pricing and activity levels. Approach potential suppliers.

6. Field research should be completely objective. Discipline yourself to draw up a representative sample of the market and to prepare formal questionnaires.

7. Arrange the topics for your questions in a logical order. Always ask questions about money at the end of the interview.

8. Ask questions in open-ended form first so that they cannot be answered just by 'Yes' or 'No'. Then ask them in structured form.

9. Include a few personal questions at the end to establish demographic identity.
10. If your research findings are negative, restructure the business concept and research again – or abandon it.

## Qualifications

11. Does the occupation you have in mind require qualifications to be successful?
12. If so, how will you qualify?

# 3

# Business Planning

Whatever kind of business you are planning to start, from a self-employed service provider to retailer or manufacturer, it is important that you begin by undertaking a disciplined planning exercise. You ought to do this even if you are funding the start-up from your own resources, and you will certainly have to do it if you aim to raise capital externally. The first step is to prove to yourself that your business concept is sound and financially sensible.

We have already made the point in Chapter 2 that it is unwise to rely on your instinct or perception of a business 'opportunity' without carrying out the basic research to support the case. Formal business planning forces you to do just that, applying the same logic and critical judgement that you would in any normal business situation. Below, in sequence, are the recommended steps in preparing your business planning.

## STEP 1: THE BUSINESS SECTOR AND YOUR MARKET

Taking on board your market research, describe the business sector and the market in which you intend to operate:

▌ What is the current size of the market you will be entering?
▌ Who are the major participants: your competitors, market leaders, and suppliers?

▌ What are the critical success factors in the sector?
▌ What do published forecasts say about the profile and future growth of the business sector?
▌ What fashions, legislation or environmental trends affect the sector?

> Build on your market research.

As an example, if you intend to open a private limousine service for business people and their families travelling to the local airport or for evening social engagements, you will need to evaluate the niche market for that service within your catchment area, the market shares of local taxi firms and other freelance operators. You will need to clarify the key ingredients of the service (eg reliability, timeliness, safety, comfort and so on) and the likely growth in demand. You must also take a view on what changes are likely in licensing and insurance legislation, and whether business travel by air is likely to increase or families will decide to drive themselves more or less often to social events in the evening.

## STEP 2: YOUR PRODUCT OR SERVICE

Write down a full description of the product or service you intend to provide and compare it with the products or service offerings of competitors. It may be helpful to open a file of photographs or drawings to illustrate the differences between your product and the competition. In the case of a service, it may clarify your mind and will certainly help third parties reading your plan to understand how your service is provided if you illustrate this section of your plan with diagrams:

▌ Fully describe the product or service. What need does it fulfil? What features will make it unique?

> Compare your product or service with those of your competitors.

■ Discuss the development of your product or service. Are there opportunities to expand the product line or service range? Is it patented or otherwise protected by copyright?

■ How will your product or service compare in quality, features and price with competitors' products?

■ Discuss the influence of new technology on your business and the technical risks (if any). What will be the next generation of derivative products or services?

**Do not overestimate your strengths or underestimate your weaknesses, or undervalue your competitors' abilities.** There will be no room for self-delusion in evaluating whether you can reach your sales goals in the face of competition.

## STEP 3: MARKETING AND SALES

This is the point where you have to identify how you will get your business off the ground, translating a bright idea into reality and generating the revenue that will provide you and your family with a sufficient income and support the development of the business.

How will you get your business off the ground?

■ Describe your prospective customers. Who are they and where are they located geographically? How sensitive are they to price, quality or service? Who has expressed an interest in your product or service?

■ Is your product or service a substitute for other products or services? Conversely, what existing products or services are substitutes for yours?

■ Describe your target market. Identify unusual market characteristics such as barriers to entry. Are you aiming for particular market segments or a quantifiable market share?

■ Explain how you will achieve your sales goals and what your marketing strategy will be. How will you identify potential customers? What customers will be the target in your initial marketing effort and how will you attract them away from the competition? How will you be using advertising or direct mail?

These first three steps incorporate the conclusions of the market research process we described in Chapter 1.

## STEP 4: RUNNING THE BUSINESS

It is now time to consider how you will run your business on a day-to-day basis. If you are self-employed, you will certainly be doing most of the income generating as well as the administrative work yourself. As the owner of a small business your role is also sure to be multi-functional:

▌ Define the production and delivery processes simply, without technical jargon. ('Production' includes the artwork if you are a graphic designer, or the client contact and report writing if you are a management consultant.) To what extent will you be dependent on key factors: suppliers, materials, and skilled labour? What will be your relationship with suppliers? What will be the capacity of your business? How will you increase it as the business grows?

▌ Personnel requirements. If you do not plan to be a self-employed sole trader, what are your employee needs in terms of skills and functions? What will be your employee costs, including benefits, and are there suitably qualified people available? Include a skills audit in your analysis.

▌ Premises. Will you be able to operate from home? If not, describe the premises you will need. How much will they cost to rent and maintain?

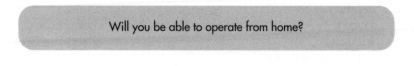

Will you be able to operate from home?

The same Barclays Bank research referred to in Chapter 1 also highlights the increasing burden of complying with regulations. On average, owner-managers are spending over 15 hours a week on administration.

# STEP 5: MANAGEMENT

The hardest part of your realistic planning process, unless you are determined to be a one-man or woman business, is to assess your own management capabilities and what additional management support you will need to be successful. Perhaps you have all the necessary creative or organization skills, but your personal sales skills are poor. The solution, as we have already suggested, may be to bring in an effective sales agent whom you can pay on commission without adding to the overhead costs of your business.

> **What additional management support will you need?**

Again, bookkeeping and accountancy may be functions that you have difficulty in performing efficiently and in a timely fashion and, in any case, feel they would be a poor use of your time. These are probably part-time tasks when you start your business and, if you are lucky, a family member can be enlisted. If not, you should plan for part-time assistance. In either case, what is important is that you should recognize your own shortcomings and plan accordingly.

As a part of your business plan be sure to include a current CV for yourself and any partner or key member of your management team.

# STEP 6: TIMING

Set down a timetable for starting your business, scheduling all key events from identifying sources of finance, setting up your place of business, and launching your product or service through to the receipt of revenue from your first month of sales. This simple exercise will give you the time frame for your financial planning. (In more complicated businesses, management consultants give this a fancy title: 'critical path analysis'.) Figure 3.1 offers a simple example. When you have done that, proceed to plan your cash flow for the first 12 month's as in Figure 3.2, being sure to include all items of revenue and expenditure in the months that they occur.

| Task | Month |
|------|-------|
| | 1 2 3 4 5 6 7 8 9 10 11 12 |
| 1. Research your business concept | x--x |
| 2. Prepare the Business Plan | x-x |
| 3. Review Business Plan with friends/family | x--x |
| 4. Secure funding | x----x |
| 5. Decide business structure and set up | x-x |
| 6. Choose & set up office (home/rented) | x-x |
| 7. Prepare and launch marketing plan | x------x |
| 8. Set up admin. and accounting | x |
| 9. Design and launch website | xx |
| 10. Prepare and print stationery | x |
| 11. Inform tax office of changed status | x |
| 12. Sales activity starts (mail/e-mail/tel.) | x--------------------x |
| 13. Negotiate/book first job (ongoing) | x-------------x |
| 14. Trading begins | x------------------x |
| 15. Review cash flow weekly | x---------------------x |
| 16. Prepare first year accounts | x |

**Figure 3.1** *Timetable for Start-up*

It is clear from Figure 3.1 that most of the actions start from the moment that funding is in place. If you can self-fund your start up or have sufficient backing from family or friends, the programme can be brought forward so that all actions from item 5 onwards in the example can be accelerated by two months or more.

# STEP 7: FINANCIAL ASPECTS

Your initial business plan for your own use will be meaningless unless you include a financial plan for the start-up and how you and your business will survive for the first 12 months. At this stage your first requirement is for a cash-flow forecast; the key elements of how to forecast your cash requirements are detailed later in Chapter 10.

Accurate cash-flow forecasting is far more important to you in starting and running your business, at least in the early years, than profit planning. The cash flow is based on when you expect to actually receive payment from your customers and when you have to pay your suppliers, and tells you what finance you need to survive. There are plenty of businesses with high profit margins that have gone bust simply because they were unable to balance revenue and expenditure timing. If you are looking to borrow working capital, the first detailed information requirement of whatever external financial source you approach will be your cash-flow forecast.

> Accurate cash-flow forecasting is far more important than project planning.

For your funding proposal to banks and other sources of funds, you will also have to produce a profit and loss account, which is easily developed from your cash-flow forecast by adjusting from cash received and paid to month of invoice for sales and dates of orders for purchases, eliminating prepayments. You should also take out VAT from your payments schedule and include depreciation as an expense item. (See Chapter 13 for an example of a profit and loss account where the elements are explained in detail.)

Finally, you should prepare a capital expenditure budget, the timing of which will affect cash flow but not the profit and loss account except in respect of depreciation.

The cash-flow forecast that you prepare now should be on a month-by-month basis for the start-up period from the time when expenditure is first required and for at least 12 months. It will show clearly what are the cash demands on your personal finances to get started and what funding you need from a bank or other source. If you are planning to grow a more substantial business involving the hiring of staff and the employment of assets, the bank may want to see your cash-flow projections for two or even three years. The format for a cash-flow forecast is illustrated in Figure 3.2.

If you are unhappy with the result, either because the cash generated is inadequate to support you or because the assumptions on which the plan is based seem over-optimistic, you have an early opportunity to rethink before 'going public' with your plan. Of course, you should be mindful of the hazards of massaging the variables to achieve a more satisfactory result at the expense of reality.

Unit £

Month 1 2 3 4 5 6 7 8 9 10 11 12

**RECEIPTS**

Cash sales

Cash from debtors

Capital injection

**Total receipts (A)**

---

**PAYMENTS**

Payments to creditors

Salaries/wages/commissions

Rent/rates/water

Heat/light/power

Insurance

Maintenance and repairs

Postage/printing/stationery

Telephone/fax/broadband

Professional fees

Capital payments

Interest and bank charges

**VAT**

**Total payments (B)**

**Net cash flow (A – B)**

**Opening bank balance**

**Closing bank balance**

Note: Sales are scheduled by the actual month when customer payment is to be received. Expenses, including prepayments (such as rent, local taxes, insurance and VAT), are scheduled by the month when they are forecast to be made.

**Figure 3.2**  *Sample cash-flow forecast*

> If you are unhappy with the result, rethink before going public with your plan.

## STEP 8: SUMMARY

The final step in your business planning exercise is a concise summary, which should be positioned as the introduction to the plan. This summary, which is sometimes given the rather grandiose title of 'executive overview', should express succinctly the uniqueness and viability of your venture. If possible, limit its length to two pages – certainly less than four. It is the most important section in that it may determine how much consideration any proposal you may make for financial support will receive or, indeed, whether your detailed plan is read at all.

> The summary may determine whether your plan is read at all.

## STEP 9: EVALUATING YOUR OWN PLAN

### Be a swot

You may find it useful to develop a one-page analysis of strengths, weaknesses, opportunities and threats in your business plan, known by its anagram as a 'SWOT' analysis. Be honest about your weaknesses and the threats you face both in your marketplace and through external factors, spelling out any mitigating circumstances and the defensive action you will take to address them. Be specific also as to how you will capitalize on your strengths to exploit the business opportunities fully. Go back to the business plan and ensure that you incorporate all the proactive and defensive measures. When you are satisfied that you have addressed all the issues raised in your SWOT analysis, you can decide whether or not to include it as a part of the business plan.

A SWOT analysis is a summary of:

- strengths;
- weaknesses;
- opportunities;
- threats.

## Friendly criticism

Now that you have a business plan with which you are comfortable, try exposing it to friendly criticism. You will certainly want your family's opinion – and they will probably give it anyway! However, it is a good idea to ask one or more of your business acquaintances whose opinion you respect to read your business plan and pass objective comment. They may well perceive weaknesses (or strengths) in the plan that you did not appreciate and help you produce a more compelling case later to third parties for whom you are an 'unknown quantity'. They will also factor into their appraisal their perceptions of your personal strengths and weaknesses.

## Sensitivity testing

Finally, try subjecting your plan to 'sensitivity testing'. See what happens to your cash-flow and profit projections if you take a more pessimistic view of sales, expenses and profit margins. A very demanding venture capitalist with whom I used to work would calculate the effects on any business plan presented to him of a fall of 30 per cent in sales and the sales-related costs. Unless the revised projections showed that the business could still survive on the amount of funding requested, he would reject the proposal. Not surprisingly, very few business plans satisfied this test and the number of ventures that he funded was small.

## Break-even analysis

Even at this early stage in your planning process, it is important to work out the break-even point of your intended business. This analysis will show what you need to generate in terms of revenue at a sustainable price in order to cover your overheads and, therefore, ensure that you are not going to trade at a loss. There are three elements in the calculation:

■ total overheads;
■ direct cost of the product or service;
■ price of product or service you are selling.

_Total overheads_ are the fixed costs of running your business from rent, community charges, insurance and utilities to stationery, telephone, interest on loans or hire charges for equipment (including motor vehicles) and associated maintenance costs. (You will find a more comprehensive definition in Chapter 15).

Include in total overheads salaries and National Insurance for yourself and any employees you plan to take on. Strictly speaking, personnel costs are semi-variable because staff can be laid off over a period, but for short-term planning purposes, they are to all intents and purposes fixed. As a self-employed person you do not receive a salary from the business, unless you have set it up as a limited company, but you are liable for National Insurance contributions (see Chapter 22) and you should cost in what you need to draw monthly from the business to cover your own household and minimum living expenses.

_Direct cost of the product or service_, sometimes referred to as variable cost, is the sum of the unit costs of the product or service you plan to sell which is volume related. In Example 1 below, the direct costs of Angela's clothing boutique are the cost to her of the garments she sells. In Example 2, the direct costs of Fred's contract gardening business, in which he and his brother Ron are the only 'employees', are the consumables for the service he provides: the tools he replaces annually, the maintenance, repairs and fuel costs of the machines they use and the running costs of the truck in which they transport their equipment from location to location.

_Price of the product or service_ is the average selling price of the garments that Angela sells in her boutique (net of VAT) or the average price charged by Fred for each gardening job.

In Angela's case, since the product sold varies, she can work out the gross profit for, say, one month's sales, ie total net sales less total direct costs. Fred's calculation is similar but simpler.

*Formulae for break-even point*

For Angela's dress shop the monthly break-even point of sales is:

$$\frac{\text{Overheads}}{\text{Price of product} - \text{direct cost of product}}$$

This gives Angela the number of items she must sell to cover her monthly overhead costs (see Example 1 below).

Fred can arrive at the same result for his gardening business in another way by a parallel calculation:

$$\frac{\text{Monthly overhead}}{\text{Gross profit margin}} \times 100$$

Gross profit margin is a percentage: the gross profit divided by the value of sales times 100. The formula gives Fred the value of sales he must make to cover the overhead costs (see Example 2).

*Example 1*
*In Angela's boutique the average price of the garments she sells is £95 and the average price she pays to her suppliers is £60 per garment, so the gross margin is £35. Her monthly overheads, including what she needs to draw from the business and payments to part-time staff (not strictly a fixed cost) are £7,500.*

*Therefore, the number of items the boutique needs to sell each month is*

$$\frac{£7,500}{£35} = 214$$

*Of course, if the sales mix of her products changes, the number of items to be sold to achieve break-even will also change; eg if Angela sells more higher price items and less lower price items so that the average gross margin is lifted to £37.50, break-even will be reached when 200 garments are sold.*

_Example 2_

_The average price that Fred charges his customers for working in their gardens twice a month is £200 (ie £100 per visit).He estimates that he and his brother working together can make 3 calls a day or 60 calls a month, but may service only 20 clients to begin with; direct monthly costs will be £1,200. On sales of £4,000 per month, Fred's gross margin is therefore £2,800 divided by 4,000, ie 70% and the gross profit per customer would be £140._

_The overheads including Fred's and Ron's minimum drawings are £4,000. Will they break-even?_

_On the second formula, the sales needed to break-even are:_

_(£4,000 divided by 70) × 100 = £5,714_

_Therefore, Fred's business is not going to be profitable unless he can raise the number of clients to 29 or charge more for his services. Working at capacity at a monthly contract rate of £200, the monthly sales would rise to £6,000, but that is only a very small profit._

We'll return to the concept of break-even analysis in Chapter 15 in the concept of marginal pricing.

## Alternative projections

An alternative approach that some experts prefer is to prepare three alternative sets of projections: one based on quite optimistic assumptions, one on pessimistic assumptions, and a 'midway' set of projections based on the entrepreneur's realistic expectation. This may be a useful internal exercise, but I don't personally favour submitting three sets of projections to funding sources or their intermediaries.

At best, it may be confusing; at worst, it may be taken as an indication of uncertainty.

### Checklist: business planning

1. The purpose of the business plan is to set out the strategy and action plan for the next one to three years.
2. Base your plan on reality. Write it as if an outsider was the reader, and keep it short.
3. Define the market in which you plan to sell. Focus on the segments in which you will compete. Include photographs or diagrams to identify the product or service.
4. Identify barriers to entry and competition.
5. Describe what your marketing strategy will be and how you will achieve your sales goals.
6. Detail how you will run the business with reference to the production and delivery processes, key skills and personnel, and premises.
7. Identify your bookkeeping and management systems, financial controls and use of IT.
8. Set down the timing for starting your business.
9. Produce financial projections concentrated on cash-flow forecasts for at least 12 months from actual start-up and add on the planning and preparation period.
10. Include a two-page summary as the introduction to the plan and a one-page SWOT analysis as an attachment. Present the plan professionally with a contents page and section numbering and put a cover on it.
11. Ask business acquaintances whom you respect and who know you well to evaluate your plan and carry out sensitivity tests.
12. Carry out a break-even analysis to satisfy yourself that you can generate sufficient cash and profit to meet your personal income requirements.

**4**

# Structuring Your Business

Before you start talking to bank managers, solicitors, accountants or tax inspectors, you will have to start thinking about what sort of legal entity the business you are going to operate will be. The kind of advice you seek from them will depend on this decision, and you have three choices. You can operate as a sole trader (ie a self-employed businessperson – it does not necessarily have to be a 'trade'), a partnership, or as a private limited company. Let us see what each of these options implies.

## SOLE TRADER

There is nothing – or at least very little – to stop you from starting a business under your own name, operating from a back room of your own house.[1] But if the place you live in is owned by someone else, you should get the landlord's permission. If the business you

> Consider trading from home.

---

[1] If your business is likely to disturb neighbours or cause a nuisance (noise, smells, clients taking up parking space) or if it necessitates your building an extension, converting an attic, etc, you must apply for planning permission. Your property may then be given a higher, commercial rateable value.

are starting in your home is one that involves a change of use of the premises, you will have to get planning permission from the local authority's planning officer. In that case you may also find that you are re-rated on a commercial basis. If you own your house, you should also check that there are no restrictive covenants in the deeds governing its use. On the whole, a business conducted unobtrusively from a private residence is unlikely to attract attention from the local authority, but, to be perfectly safe, it is as well to have a word with the authority's planning department since any change of use, even of part of your residence, requires planning permission.

## Taxation

The next step is to inform your local tax inspector or to get your accountant to do so (see Chapter 6 on choosing professional advisers). This is always advisable if the nature of your earnings is changing and imperative if you are moving from employee to full-time self-employed status, because it changes the basis on which you pay tax.

Some allowable business expenses can be set off against your earnings for tax purposes. These will not include entertainment of potential customers but will cover items 'wholly and exclusively incurred for the purposes of business'. These are spelt out in more detail in Chapter 22.

Some things, of course, are used partly for private and partly for business purposes – your car or your telephone, for instance. In these cases only that proportion of expenditure that can definitely be attributed to business use is chargeable against tax. Careful records of such use must, therefore, be kept, and its extent must also be credible. If you are not exporting anything in the way of a product or service, you may be unable to convince the inspector that a weekend in Paris was in the course of business! But if you are, he is unlikely to quibble about a modest hotel bill.

More importantly, if you are carrying out your business from home, you will be able to charge against income, for tax purposes, a proportion of the running costs of your home. More information is available in Chapter 22.

> Some business expenses are allowable before tax.

## Personal liability

The principal cautionary point to bear in mind about operating as a sole trader is that you are personally liable for the debts of your business. If you go bankrupt your creditors are entitled to seize and sell your *personal* possessions, not just equipment, cars and other items directly related to your business.

You may decide to trade under a business name, and the registration of business names is discussed below. Using a business name helps to create an identity for your business and you will be able to use that name when registering your business for VAT (see Chapter 20).

# PARTNERSHIPS

Most of the above points are also true if you are setting up in an unlimited partnership with other people. Once again, there are very few unlimited restrictions against setting up in partnership with someone to carry on a business, but because all the members of a partnership are personally liable for its debts, even if these are incurred by a piece of mismanagement by one partner which was not known to his or her colleagues, the choice of partners is a step that requires very careful thought.

> All members of a partnership are personally liable for its debts.

## Should you have a partner at all?

Certainly it is not advisable to do so just for the sake of having company, because unless the partner can really contribute something to the business, you are giving away a part of what could in time be a very valuable asset to little purpose.

A partner should be able to make an important contribution to running the business in an area which you are unable to take care of. He or she may have some range of specialized expertise that is vital to the business; or a range of contacts to bring in work; or the work may be of such a nature that the executive tasks and decisions cannot be handled by one person.

Be sure that your skills and capabilities complement each other.

He or she may even be a 'sleeping partner' who is doing little else apart from putting up some money in return for a share of the eventual profits. It is not uncommon for colleagues who have been made redundant from the same company to set up in business together. If you are thinking of doing that, be sure that your skills and capabilities truly complement each other. 'Drowning' men (or women) clutching each other for comfort are unlikely to survive.

## Choosing your partner

But whatever the reason may be for establishing a partnership as opposed to going it alone and owning the whole business, you should be sure that your partner (of course, there may be more than one, but for the sake of simplicity we will assume that only one person is involved) is someone you know well in a business, not just a social, capacity.

Before formally establishing a partnership it may be advisable to tackle, as an informal joint venture, one or two jobs together, carrying at the end of the day an agreed share of the costs and profits. That way you will learn about each other's strengths and weaknesses, and indeed whether you can work together harmoniously at all. It may turn out, for instance, that your prospective partner's expertise or contacts, while useful, do not justify giving him or her a share of the business and that in fact a consultancy fee is the right way of giving remuneration. If your colleague's contribution is simply to bring in business, then a sales commission may be the most appropriate arrangement.

## Formal partnership agreements

Even if all goes well and you find that you can cooperate, it is vital that a formal partnership agreement should be drawn up by a solicitor, **even in the case of husband-and-wife partnerships.** The agreement should cover such points as the following:

1. Who is responsible for what aspects of the operation (eg production, marketing)?
2. What constitutes a policy decision (eg whether or not to take on a contract) and how is it taken? By a majority vote, if there is an uneven number of partners? By the partner concerned with that aspect of things? Only if all partners agree?
3. How are the profits to be divided? According to the amount of capital put in? According to the amount of work done by each partner? Over the whole business done by the partnership over a year? On a job-by-job basis? How much money can be drawn, on what basis, and how often in the way of remuneration?
4. What items, such as cars, not exclusively used for business can be charged to the partnership? And is there any limitation to the amount of money involved?
5. If one of the partners retires or withdraws, how is his or her share of the business to be valued?
6. If work is done in office hours, outside the framework of the partnership, to whom does the income accrue?
7. What arbitration arrangements are there, in case of irreconcilable differences?
8. If one of the partners dies, what provisions should the other make for his dependants?

There are obviously many kinds of eventualities that have to be provided for, depending on the kind of business that is going to be carried on. Some professional partnerships, for instance, may consist of little more than an agreement to pool office expenses such as the services of typists and telephonists, with partners drawing their own fees quite independently of each other.

The best way to prepare the ground for a solicitor to draw up an agreement is for each partner to make a list of possible points of dispute and to leave it to the legal adviser to produce a form of words to cover these and any other points he or she may come up with. Partnerships offering services, particularly professional firms, are more likely to trade under the name of two or more of the partners.

Leave it to the legal advisor to produce a form of words.

## PRIVATE LIMITED COMPANIES

Tax legislation over the last 10 years has made it less attractive to start out trading as a limited company unless you are in a form of business that might leave you at risk as a debtor – as might be the case, for instance, if you were a graphic designer commissioning processing on behalf of a client.

The reason for this is that, in law, a limited company has an identity distinct from that of the shareholders who are its owners. Consequently, if a limited company goes bankrupt, the claims of the creditors are limited to the assets of the company. This includes any capital issued to shareholders which they have **paid for either in full or in part**. We shall return to the question of share capital in a moment, but the principle at work here is that when shares are issued, the shareholders need not necessarily pay for them in full, though they have a legal obligation to do so if the company goes bankrupt.

Shareholders are not liable as individuals. Directors who give guarantees are not protected.

Otherwise, shareholders are not liable as individuals, and their private assets outside the company may not be touched unless their company has been trading fraudulently. On the other hand, if creditors ask for personal guarantees, directors of limited companies who give them are not protected and **personal** assets to the amount of the guarantee as well as business assets are at risk in the event of bankruptcy.

There is also another important area where the principle of limited liability does not apply. Company directors are liable, in law, for employees' National Insurance contributions. This is a

Directors have other liabilities.

personal liability which is being enforced by the Department for Work and Pensions in the same way as bank guarantees. There have even been cases of non-executive directors of insolvent companies being pursued for non-payment of NI contributions by companies with which they were involved, though the Social Security Act of 1975 stated that the directors are only responsible in such circumstances if they 'knew or reasonably could have known' that these were not being paid. Company directors can also be held guilty of 'wrongful trading', which essentially means trading while they know their company is insolvent. In that case they may be obliged to contribute personally to the compensation of creditors.

## Company formation requirements

Under EU legislation, a limited company can be formed by a single shareholder who must be a director. It must also have a company secretary, who can be an outside person such as your solicitor or accountant. Apart from this, the main requirements relate to documentation. Like sole traders or partnerships, a limited company must prepare a set of accounts annually for the inspector of taxes and it must make an annual return to the Registrar of Companies, showing all the shareholders and directors, any changes of ownership that have taken place, a profit and loss account over the year and a balance sheet.

## Advantages and disadvantages of limited companies

Apart from the more exacting requirements regarding documentation, a significant disadvantage of setting up a limited company as compared to a partnership or sole trader is that sole traders and partnerships can set off any losses they incur in the first four years' trading retrospectively against the owners' income tax on earnings in the three preceding years. This may enable you to recover tax already paid in earlier years of ordinary employment.

Losses can only be set off against a company's corporation tax when it makes a profit.

This concession does not, however, apply to investment in your own limited company, or to investments made in such a company by those closely connected with the shareholders. If it makes losses, those losses can only be set off against the *company's* corporation tax in other years when it makes a profit. If it fails altogether, then the loss of your investment is a *capital* loss which can only be set off against other capital gains you make – not against other earned income.

Therefore, if the nature of your business is a service which does not involve exposure to liabilities that you need to protect – for instance, if you are a consultant, rather than a shopkeeper or a manufacturer incurring liabilities to suppliers – there may be a distinct advantage in opting for partnership or sole trader status rather than establishing a limited company.

There may, for instance, be factors other than trading risks which need to be protected by limited liability. Highly profitable ventures can also benefit from limited company status because their profits are taxed at corporation tax rates rather than the higher personal income tax rate of 40 per cent. As your start-up business prospers you should review the alternative taxation status of a limited company to self-employment at regular intervals. In any case, taking professional advice is recommended.

## Cost of company formation

The cost of forming a company, including the capital duty which is based on minimal issued capital (the distinction between this and nominal capital is described later), is likely to be around £250, depending on what method you use to go about it. Buying a ready-made ('off the shelf') company from one of the registration agents who advertise their services on the internet costs less than £40. Such a company will not actually have been trading, but will be properly registered by the agents. All that has to be done is for the existing 'shareholders' (who are probably the agent's nominees) to resign and for the purchasers to become the new shareholders and to appoint directors. You can also form your company direct through Companies House.

Alternatively you can start your own company from scratch, but whichever course you choose, professional advice is vital at this stage. The technicalities are trickier than they sound, though simple enough to those versed in such transactions.

Ultimately, the decision on whether or not to form a limited company depends on your long-term objectives. If you are planning to become an entrepreneur, and to build a business for significant capital growth, a limited company structure and the creation of shares has to be considered at an early stage. It will, for instance, be essential if you want to raise serious amounts of money from outside investors, as we will show in Chapter 5. But if you are thinking about what is essentially a salaried income replacement venture, a sole trader or partnership structure would usually be the better and simpler option.

> Deciding whether or not to form a limited company depends on long-term objectives.

# REGISTRATION OF BUSINESS NAMES

One problem you may encounter with an 'off the shelf' company is when it has a name that does not relate meaningfully to the activity you are proposing to carry on. In that case you can change the company name by contacting the Companies Registrations Office on 029 2038 0801 or online and they will guide you through the procedure, which is straightforward and costs around £50. You can also contact the new companies section on the same number, and register a new company. This again is a straightforward procedure and costs £20 or £15 online. You can also write to the Registrar of Companies for information (The Registrar of Companies, Companies House, Crown Way, Cardiff CF14 3UZ). If your enquiry is about registering a new company, address it to The Registrar of Companies – New Companies Section.

## Trading under a different name

The other option is to trade under a name which is different from the company's official one; for instance, your company may be called 'Period Investments Ltd', but you trade as 'Regency Antiques'. Until 1982 you had to register your business name with the Registrar of Business Names, but that office has since been abolished. Instead, if you trade under any name other than your own – in the case of a sole trader or partnership – or that of the name of the company carrying on the business in the case of a company, you have to disclose the name of the owner or owners and, for each owner, a business or other address within the United Kingdom.

**The rules of disclosure for sole traders and partnerships are quite far-reaching and failure to comply with them is a criminal offence.** You must show the information about owners and their addresses on all business letters, written orders for the supply of goods or services, invoices and receipts issued in the course of business, and written demands for payment of business debts. Furthermore, you have to display this information prominently and readably in any premises where the business is carried on and to which customers and suppliers have access.

## Choice of business name

It is worth giving a good deal of thought to the choice of a business name. Clever names are all very well, but if they do not clearly establish the nature of the business you are in, prospective customers leafing through a telephone or business directory may have trouble in finding you; or, if they do find you, they may not readily match your name to their needs. For instance, if you are a furniture repairer, it is far better to describe yourself as such in your business name than to call yourself something like 'Chippendale Restorations'. However, if your name already has a big reputation in some specialized sector, stick with it.

Protect your business name by registration.

Legislation makes it possible to protect a trading name by registering it with the Trade Marks Registry at the Patent Office. The advantage of this is that you can prevent other traders from using your name – or something very similar – and cashing in on your goodwill. You can also register a trade mark – the sign or logo that identifies your business on letterheads, packaging and so forth.

The activities for which marks can be registered include service industries as well as manufacturing ones.

There are, it should be said, certain words that the Registrar of Companies has proved likely to object to: those that could mislead the public by suggesting that an enterprise is larger or has a more prestigious status than circumstances indicate. Cases in point are the use of words such as Trust, Global, Universal, University and Group. National adjectives ('British') are also unpopular. When you get to this stage the names of the proprietors have to be shown not only on letterheads, but also on catalogues and trade literature.

## Limited company requirements

Limited companies have to show their registration number and the address of their registered office on such stationery. This address may not necessarily be the same as the one at which business is normally transacted. Some firms use their accountant's or solicitor's premises as their registered office. You will probably see quite a number of registration certificates hanging in their offices (they are required by law to be so displayed) when you go there. This is because it is to that address that all legal and official documents are sent. If you have placed complete responsibility for dealing with such matters in the hands of professional advisers, it is obviously convenient that the related correspondence should also be directed there. Bear in mind, though, that this does involve a certain loss of control on your part. Unless you see these documents yourself, you will have no idea, for instance, whether the important ones are being handled with due dispatch.

## LIMITED COMPANY DOCUMENTS

When you set up a limited company, your solicitor or accountant will be involved in drafting certain papers and documents which govern its structure and the way it is to be run. When this process has been completed you will receive copies of the company's Memorandum and Articles of Association, some share transfer forms, a minute book, the company seal and the Certificate of Incorporation.

## The Memorandum

This document sets out the main objects for which the company is formed and what it is allowed to do. There are standard clauses for this and your professional adviser will use these in drafting the

> Do not be too specific in setting out the limits of the operation.

document. The main thing to watch out for is that he should not be too specific in setting out the limits of the proposed operation, because if you change tack somewhere along the line – for instance, if you move from mail order to making goods for the customers you have built up – you may lose the protection of your limited liability unless the Memorandum provides for this. There are, however, catch-all clauses which allow you to trade in pretty much anything or any manner you like. Furthermore, the 'objects' clauses can be changed by a special resolution, passed by 75 per cent of the shareholders.[1]

> Understand the definitions of nominal and share capital.

The Memorandum also sets out the company's nominal or authorized share capital and the par value per share. This is a point which many newcomers may find very confusing. The thing to remember is that in this context the value of share capital is a purely *nominal* value. You can have a company operating with thousands of pounds' worth of nominal share capital. This sounds very impressive, but what counts is the *issued* share capital, because this represents what the shareholders have actually put into the business or pledged themselves so to do. It is quite possible to have a company with a nominal capital of £1,000, but with only one issue share of £1 to the one shareholder that is required by law.

---

[1] For new companies registering under the 2006 Act, the objects of a company will be deemed to be unrestricted, unless there is contrary provision in the Articles of Association.

The issued share capital also determines the ownership of a company. In the case we have just quoted, the one shareholder would own the company absolutely. But if a second £1 share is then issued to another person, making 2 shares in total, he or she would now own only half of the company. This is a vital point to remember when raising capital by means of selling shares.

## Implications of issued share capital

Apart from determining proportions of ownership, issued share capital also signifies how much of their own money the shareholders have put into the company or are prepared to accept liability for. Therefore, in raising money from a bank or finance house, the manager there will look closely at the issued share capital. To the extent that he or she is not satisfied that the liability for the amount being asked for is adequately backed by issued share capital, he or she is likely to ask the shareholders to guarantee a loan or overdraft with their own personal assets – for instance, by depositing shares they privately hold in a public quoted company or unit trust as security or signing a legal charge over your house in favour of the bank. In the case of a new company without a track record this would, in fact, be the usual procedure.

> Where issued share capital is inadequate, banks will require personal guarantees.

The nominal share capital of a new small-scale business is usually £100. It can be increased later, as business grows, on application to the Registrar of Companies. The point of such a move would be to increase the **issued** share capital, for instance if a new shareholder were to put money into the company. But, once again, it should be borne in mind that if the issued share capital was increased from £100 to £1,000, and a backer were to buy £900-worth of shares at par value, the original shareholders would only own one-tenth of the business; the fact that they got the whole thing going is quite beside the point.

## Part payment for share subscriptions

One last question about issued share capital which sometimes puzzles people: must you actually hand over money for the shares when you start your own company, as is the case when you buy shares on the stock market, and what happens to it? The answer is yes. You pay it into the company's bank account because, remember, it has a separate legal identity from the shareholders who own it. However, you need not pay for your shares in full. You can, for instance, pay 50p per share for a hundred £1 shares. The balance of £50 represents your liability if the company goes bankrupt, and you actually have to hand over the money only if that happens or if a majority at a shareholders' meeting requires you to do so. The fact that you have not paid in full for shares issued to you does not, however, diminish your entitlement to share in the profits, these being distributed as dividends according to the proportion of share capital issued. The same applies to outside shareholders, so if you are raising money by selling shares to people outside the firm, you should normally ensure that they pay in full for any capital that is issued to them.

> Part payment for shares issued does not diminish the entitlement to share in profit.

## The Articles of Association

These are coupled together with the Memorandum, and set out the rules under which the company is run. They govern matters such as issue of the share capital, appointment and powers of directors and proceedings at general meetings. As in the case of the Memorandum, the clauses are largely standard, but those relating to the issue of shares should be read carefully. It is most important that there should be a proviso under which any new shares that are issued should be offered first to the existing shareholders in the proportion in which they already hold shares. This is particularly so when two or more shareholders are involved, or when you are buying into a company; otherwise the other shareholders can vote to water down your holding in the company whenever they see fit by issuing further shares. For the same reason, there should be a clause under which any shareholder who wants to transfer shares should offer them first of all to the existing shareholders.

> Any new shares that are issued should be offered first to the existing shareholders.

## Effects of share valuation

The Articles of Association also state how the value of the shares is to be determined, the point here being that if the company is successful and makes large profits, the true value of the shares will be much greater than their par value of £1, 50p or whatever. It should be noted, though, that the market valuation of the shares does not increase the liability of shareholders accordingly. In other words, if your £1 par shares are actually valued at, say, £50, your liability still remains at £1.

Table A of the Companies Act of 1985, which applies to companies that registered before January 2007 and can be purchased at any Stationery Office branch, sets out a specimen Memorandum and Articles, which are used widely by those forming companies.

The new Companies Act 2006 introduces model or 'default' articles in place of Table A of the 1985 Act for private companies limited by shares. Existing companies are free to choose whether to adopt the new model articles or to retain the present articles with or without modification.

## The Minute Book

Company law requires that a record be kept of the proceedings at both shareholders' and directors' board meetings. These proceedings are recorded in the Minute Book, which is held at the company's registered office. Decisions made at company meetings

> Important matters such as who signs cheques can be minuted at the first board meeting.

are signed by the Chair and are legally binding on the directors if they are agreed by a majority.[2] Therefore, any points of procedure that are not covered by the Memorandum and Articles of Association can be written into the minutes and have the force of law, provided that they do not conflict with the former two documents. Thus, the various responsibilities of the directors can be defined and minuted at the first board meeting; so can important matters such as who signs the cheques. It is generally a good idea for cheques to carry two signatures to be valid.

## The common seal

This used to be a stamp affixed with the authority of the directors, but nowadays formal documents can be executed by the signatures of two directors. That has the same legal effect as the seal used to have, but it may still be used in some special circumstances.

## The Certificate of Incorporation

When the wording of the Memorandum and Articles of Association has been agreed and the names of the directors and the size of the nominal capital have been settled, your professional adviser will send the documents concerned to the Registrar of Companies, who will issue a Certificate of Incorporation which is, as it were, the birth certificate of your company.

# COMPANY DIRECTORS

When your Certificate of Incorporation arrives, you and your fellow shareholders are the owners of a fully fledged private limited company. You will almost certainly also be the directors. This title in fact means very little. A director is merely an employee of the company, who is entrusted by the shareholders with the running of it. He or she need not personally be a shareholder at all, and can be removed by a vote of the shareholders which, since each

---

[2] Under the Companies Act 2006 private companies are no longer required to hold shareholders' Annual General Meetings (AGMs), nor to lay a Report and Accounts in general meetings.

share normally carries one vote, is a good reason for not losing control of your company by issuing a majority shareholding to outsiders.

> Without control, even a managing director is only an employee.

Another good reason is that since the ownership of the company is in proportion to the issued share capital, so also is the allocation of profits, when you come to make them. If you let control pass to an outsider for the sake of raising a few hundred pounds now – there are other means of raising capital than the sale of shares as you will see in Chapter 5 – you will have had all the problems of getting things going, while only receiving a small part of the rewards. Remember, furthermore, that without control you are only an employee, even if you are called 'managing director'.

## Checklist: structuring your business

_Sole trader_
1. Do you need planning permission to operate from your own home?
2. Does your lease allow you to carry on a trade from the premises you intend to use?
3. If you own the premises, whether or not they are your home as well, are there any restrictive covenants which might prevent you from using them for the purpose intended?
4. Have you notified your tax inspector that the nature of your earnings is changing?
5. Are you aware of the implications of being a sole trader if your business fails?
6. Have you taken steps to register a business name?

_Partnerships_
1. Points 1 to 6 above also apply to partnerships. Have you taken care of them?

2. How well do you know your partners – personally and as people to work with?
3. If you do not know them well, what evidence do you have of their personal and business qualities?
4. What skills, contacts or other assets (such as capital) can they bring into the business?
5. Have you asked your solicitor to draw up a deed of partnership and does it cover all the eventualities you can think of?
6. Have you talked to anybody who is in, or has tried, partnership in the same line of business, to see what the snags are?

*Private limited companies*
1. Do you have the requisite shareholders or you will be the sole shareholder?
2. Do you have a competent company secretary, who can carry out the legal duties required under the Companies Acts?
3. Are you yourself reasonably conversant with those duties?
4. Have you registered, if this is required, a company name and a business name?
5. Has permission been granted to use the names chosen?
6. Have the necessary documents been deposited with the Registrar of Companies? (Memorandum and Articles of Association, a statutory declaration of compliance with registration requirements, a statement of nominal share capital.)
7. Have you read and understood the Memorandum and Articles? Do they enable you to carry out all present and any possible future objects for which the company is formed?
8. Do your stationery, catalogues, letterheads, etc show all the details required by the Companies Acts?
9. Is the Registration Certificate displayed in the company's registered office, as required by law?
10. Do you understand the wide range of benefits – company cars, other business expenses, limited liability, self-

administered pension schemes, etc – enjoyed by limited companies?
11. Points 1 to 3 of the 'Sole trader' checklist may also apply to you. If so, have you taken care of them?

# 5

# Funding Your Business

## OWN FUNDS

Starting your own full-time business usually requires the provision of working capital, if only to cover the gap between your previous income ceasing and a positive cash flow from your self-employed activities, or your ability to make drawings from the partnership or to take a salary if you set up a company. Most people setting out in business on their own account provide the initial funding from their own financial resources, using personal savings, cashing in on a pension or insurance policy, borrowing against the surrender value of an endowment insurance policy or borrowing from family and friends. Even personal credit cards are a common source of finance to support initial cash flow.

If you do need to turn to external sources, a variety are available depending on the size and nature of your business and its requirements. However, in the wake of the global financial crisis external sources are thin on the ground, and those who cannot start up their chosen business wthout significant funding are disadvantaged.

# DEBT FINANCE

## Types of borrowing

In more recent times, the banks have formed the most important source of external finance for the self-employed and small businesses in the United Kingdom and their dominance of business funding seems sure to continue in spite of credit crunches and squeezes. Bank lending takes the form of term loans (repayable by instalments over a period of time) and overdrafts, and banks rely heavily on taking security for lending any significant sum. The owners of small businesses should expect to provide security over personal assets when negotiating bank funding for start-up or early-stage development.

In recent years there has been an increase in other bank products, such as factored debt and asset-based finance.

## Factoring

Factoring is, effectively, the discounting of trade debtors whereby you receive a proportion of the face value of your invoices to credit acceptable customers and the bank or factoring company takes on the financial risk and the responsibility of collection. Plainly, this means of raising cash applies to your operation only when you have built up a sufficient level of business; it is not normally available within the first 18 months of trading until you can produce your first 12 months accounts and show a satisfactory level of business and a sound debtor payment record.

## Asset finance

Asset finance is applied particularly to the acquisition of office or manufacturing equipment and motor vehicles; it can take the form of hire purchase, finance leasing or operating leasing. Before choosing which route to take, you should consult with your accountant regarding the real cost of each alternative and the implications for tax allowances and ownership of the asset. Even the supply of these facilities is limited in today's conditions.

## Bank borrowing

If you do borrow from the bank in the name of the company you have set up for your business, it is likely that the bank will require your personal guarantee. Likewise, 'joint and several liability' will probably be a prerequisite of borrowing in the name of a partnership, which means that each partner will have liability to the bank in respect of the total partnership debt.

> Understand the meaning of 'joint' and 'several' guarantee.

If things go wrong, the bank calls in the partnership debt, and if some partners are unable to pay or have given security that is inadequate or not easily realizable, it will look to those whom they identify as being most able swiftly to repay the partnership's borrowings in full. Those who pay up more than their share of the total amount will have recourse against those who do not, but pursuit will be extended and may be fruitless. The same problem can arise for the directors of a private limited company who provided their guarantees jointly for the company's borrowings or a debt.

Commonly, if the sum you wish to borrow is substantial and the only significant asset you hold is the equity interest in your house, the bank may ask for a second charge on the house (after the mortgage provider). This involves you and your family in an unwelcome decision that you should not take without seeking advice from a solicitor who will explain the full implications, nor without ensuring that there is family unanimity. If the family are not in agreement, rethink your plan. Dissent on this issue is likely to put unwelcome stress on family relationships. The last thing you need if you are starting up on your own is family stress.

> If the bank asks for a legal charge on your home, ensure that your family agrees.

## Private loans

You may have friends or relatives who are prepared to lend you money, but private loans are a rich source of misunderstanding and so you should be clear about all the implications of such an arrangement. The best plan is to have a solicitor draw up the terms of the loan, covering the rate of interest, the period over which the loan is repayable and the circumstances under which it can be withdrawn. It must also be made clear to what extent, if any, the lender has any say in the running of the business and what the nature of this control is. Normally, however, lenders should not be entitled to participation in management matters; nor does the existence of the loan entitle them to a share of the profits, no matter how strong a moral claim they think they might have once your business starts making real money.

> The best plan is to have a solicitor draw up the terms of the loan.

In the case of a limited company, you must explain to the lender that a loan is not the same thing as a shareholding, although, of course, the offer of a loan might be conditional on acquiring shares or the option to acquire them. You should be clear that a shareholding entitles the shareholder to a percentage of the profits in proportion to his or her holding and though loans can be repaid, it is virtually impossible to dismantle issued share capital in this way.

Often private loans are not offered directly but in the form of guaranteeing an overdraft, on the basis that if the recipient of the overdraft is unable to repay it, the guarantor is liable for that amount. Losses incurred by the guarantor of a capital loan can be treated as a capital loss, to be set off against capital gains.

## The Small Firms Loan Guarantee Scheme

There is one third-party source of relief for small firms located in England with viable business proposals that are unable to secure conventional finance because they and their owners lack assets as collateral security to offer against a loan. The Small Firms Loan

Guarantee Scheme is a joint venture between the Department for Business, Enterprise and Regulatory Reform (BERR) and a number of participating lenders. The SFLG provides a guarantee against default that encourages lenders who are otherwise satisfied with the business proposal but will not advance funds without adequate security.

Participating banks and other financial institutions that take responsibility for commercial decisions regarding borrowers provide loans over 2 to 10 years. The SFLG provides a 75 per cent guarantee on loans of up to £250,000 for established businesses that have been trading for two years or more at the time of application.

The SFLG scheme is available to businesses in most sectors that are less than five years old with an annual turnover of up to £5.6 million, and for most business purposes.

The annual premium is 2 per cent per year on the balance of the outstanding loan payable to BERR.

To make an application you should approach one of the approved lenders, who will consider whether to lend you money, either by way of a conventional loan or overdraft or the SFLG. The lender will apply to BERR for a guarantee.

Of course, not every application for the SFLG succeeds. However, in the first 20 years since the start of the scheme in 1981 over 76,000 loans, valued at more than £2.7 billion, were guaranteed. For more details of the scheme visit www.businesslink.gov. uk.sflg. A temporary 20 per cent increase in the funds available under the SFLG was announced in the March 2008 Budget. The availability of further funds or guarantees for small business loans has been announced by the government more recently. However, the terms and actual availability remain uncertain.

## Grants

A variety of grants are available from a number of sources: from local government and development agencies, regional development agencies, Chambers of Commerce, County Enterprise Boards, the UK government and the EU. A capital fund of 12.5 million was also introduced in the 2008 Budget to encourage more women to go into business. For details visit the Business Link website at www.businesslink.gov.uk.

# EQUITY FINANCE

Since the mid-1990s the supply of risk capital to enterprises from both formal venture capital funds and informal investors, known as 'business angels', has grown considerably. Although it still accounts for only a small proportion of total small business financing in the United Kingdom, risk capital plays an important role in financing higher-growth small firms.

## Formal venture capital finance

Formal venture capital finance usually takes the form of a mixture of loan capital and equity (ordinary shares and, perhaps, preference shares). The loan capital is generally combined with conventional bank borrowing to provide most of the funding, while the investment in ordinary share capital is a relatively small proportion of the total, normally representing less than a third of the company's equity. Such a financing structure, which is designed to leave the owners of the business with a majority shareholding and to provide a high rate of return on investors' equity, is described as 'highly geared'. However, formal venture capital is seldom made available for investment propositions involving less than £1 million financing, although deals involving less than £500,000 have become quite common. Unless working for yourself involves participation in a management buy-out (MBO) or management buy-in (MBI), your business is unlikely to attract this category of investor. For the investor, venture capital trusts are an attractive form of investment. Income tax relief at up to 30 per cent is available on qualifying investments of up to £200,000 per year, and dividends and capital gains are exempt from tax.

> Deals involving less than £500,000 have become quite common.

One deterrent for small companies and entrepreneurs seeking formal venture capital is the high cost. Specialist advice is required from lawyers and accountants and, perhaps, from a professional corporate finance adviser, unless that role is provided by the accountancy firm with which you work. Overall cost can rise to as much as 10 per cent of the finance raised, and 4 or 5 per cent is commonplace.

Nevertheless, the government has augmented the supply of risk capital for small and medium-sized enterprises (SMEs) that demonstrate growth potential by setting up Regional Venture Capital Funds (RVCFs) in each of the nine English regions to focus on sub-£500,000 investments. The first to launch were in the North East and East Midlands in January 2002. By January 2003 the nine RVCFs had reached collectively fund totals at their first and final closing of £218 million. Additional enterprise capital funds as support for mezzanine finance were provided in the 2008 Budget.

## Business angel investment

Raising equity capital in the amounts required by smaller businesses can be especially difficult, not only because of the high risks but also because of the high costs of making such investments.

> You may be able to attract a business angel, but you will have to make up to 30 per cent of your share capital available.

However, business angels provide smaller amounts of risk capital to businesses with growth potential, particularly start-up and early-stage businesses. In 2008, the supply of UK business angel investment was estimated at between £500 million to £1 billion per year, from some 20,000 to 40,000 actual and potential business angels, spread over some 3,000 to 6,000 companies. However, this source of funds has temporarily dried up.

If your business concept is innovative and your business plan indicates that high profitability and a rapid rate of growth can be achieved, you may still be able to attract a business angel. The same kind of 'gearing' between loan capital and equity may be appropriate as for formal venture capital, and you will certainly have to make available up to 30 per cent of the ordinary share capital of your company to the investors. Before setting out to attract an investor, you should be aware of what business angels are likely to demand.

## Business angel profile

▪ Business angels are very often successful businesspeople who have built up their own businesses from scratch, as you intend to do.

▪ Their preferences for the kind of business in which they want to invest are conditioned by experience, and may seem quite idiosyncratic.

▪ They will expect a sufficient personal investment from you to ensure your commitment (but not to cripple you financially).

▪ They will require the return of their investment and profit within three to five years, or a shorter time, if you need to go for secondary funding to grow the business.

▪ They may want to play an active part in the business (whether or not this is a good thing from your point of view depends on personal chemistry, whether they can make a genuine contribution and whether the terms of participation have been clearly set out).

There is a National Business Angels Network (NBAN), supported by the Enterprise Directive, a number of clearing banks and other sponsoring organizations. NBAN works with the local Business Angel Networks (BANs), to which many groups and individual investors belong, and with local banks, accountants and solicitors who help to operate this informal market. If you decide to seek investment from this sector, contact the NBAN or your local BAN to be put in touch with investors.

Potential business angel investors are also identified in a directory published by the British Venture Capital Association (3 Clements Inn, London WC2A 2AZ; 020 7025 2950; website: www.bvca.co.uk). As a further alternative, you can take a proactive approach by registering with a Business Introduction Service, which sets out to help firms looking for finance present their case in a way that is likely to attract investors.

## BERR Equity Initiatives

The BERR plays an active role in promoting an increased supply of equity finance to SMEs through the RVCFs and Early Growth Funding. The second of these initiatives targets businesses seeking to raise up to £50,000 for innovative and knowledge-intensive businesses, as well as smaller manufacturers needing fresh investment for growing new opportunities.

### Checklist: different sources of capital

1. Most people starting to work for themselves provide initial funding from their personal resources.
2. If you do need to turn to external sources, such as a bank, be prepared to provide security over personal assets for start-up or early-stage development. Ensure that you understand the full implications and that there is complete family unanimity.
3. Decide on appropriate types of finance; an overdraft is for working capital.
4. Consider if additional capital is needed. If so, look for a grant, a private loan or equity finance.
5. Factoring may be an alternative to overdraft borrowing, but only if you have a good debtor book, strong credit controls and a track record of two years or more.
6. The Small Firms Loan Guarantee (SFLG) Scheme may be available to viable businesses located in England where the banks' requirement for security cannot be met.
7. BERR promotes equity finance through Regional Venture Capital Funds and Early Growth Funding. The BERR website is the first source of information on both schemes.
8. Investigate the multitude of other grants that could be available by visiting www.businesslink.gov.uk.
9. 'Business angel' capital can be attracted for smaller amounts of capital for early-stage businesses, even start-ups, provided that you can demonstrate innovation and that high growth and profitability are achievable.

However, business angels may wish to play a more active role in your business than you would like.

10. Formal venture capital finance is often not available for financing requirements of less than £1 million, and is costly for small companies.

11. All venture capitalists will expect the return of their investment and profit within three to five years, and most will require representation on the board of your company.

Note: If you are planning an MBI or MBO or require substantial funding for your business a more comprehensive overview of financing is provided by Reuvid, J M (2002) *Corporate Finance Handbook*, Kogan Page, London.

# 6

# Choosing Your Advisers

We have already touched on the importance of the role that professional advisers, particularly accountants and solicitors, are going to play in the formation of your business, whether it is to be a limited company or some other form of entity. You are going to be using their advice quite frequently, not only at the beginning but also later, in matters such as acquiring premises or preparing a set of accounts. Obviously, therefore, how you choose and use these advisers is a matter for careful thought. There are others whom you may consult who may be able to give you useful help in the start-up of your business.

## MAKING THE RIGHT CHOICE

Many people think that there is some kind of special mystique attached to membership of a profession and that any lawyer or accountant is going to do a good job for them. The fact is, though, that while they do have useful specialist knowledge, the competence with which they apply it can vary widely. A high proportion of people who have bought a house, for instance, can tell you of

> The competence with which lawyers and accountants apply their knowledge varies widely.

errors and delays in the conveyancing process, and some accountants entrusted with their clients' tax affairs have been known to send in large bills for their services while overlooking claims for legitimate expenses that were the object of employing them in the first place.

So do not just go to the solicitor or accountant who happens to be nearest; nor should you go to someone you only know in a social capacity. Ask friends who are already in business on a similar scale and, if possible, of a similar nature to your own, for recommendations. (If you already have a bank manager you know well, he or she may also be able to offer useful advice.) The kind of professional adviser you should be looking for at this stage is not in a big office in a central location. They will have bigger fish to fry and after the initial interview you may well be fobbed off with an articled clerk. Apart from that they will be expensive, for they have big office overheads to meet. On the other hand, a solo operation can create a problem if that person is ill or on holiday. The ideal office will be a suburban one, preferably close to where you intend to set up business, because knowledge of local conditions and personalities can be invaluable, with two or three partners. Apart from that, personal impressions do count. You will probably not want to take on an adviser who immediately exudes gloomy caution, or one who appears to be a wide boy, or somebody with whom you have no rapport. We recommend that you should make a shortlist of two or three possibles and go and talk to them before making your choice.

> The ideal professional firm will be a local one with two or three partners.

Professional associations will also have details of members in your area. The Law Society runs a scheme, Lawyers for Your Business (LFYB), to help small companies assess their legal needs by offering a free consultation with a local member. The LFYB telephone hotline is 020 7405 9075 and free guides are available at 020 7316 5521. Details can also be found on the Law Society's website at www.lawsoc.org.uk. The Institute of Chartered Accountants in England and Wales (ICAEW) also provides details of local practitioners to members of the public. Its Practitioner Bureau can be contacted direct on 01908 248090 and its website address is www.icaew.co.uk/. The Institute of Chartered Accountants Scotland also publishes a list of members which can be ordered on 0131 347 4883, with details shown on the website www.icas.org.uk.

## WHAT QUESTIONS DO YOU ASK?

Later on you will be approaching your adviser about specific problems, but at the outset you and he or she will be exploring the potential help you can be given. Begin by outlining the kind of business or service you intend to set up, how much money you have available, what you think your financial needs are going to be over the first year of operation, how many people are going to be involved as partners or shareholders and what your plans are for the future. An accountant will want to know the range of your experience in handling accounting problems and how much help you are going to need in writing up the books, and he or she will advise you on the basic records you should set up.

Remember to ask for advice on your year end/year start; this does not have to be 6 April to 5 April, and there may be sound tax reasons for choosing other dates. Your advisor may even be able to recommend the services of a part-time bookkeeper to handle the mechanics, but, as we shall show in Chapter 11, this does not absolve you from keeping a close watch on what money is coming in and going out.

It should be stressed at this point that, certainly in the case of a private limited company, the accountants you are talking to should

Accountants you talk to should be qualified professionally.

be qualified, through membership of either the Institute of Chartered Accountants or the Chartered Association of Certified Accountants. Someone who advertises his services as a bookkeeper or merely as an 'accountant' is not qualified to give professional advice in the true meaning of that term, though someone good if unqualified can do a very adequate job in preparing tax returns for something like a small freelance business.

Solicitors will also want to know the kind of business you are in and your plans for the future. But they will concentrate, obviously, on legal rather than financial aspects (so do not go on about money – they are busy people and this is only an exploratory visit). Your solicitor is interested in what structure the operation is going to have and, in the case of a partnership or limited company, whether you and your colleagues have made any tentative agreements between yourselves regarding the running of the firm and the division of profits. He or she will also want to get some idea of what kind of property you want to buy or lease and whether any planning permissions have to be sought.

## HOW MUCH ARE ADVISERS GOING TO CHARGE?

This is rather like asking how long is a piece of string. It depends on how often you have to consult your advisers, so it is no use asking them to quote a price at the outset, though if you are lucky

> Your accountant may suggest an annual retainer for basic services.

enough to have a very clear idea of what you want done – say, in the case of an accountant, a monthly or weekly supervision of your books, plus the preparation and auditing of your accounts – they may give you a rough idea of what the charges will be. Alternatively, they may suggest an annual retainer for these services and any advice directly concerned with them, plus extra charges for anything that falls outside them such as a complicated wrangle with the inspector of taxes about allowable items. When calculating the likely cost of using an accountant remember that his or her fees are tax-deductible.

An annual retainer is a less suitable way of dealing with your solicitor because your problems are likely to be less predictable and

> Check at the outset what the procedure and costs are for telephone advice.

more sporadic than those connected with accounting and book-keeping. A lot of your queries may be raised, and settled, on the telephone: the 'Can I do this?' type. Explaining that kind of problem on the telephone is usually quicker and points can be more readily clarified than by writing a letter setting out the facts of the case (though you should ask for confirmation in writing in matters where you could be legally liable in acting on the advice you have been given!). However, asking advice on the telephone can be embarrassing for both parties. You will be wondering whether your solicitor is charging you for it and either way it could inhibit you from discussing the matter fully. You should therefore check at the outset what the procedure is for telephone enquiries and how these are accounted for on your bill.

## A GUIDE – NOT A CRUTCH

For someone starting in business on their own, facing for the first time 'the loneliness of thought and the agony of decision', there is a temptation to lean on professional advisers too much. Apart from the fact that this can be very expensive, it is a bad way to run a business. Before you lift the telephone or write a letter, think. Is this

> Only get in touch with your advisors when you are genuinely stumped for an answer.

clause in a contract something you could figure out for yourself if you sat down and concentrated on reading it carefully? Would it not be better to check through the ledger yourself to find out where to put some item of expenditure that is not immediately classifi-able? Only get in touch with your advisers when you are genuinely stumped for an answer, not just because you cannot be bothered to think it out for yourself. Remember, too, that nobody can make up your mind for you on matters of policy. If you feel, for example, that you cannot work with your partner, the only thing your solici-tor can or should do for you is to tell you how to dissolve the part-nership, not whether it should be done at all.

# YOUR BANK MANAGER

Traditionally, the other person with whom you might make contact when starting up your business was your bank manager. The importance of picking a banking service of the right quality, which we have mentioned in connection with professional advice, holds true with your choice of bank. However, the first question to consider is whether you actually need face-to-face contact with a bank manager, rather than an organization that can answer your questions promptly when they arise.

> Do you actually need face-to-face contact with a bank manager?

The direct banking revolution and electronic communication have made the distance management of bank accounts a time-saving and cost-effective alternative for the small business. Possibly you will want to consider the bank that holds your personal account, or your accountant may offer to introduce you to the local branch of another high street bank. However, if you are trying to arrange a sizeable overdraft or business loan, any bank, whether it is a high street branch or a direct bank, will want to examine your track record when considering an application. Effective bank account management is discussed in greater detail in Chapter 9.

If you do decide to offer your business to your personal bank, you must inform your bank manager of your intention to set up in business, providing him or her with much the same information as you gave to your accountant.

> Keep your personal and business bank accounts separate.

You may be operating a small-scale freelance business that does not call for bank finance. It is very important, in that case, to keep your personal and business accounts separate, with separate cheque and paying-in books for each one. Mixing up private and business transactions can only lead to confusion, for you as well as your accountant. Even if you are simply, say, a one-person freelance consultancy, it is worth keeping your bank well informed about your business. Your cash flow as a freelance might well be highly erratic and unless your bank knows you and your business well it will be firing off letters or telephoning you about your unauthorized overdraft as well as making penalty charges for overruns. In today's environment of electronic banking where 'managers'' letters are written automatically when limits are exceeded, you may not avoid this kind of prompting anyway.

## INSURANCE

If you are setting up a photographic studio and an electrical fault on the first day destroys some of your equipment, you are in trouble before you have really begun. If you are a decorator and a pot of paint falling from a window sill causes injury to someone passing below you could face a suit for damages that will clean you out of the funds you have accumulated to start your business. Insurance coverage is, therefore, essential from the start for almost all kinds of business.

> Use an insurance broker to select your insurance company.

Insurance companies vary a good deal in the premiums they charge for different kinds of cover, and in the promptness with which they pay out on claims. The best plan is not to go direct to a company, even if you already transact your car or life insurance with them, but to an insurance broker. Brokers receive their income from commissions from the insurance companies they represent, but they are generally independent of individual companies and thus reasonably impartial. Here again, your accountant or solicitor can advise you of a suitable choice, which would be a firm that is big enough to have contacts in all the fields for which you need cover (and big enough to exert pressure on your behalf when it comes to making a claim), but not so big that the relatively modest amounts of commission they will earn from you initially are not worth their while taking the trouble when, for instance, it comes to reminding you about renewals. Apart from these general points you will have to consider what kinds of cover you need and this will vary somewhat with the kind of business you are in. The main kinds are:

## Types of insurance

1. Insurance of your premises.
2. Insurance of the contents of your premises.
3. Insurance of your stock.
   (The above three kinds of cover should also extend to 'consequential loss'. For instance, you may lose in a fire a list of all your customers. This list has no value in itself but the 'consequent' loss of business could be disastrous. The same is true of stock losses. If a publisher loses all their books in a fire it is not only their value that is lost, but also the consequent loss of business while they are being reprinted, by which time the demand for them may have diminished.)
4. Employer's liability is compulsory if you employ staff on the premises, even on a part-time basis.
5. Public liability in case you cause injury to a member of the public or their premises in the course of business. You will also need third-party public liability if you employ staff or work with partners.
6. Legal insurance policies, which cover you against prosecution under Acts of Parliament which relate to your business (eg those covering unfair dismissal and fair trading).
7. Insurance against losing your driving licence – important if your business depends on your being able to drive.
8. Insurance of machinery, especially mechanical failure of computers, the consequences of which can be disastrous for most kinds of business.
9. Professional indemnity insurance. If you are offering a service, such as consultancy, many clients will demand that you are covered for loss that they might incur as a result of your advice.

10. Product liability insurance. The same principle as the above applies if you are manufacturing or supplying goods. Your customers will expect you to be covered against claims from faulty products.
11. Personal accident insurance, particularly if you are in a hazardous occupation such as the fitting of TV aerials and satellite dishes on buildings.

Your broker will advise you on other items of cover you will need. You should check, for instance, that your existing policies, such as home and vehicle insurance, cover commercial use if that is what you envisage, but do not leave the whole business of insurance in his or her hands. Read your policies carefully when you get them and make sure that the small print does not exclude any essential item.

Insurance is expensive (though the premiums are allowable against tax inasmuch as they are incurred wholly in respect of your business), and you may find that in the course of time you have paid out thousands of pounds without ever making a claim. However, it is a vital precaution, because one fire or legal action against you can wipe out the work of years if you are not insured. For this reason you must check each year that items like contents insurance represent current replacement values and that your premiums are paid on the due date. Your broker should remind you about this, but if he or she overlooks it, it is you who carries the can.

> Insurance is expensive but a vital precaution.

Membership of the Federation of Small Businesses (see Appendix 2) includes automatic free legal insurance which covers legal and professional insurance of up to £1 million to protect your business against various legal actions including: HM Revenue & Customs investigations, VAT tribunals, employment disputes, Health and Safety at Work prosecutions, Consumer Protection Act prosecutions and claims against your business for personal injury. This service also includes a free legal helpline open 24 hours a day, 365 days of the year.

# OTHER ADVISERS AND SUPPLIERS

## Local Enterprise Agencies (LEAs)

There are LEAs throughout the country – a complete list is available from Business in the Community (see address in Appendix 2). LEAs are sponsored by local firms or local branches of national companies, banks, accountancy practices and various public sector bodies. Apart from underwriting the running costs, sponsors often second members of their staff to them. Sometimes these are experienced managers on the eve of retirement, but quite often they are young high-flyers on the way up, being exposed, as part of a career development plan, to a wider variety of business problems than they would get in their own offices.

The quality of advice and their general helpfulness is high – for instance, they will help you to prepare a business plan and advise you on methods of obtaining finance. LEAs also run courses on basic topics like marketing and finance. They are less able to advise on the conduct of specific types of business activity, unless it is one that a seconded member of the LEA's staff happens to know about. However, many do operate 'marriage bureaux', putting small businesses in touch with potential customers or investors. Some also maintain registers of suitable properties for small businesses.

Calling in to your Local Enterprise Agency in the early stages of setting up business increasingly ranks with visiting your bank manager as one of the vital first steps of working for yourself.

## Business Link and the Small Business Service

The Small Business Service (SBS) was set up by the Department of Trade and Industry (DTI), now the Department for Business Enterprise and Regulatory Reform (BERR), to help start-ups, and operates through regional Business Links throughout England (Business Connect in Wales and Business Shop in Scotland).

In mid-2007, the SBS was renamed the Enterprise Directive and given a new focus. SMEs can now connect Business Link direct. This is an impressive resource offering headline advice on all aspects of business start-up. Many of the topics in this book, ranging from business structure and business planning through sources of finance and start-up action planning to marketing, sales and taxation are covered. Enter your data into the website, and you will be directed to your local Business Link.

For more information on their range of services, visit www.businesslink.gov.uk.

## The Prince's Trust

Young entrepreneurs up to the age of 30 seeking help to start new ventures should consider approaching The Prince's Trust (website: www.princes-trust.org.uk). Applications for grants will almost certainly fail unless they are supported by a sound business plan.

## The Federation of Small Businesses

Representing 190,000 members through 13 regional offices and 230 branches in England and Scotland, and with press offices in Cardiff, Belfast, London and Brussels, the Federation of Small Businesses (FSB) offers a wide range of services and information on all aspects of business in the areas of regulation and business practice. Formed in 1974, the FSB fights for a better deal for small businesses and lobbies government and politicians in Westminster and Whitehall and at constituency levels through its Press and Parliamentary Offices.

Among the many benefits the FSB offers its members are:

I   legal advice, insurance and information;
I   tax information;
I   representation in VAT and PAYE (employer compliance) disputes;
I   FSB distribution and delivery service;
I   FSB business banking and credit card services;
I   independent financial planning;
I   FSB internet broadband services;
I   cost-saving telecom fixed-line and mobile services;
I   motoring solutions;
I   members-only online directory and member-only website areas.

To explore these services and the cost of membership, telephone

020 7592 8100 or fill in a membership requirement form by visiting the FSB website at www.fsb.org.uk/benefits.

## Other services and supplies

In the course of setting up your business, you will probably need other types of services: builders to maintain and, perhaps, refurbish your premises; printers to produce letterheads, advertising material, etc; surveyors and valuers to assess your property; courier services for fast delivery; and so on. You should apply the same criteria to these as to your professional advisers. The services should be reasonably priced and performed to the required standard. If the service is of a professional nature, the provider should be a member of the relevant professional body. If not, you can seek recommendations from others in business locally, from your nearest Business Link or from the local Chamber of Commerce.

### Checklist: professional advisers

_Solicitors_
1. How well do you know the firm concerned?
2. What do you know of their ability to handle the kind of transactions you have in mind?
3. Is their office convenient to the place of work you intend to establish?
4. Do they know local conditions and personalities?
5. Are they the right size to handle your business affairs over the foreseeable future?
6. Have you prepared an exhaustive list of the points on which you want legal advice at the setting-up stage?

_Accountants_
1. Have they been recommended by someone whose judgement you trust and who has actually used their services?
2. Are the partners members of one of the official accountants' bodies?
3. Is their office reasonably close by?

4. Does it create a good and organized impression?
5. Can they guarantee that a member of the firm will give you personal and reasonably prompt attention when required?
6. Have you thought out what sort of help you are going to need?
7. Have you prepared an outline of your present financial position and future needs?
8. Have you considered, in consultation with your solicitor and accountant, whether you want to set up as a sole trader, a partnership or a limited company?

*Bank manager*
1. Is your present bank likely to be the right one for you to deal with in this context?
2. Have you informed your bank manager of your intention to set up a business?
3. Have you established a separate bank account for your business?
4. Have you discussed with your bank manager the possibility of switching your account to a local branch?
5. Do you need face-to-face contact with your bank or are you content to bank online or over the telephone?

*Insurance*
1. Do you have a reliable reference on the broker you intend to use?
2. Is he or she efficient, according to the reports you receive, about reminding you when policies come up for renewal?
3. Has he or she any track record of paying promptly on claims?
4. Have you prepared a list of the aspects of your proposed business which require insurance cover?
5. Are you fully insured for replacement value and consequential loss?
6. Have you read the small print on your policies or checked them out with your solicitors?

# 7

# Making Your Case for Raising Capital

Banks make money by lending out the funds deposited with them at rates of interest which vary according to government policy. During periods of economic expansion that rate will be lower – and money easier to get – than during the 'stop' parts of the 'stop and go cycle' of the British economy. But banks, like everybody else, have to continue to trade even through less prosperous times.

You will find, therefore, that bank managers will normally be willing to discuss making money available to you, because potentially you are a source of income to them. How much that will be depends somewhat on the size of the branch you are approaching. This is an argument in favour of going to a large branch if you need a sizeable sum; on the other hand, in a smaller community, your professional adviser may well have a shrewd idea of what the bank manager's lending limits are. Increasingly, decisions on the availability of loans and overdrafts are taken according to a more rigid Head Office formula and the manager's decision-making discretion is limited. This is particularly true at the present time when the flood of funds available to small business has slowed to a trickle.

> Managers' discretion to make decisions is restricted by formula.

# EXISTING BUSINESS

Whether you can convince your bank that your business is a good risk depends on how well you have thought out your approach. To some extent the bank will go on personal impressions and on what it can gather of your previous business experience. If you have already been running your own firm for a year or two, the bank will have some hard evidence to go on in the shape of your profit and loss account, your balance sheet and how you have managed your bank account. It will look at the financial position of your firm, particularly the relationship of current assets to current liabilities and of debtors to creditors (see Chapter 13). It will want to be satisfied that you are valuing your stock realistically and will want to know how much money you (and your partners, if you have any) have put into the business from your own resources. In the case of a limited company it will want to know what is the issued share capital.

> The bank will want hard evidence on how you have managed your bank account.

If a business has been operating for several years, a bank will want to look at its historic cash flow in order to see if it is able to meet the repayments of future loans. Michael Brand in *A Guide to Sources of Finance for SMEs* (Kogan Page) describes this approach as 'driving by looking in the rear view mirror'. However, this does have the advantage over start-ups in providing hard facts for banks to base their decisions on, rather than projections of future earnings.

# NEW BUSINESS

While businesses that are able to show evidence of previous trading are advantaged, the banks do normally still lend to start-ups even though the amount tends to be less and a number of other factors will need to be taken into account. Proposals for lending to a new business will need to be fully worked out and have realistic and thorough cash-flow projections.

The bank will be looking to see whether your business satisfies three criteria:

## Bank criteria for new businesses

1. That its money is secure, and in the case of a new business it will probably ask for security to be in the shape of tangible items like fixed assets within the business, or shares and other assets belonging to the owners in their private capacity in a ratio which may be as high as 1:1.
2. That your firm is likely to have inflow of enough liquid assets to enable the bank to recall its money, if necessary.
3. That you will be able to make profitable use of the business and pay the interest without difficulty.

There is a saying that banks will only lend you money if you do not need it, and reading these requirements you may be coming to the conclusion that there is an element of truth in this. But what it really means is that there is no use going to a bank these days to bail you out of trouble. A business in trouble generally requires assistance on the management side at the very least and banks are just not in a position to provide such assistance, no matter how glowing the prospects might be if the firm could be brought back on track. So the bank manager is only going to be looking at present and quantifiable situations. He will not be very interested in often vague assets such as goodwill and will be even less interested in your hopes for the future.

> There is no use in going to a bank to bail you out of trouble.

If you have only just set up in business you may not have much more than hopes for the future to offer; the bank manager will obviously be cautious in such cases. But can these hopes be quantified and have you outlined a thorough cash-flow budget? If you are opening, say, a new restaurant, facts such as that you and your spouse are excellent cooks, have attended courses in catering and have established that there would be a demand for a good place to eat in a particular locality, are relevant. But the bank also wants further information.

## Additional bank information

■ What your start-up costs are going to be.
■ Whether you have fully worked out what your overheads and direct costs are (ie items like rent, rates, gas and electricity, equipment, staff wages and the cost of food).
■ What relation these are going to have to your charges for meals.
■ What levels of seat occupancy you need to achieve to make a profit.

This might take quite a lot of working out and you are advised to consult closely with your accountant in preparing your case for the bank. Indeed, it may be a good idea to take your accountant along with you when you are approaching the bank for financial help.

It is, however, not impossible to do this by yourself. What you need is a 'business plan' of the kind detailed in Chapter 3, and if you haven't made yours already, all the banks actually have kits

Banks actually have kits which show you how to prepare business plans.

which show you how to prepare them. As we have already noted, even if you do not need finance it is a good idea to prepare a business plan because it will focus your mind on the main issues that are likely to determine the success of your venture. The salient points for the bank manager are as follows:

■ your business experience;
■ your existing assets and liabilities;

- the product or service you are proposing to offer, the geographical market for it and how you propose to reach it;
- the likely demand for it – ie whether it is continuing and to what extent it is seasonal or susceptible to technological obsolescence;
- competition: where it is and how you propose to counter it by means of price, service, etc;
- requirements for and likely costs of premises and/or equipment;
- how much of your own money you are proposing to put in;
- the amount of finance required and what it is going to be used for;
- what security you are able to offer;
- cash-flow and profit and loss forecasts for the first 12 months.

A business plan should always be kept as clear as possible and the information should be structured in a way that enables the reader to follow it easily. Lenders and investors are looking for hard facts, and figures need to be included to back up your case. A lender may want to see projections that include the worst-case scenario as well as the best and you will need to show that you have anticipated some of the pitfalls that might occur, and that you have an idea of how you might deal with them (ie a SWOT analysis of the kind discussed in Chapter 3).

> Include the worst-case scenario as well as the best and how you might deal with pitfalls.

Above all, you must demonstrate that you have a good grasp of your business and understand the nature of the industry into which you are proposing to enter. Your advisers should be able to provide an objective view before you submit the business plan to the bank and should point out any areas where the detail is unclear.

On the basis of this information the bank manager will decide what form of help, if any, he or she is able to offer or will recommend if a superior decision-making authority is required.

## Checklist: presenting your case

1. Have you prepared a written description of your firm?
2. Have you described what skills the key people in your firm have to offer?
3. Have you identified your objectives?
4. Have you described how your product or service compares with the competition's?
5. Have you included what firm orders you have secured?
6. Have you identified what your realistic expectations, opportunities and goals are?
7. Do you have supporting evidence on orders you have obtained or are likely to obtain?
8. Have you (and your associates if any) made as full a commitment to your enterprise in terms of time and money as can reasonably be expected of you?
9. Have you previously obtained financial help for this or any other business? Have you repaid it within the period due?
10. If you have any loans outstanding on the business, how much are they for, for what purpose and how are they secured?
11. Can you produce an up-to-date balance sheet showing the present financial state of your company?
12. Do you have a detailed cash-flow projection, monthly over the first two years and quarterly thereafter, showing cash flow over the period of the loan?

# 8

# Self-Employment Alternatives to Starting a Business

Self-employment has traditionally taken the form of running a full-time business as either a limited company, partnership or sole trader as described in Chapter 4. However, recent years have witnessed the rise in forms of work that are alternatives to starting up your own business. Not only can the number of hours that you work be a question of choice, but also who you supply and the form that the working relationship takes has become more flexible. For example, the rise in outsourced and contract work has also opened up opportunities for the self-employed to work in a freelance capacity and this has become the choice of a growing number of people. At the other end of the spectrum, taking up a franchise or participating in a management buy-out can provide opportunities for self-employment of a different kind in national organizations with high turnovers. This chapter will examine the pros and cons of each of these opportunities.

## PART-TIME WORK

Part-time work has become a significant part of the UK economy. Official figures show that one-third of the workforce is employed on this basis. Indeed, in this recessionary period, part-time work may be all that is on offer to former full-time employees.

The variety of ways in which people work part time is also wide.

## Varieties of part-time work

■ 'Portfolio' part-time work – doing part-time jobs for several different employers on a regular basis.

■ Working part time for a single employer – for instance, the human resource strategy director for the employment agency Reed Executive works there only three days a week.

■ Doing a part-time job as a spare-time activity, usually to earn extra money. Sometimes this takes the form of extending the job you do for your employer into private work in your spare time – a matter we will cover in a little more detail shortly.

■ Casual work – occasionally taking on work to help out a friend or to augment one's income.

HM Revenue & Customs suspects that a significant part of the black economy, through which at least £40 billion a year is lost to the Exchequer, flourishes through casual and spare-time work. Anecdotal evidence suggests it could be much more. Many trades-people commonly express a strong preference to be paid in cash by private customers. Such payments are extremely difficult for tax inspectors to trace.

People often fail to declare their part-time income to remain eligible for unemployment benefit.

It is likely, however, that people who fail to declare their income from part-time work are more concerned to conceal their activities from the Department for Work and Pensions than from HM Revenue & Customs. It is very easy to cease to be eligible for un-employment benefit by earning income of more than the basic unemployment benefit for any given six-day period. If this source of earned income does not continue and you wish to sign on again, there can be considerable delays before you receive unemployment benefit. Therefore there is a strong temptation, if you do something that brings in a few pounds a week while you are unemployed, not to declare it.

The government recognizes the fact that income from a new business is usually less than the dole and the Business Start-Up scheme helps to bridge the gap.

## Tax advantages of part-time employment

If you are married with another source of income, not declaring your earnings from part-time work might be a very unwise move – apart from being illegal. In the first place it is usually possible to avoid paying tax on it at all because of the single person's earned income allowance, currently set at £5,435 for the 2008/09 tax year (£9,030 for those aged 65 to 74 and £9,180 for those over 75). This means that the first £5,435 of everyone's earnings is free of tax; so if you can arrange for your spouse to earn that amount of money from your source of extra income, you will not pay any tax on it – assuming he or she does not already have a job and is taxed separately. Remember, it is the profit that is taxed, not the total earnings.

> Arrange, if you can, for your spouse to earn from your source of extra income up to the amount of the current earned income allowance.

If you cannot get that figure close to £5,435 by setting off against gross earnings all the allowable expenses described in Chapter 22, then you are either doing so well as to make it worth considering converting your spare-time occupation into a full-time activity, or you should get an accountant, or you should change the accountant you have. However, you do have to prove, to the satisfaction of the tax inspector, that your spouse really is working in the business – taking messages, typing invoices, bookkeeping, or whatever. Holding the fort by looking after the kids and doing the shopping so that you can get on with it does not count.

All this is reinforced by the fact that even if you do not pay tax on them, there are definite advantages in earnings that are taxed under Schedule D. You will be able to claim allowances on services (gas, electricity and water) for the use of part of your house, plus a proportion of your bill for the telephone, stamps and stationery – whatever, in fact, can be shown to be reasonably related to the nature of the activity you are carrying on, including motoring expenses. Small is beautiful, provided you declare it.

## Planning and other permissions; insurance

### Planning consent

Strictly speaking, if you carry on a business from home you have to apply for planning permission. In practice, very few people bother when it comes to part-time work, though if what you are intending to do creates a noise, a nuisance or a smell (and some crafts and home repair activities do some or all of these things even when carried on in quite a small way) you should inform the local authority of your intentions. Complaints from neighbours not only cause embarrassment but can also result in your being required to find proper premises, the cost of which may invalidate your whole idea. Applying for planning permission will highlight such potential problems, and forewarned is forearmed. By the same token, if planning permission has been granted you will be able to face most complaints with equanimity. On the other hand, the local planning officer may tell you that it is unnecessary to apply.

### Health and safety regulations

If you are doing anything with food – making pâtés for your local delicatessen, for instance – you should inform the environmental health inspector. Here again, very few people bother and, in fact, the health officials are more concerned with commercial kitchens than domestic ones, which are generally cleaner; on the other hand, you could be liable for prosecution if it turns out, for instance, that the cause of someone being made ill by your pâté was a breach of the health regulations.

### Insurance

One important precaution you should not neglect if you are planning to work from home, whatever that work is, is to tell your insurance company. This is because your normal house and contents policy covers domestic use only and if you change the circumstances without telling the insurers they could fail to pay you in the event of a claim – and would probably do so if the loss was caused by the undeclared activity. Additional insurance cover will not normally cost you much, which is often more than could be said for any loss that occurs.

## Assessing the market

From the point of view of anyone still in employment contemplating full-time self-employment, the principal advantage of part-time work is not really that it is a source of extra income, however valuable that may be, but that it serves as a trial run for the real thing. The most important thing is to assess whether there is a market for the goods or services you are proposing to offer, at a price that will bring you a worthwhile profit. Working part-time at something will give you an idea of whether the demand and the competition will enable you to do that.

> Extra part-time working while in employment will help you test the market.

For instance, if working 12 hours extra a week, evenings and weekends produces a gross £125 a week – £6,000 a year, allowing for four weeks' holiday – and your present income is, say, £22,000, there is a marginal case for considering full-time self-employment. By working 48 hours a week you could, on that evidence, gross about £24,000 in a 48-week year provided that you are able to increase your income pro rata to the number of hours worked.

Of course, it would depend on what your costs were, but some of the fixed ones – tools or your personal computer (PC), for instance – would not change if you expanded your activities. If there was evidence of a very strong demand, you might even consider raising your prices, especially if the experience you have gained about the market indicates that you are appreciably cheaper than the competition. Alternatively, you might discover that by making one or two modifications you could either charge more than the competition or create a stronger demand for your original concept. It is much easier to make these adaptations to market conditions while still operating at a modest level and with a main income from another source. Take into account also that any short-fall in gross income between full-time self-employment and employment may be more than offset by the tax-free 'salary' that you can pay your spouse and the tax allowable expenses that you may charge against gross income.

In order to weigh up the opportunity, carry out your own break-even analysis, as described in Chapter 3.

## Objectives

Whether the person in a £22,000-a-year secure job throws his or her hand in for a potential £24,000-worth of insecurity depends not only on financial factors but also on personal objectives. Here again, working part-time before making the commitment to full-time self-employment will help you to shape your thinking about what those objectives are and what they are worth to you. If independence is the overriding factor, you might feel that even a size-able financial sacrifice is worth making. On the other hand, if money is the main objective and you are secure in your main job, then clearly, in the instance we have given you, you are much better off earning an extra £6,000 a year from your part-time job, plus £22,000 a year from your main one, than giving up the latter alto-gether if you are prepared to work the longer hours – unless you could see a way of doing much better on your own.

Another uncertainty that could be tested is whether you can work with an intended partner. Some very successful businesses are run by people who have little in common except a respect for each other's abilities, but it is usually difficult to test your compat-ibility unless you have actually worked closely with someone. Trying out a partnership arrangement on a part-time basis is a good way of doing this.

## Assessing yourself

There is also the question of assessing your own suitability, which we have already discussed, but which you should review again before taking the self-employment plunge. There is a big gap between pipe dreams of independence and the reality, even when it comes to working full-time at something you have previously enjoyed doing as a hobby.

Apart from the fact that what is fun as a hobby can sometimes be quite another proposition when undertaken hour after hour and day after day, there is often a huge difference between amateur and professional standards. For instance, it may take you all day to turn out a widget – that mythical, all-purpose British unit of manufacture – or erect a television aerial and satellite dish, whereas a professional can do it in a couple of hours. That is fine when you are doing it part time more or less for fun, but fatal if you are trying to earn a living, unless you are confident you can get to professional standards fairly quickly.

> Can you get to professional standards quickly? How good are you at working very long hours?

Whether you can actually do so usually depends on how good you are at working for very long hours, initially for not much money, and spending a great deal of your 'spare time' on administration: keeping records, writing letters and preparing quotes. You will not know your capacities in this respect until you try, but working part time will give you an inkling.

> Workaholism is a great source of family friction.

It will also give you some indication of your family's attitudes to your work. If you are working part time on top of a full-time job, you are probably reasonably close to putting in the sort of hours that are needed to make a success of self-employment at least for an initial – and usually prolonged – period of time. In other words, your family will not see a great deal of you unless they are able and willing to pitch in as well. They may view this prospect with equanimity; on the other hand, workaholism, like alcoholism, can be a great source of family friction. When working part-time, it is quite easy to cut down the hours you are putting in, or even to stop altogether. If your living depends on it, the case is completely different.

## Financial commitment

One of the advantages of part-time work is that you are keeping your overheads, or fixed costs, low. You can work from home instead of renting premises or offices. You can hire equipment instead of buying it. You may even be able to use facilities available at your place of work – photocopying, for instance – though to what extent that is a wise move depends on the attitude of your employer. Some take it as a sign of initiative, provided that it does not interfere with your regular job. Others hate it, in which case you will have to be very careful how you go about it, and at least account for everything you use. The point is, though, that for part-time work you will not have to 'tool up' expensively and, indeed, you should avoid irreversible financial commitments as much as possible. Do not, for instance, rent a van until you are sure you are going to get profitable use out of it, or unless you want one anyway. Do not, to take another case, buy a knitting machine – hire it and see whether you really can make knitting pay.

> With part-time work, never buy anything unless you have to and have a need for it.

The principle can be extended to any given activity. You should never buy anything unless you have to and until you have established an ongoing need for it. This is so with full-time activities, and it is even more the case with part-time work because, by definition, the number of hours you have in which to amortize the cost – to make a profit and get your money back – are far fewer.

## Opportunities

### Extension of full-time employment

In the previous section we referred to the situation where someone is carrying on into evenings and weekends private work similar to that normally done for an employer in the daytime: typical examples might be repair and building work, some forms of design, and teaching extended into exam coaching. The great advantage of this type of work is that it can give you a direct access to the market.

> Extra part-time work for your employer gives you access to the market.

Everybody who walks through the door at your place of employment is a potential private customer, whereas in other forms of part-time work, finding the market is an important but difficult part of the total concept. Furthermore, private, part-time clients can later be turned into sources of work on a larger scale, either directly or as leads to other work. Even suppliers can be useful people to get to know, both in terms of establishing your credibility when it comes to asking for credit and in the matter of sorting out good and reliable suppliers from the many other varieties.

The principal risk in this type of work is that it can lead to conflicts of interests. The temptation to steer work your way rather than towards your employer can be very strong. It need not be anything as blatant as buttonholing your employer's customers at the door. There are subtler ways of bending the rules. The best way to avoid such temptations is to develop your own clients and contacts as soon as possible.

## Turning a hobby into a source of income

This is usually the most satisfying form of part-time work because people generally perform best at what they most enjoy doing. Furthermore, many people, especially the over-30s, find that they have gone or been pushed into careers that do not reflect their real interests or skills, or that they have simply developed new ones that they find more satisfying than what they do for a living. Practising crafts of various kinds is a case in point.

The trap here is the one that we have referred to earlier – that there is a world of difference between doing something for fun and working at it full-time. Professional craftspeople have years of experience which enable them to turn out work quickly and economically. They also know the market: who buys what, at which price; what sells and what does not. In the case of photography, to take another instance, the good amateur turned

> Paid part-time work at your hobby may be more satisfying than what you do for a living.

professional is competing in a field where contacts are all-important and where high standards of work depend not only on individual skill, but also on having the latest equipment.

## Learning a new skill

Sometimes people learn a new skill, perhaps at an evening class, which is capable of being turned to commercial use – particularly these days when the range of services available from shops and manufacturers has become increasingly scarce and expensive. Popular examples are picture framing and upholstery.

> Non-manual skills can be turned to good account too.

There are also non-manual skills which can be turned to good account, such as selling; quite a number of people are engaged in party plan or catalogue selling. The problem there, however, is that it is difficult to go into a higher, full-time gear to make a living from that type of work, because commissions are fixed percentages and, in the case of catalogue selling, quite small ones.

## Reviving an unused skill

This is also very popular, especially with women thinking of returning to work. The most frequently cited example is word processing and other PC tasks, which can be performed just as well in the home as at a place of work. As it happens, this one neatly illustrates the importance of observing the laws of supply and demand in choosing even a part-time source of income. Because there are many women available for such work, the rates are not particularly good. The only way you can lift yourself into a higher bracket is by identifying a service which few other homeworkers in IT services offer and for which there is also a demand: in a university town, for instance, there might be a call for someone who can

> The rates paid for part-time homework observe the laws of supply and demand.

process theses quickly and accurately or carry out online record keeping and data processing. An exporter, to take another example, might have a demand for someone who can process quotations, orders, shipping documents and customer correspondence accurately in another language.

The same supply-and-demand principle also applies to translating. There are many graduates around who can translate from one of the main European languages into English, but rather fewer who can do the more difficult, reverse kind of translation: from English into idiomatic French, German or Spanish. Even rarer, and therefore more marketable, is fluency in another language *plus* a qualification in a specialist subject such as law or science.

# USING AN EXISTING ASSET AS A SOURCE OF INCOME: ACCOMMODATION

By far the biggest asset that most people own is their house. When there is a need for more money, or as members of the family grow up or move away, that asset can be a source of income: rooms can be let, the house can be subdivided into flats or even – ultimately – the whole place can be turned into a guest house. The advantage of these courses of action is that little skill or training is required to turn them into money-making activities. The disadvantage is that they are full of legal pitfalls which deter a great many people. The common option is to circumvent the law by moving into a cash only, black economy relationship with tenants, but by that token you also lose much legal protection that would be available if there was a dispute. By getting a tenancy agreement drawn up you can protect yourself to a large degree, especially if you are also the kind of student of human nature who can spot a potential troublemaker before he or she crosses your threshold.

Letting out part of your house requires little skill or training, but is full of legal pitfalls.

## Letting rooms

In recent years, and especially since the 1980 Housing Act, there have been many horror stories about the difficulty of getting rid of unwanted tenants, even, on occasion, when they have been well behind with the rent. For this reason it is very unwise to let rooms without having an agreement drawn up by a solicitor; even the Citizens' Advice Bureau, staffed, in general, by people whose natural sympathies lie with the tenant, recommend this. It is usually unwise, incidentally, to have a room-letting agreement which runs much longer than on a month-to-month basis because, except in extreme circumstances, the courts are likely to take the view that an agreement will have to run its full course before being terminated.

> It is unwise to have a room-letting agreement on more than a month-to-month basis.

The other piece of legislation to beware of is the Rent Act of 1977, and subsequent updates, which gives the tenant the right to go to a tribunal and ask for a 'reasonable' rent to be applied if he or she thinks you are asking too much. A register of reasonable rents is kept at your local authority's Rent Assessment Panel office, if you want to check what these are, but you will often find that these do not allow for subtle shades of amenity value – the social difference between nearby streets, for instance.

> The best way to get good tenants in is to ask for written references from previous landlords.

The best way to get good tenants is to select them – not by race or sex, which is illegal – but by asking for written references from their previous landlord.

If you let a room or part of your house and you have a mortgage, you should contact the mortgage lender to make sure you are not breaching your contract with them. Most lenders will not have a problem if your letting income falls within the 'rent a room' scheme. Under this scheme, you may be able to claim tax relief up to £5,435 against the income from your tenant.

# FREELANCING

There are obviously overlaps between working part time and working as a freelance. A person contributing regular articles to journals and newspapers could be doing so part time and still be described as a freelance. In general, though, a freelance is regarded as someone who is self-employed full time, providing a service to a range of different principals as the demand occurs, or as he or she can persuade them to buy the service that is being offered.

Some occupations have a very high freelance content because of the unpredictability of the flow of work. The prime example is the world of films and television. Over a third of the members of BECTU (Broadcasting, Entertainment, Cinematograph and Theatre Union), the principal trade union in this sphere, are free-lancers, employed by a variety of different companies for anything from a day to six months, according to the duration of a particular project. Performing artists, too, tend almost exclusively to be free-lancers, even though they may have spells when they are attached to a particular orchestra or a repertory company.

> In the media and parts of industry the tendency to put work out to freelancers has grown rapidly.

In the media and even in certain parts of industry, the tendency to put work out to freelancers and other suppliers of ad hoc labour has grown rapidly. When trading conditions are uncertain, employers are reluctant to commit themselves to taking on people full time. It makes more sense to bring them in as and when they are needed or to commission them – even to the point of subcontracting whole jobs to them. In addition, the effect of an increasing number of additions to employment law (see Chapter 21) have made the employment of staff by small businesses, as an alternative to part-time workers, unattractive.

There are also many tasks in many firms which need to be done but where the in-house demand is neither large nor constant enough to justify the employment of a full-time member of staff. It is people in such occupations, which can range from manual jobs like that of the firm's carpenter to services like public relations, who may find themselves at risk when times get hard. Yet, operating as freelancers for their own firm, plus other clients, they often have a highly profitable new lease of working life.

## How freelancers find work

The circumstances just described bring out a number of points about freelance work. It is often very difficult, for instance, simply to decide to 'go freelance', as many redundant executives have found to their cost when they wanted to set up as consultants. You need to have contacts, reliable sources of work and a known track record in your chosen area. Many freelancers report, in fact, that their first client was their previous employer or someone whom they got to know through their former workplace.

> The first client of many freelancers was their previous employer.

Even so, freelance work is patchy and unpredictable. The elements of self-marketing and constant self-motivation are vital. Freelance management consultants, for instance, reckon to spend at least 40 per cent of their time hunting for work: identifying opportunities from reports in the business, trade or professional press, and following them up with letters, phone calls or proposals. The same pattern can be seen in other freelance occupations: photographers and entertainers check in with their agents; writers prepare material 'on spec' for book and magazine publishers. It is a fairly insecure life until you get established and clients start ringing you, rather than the other way round. Indeed, many freelancers are of the opinion that to make a success of it, you need at least one reliable source of regular work – someone who brings you in for one day a week, for instance.

For aspiring novelists life has become tougher. Most publishers now require complete manuscripts in a prescribed format rather than one or two chapters and a synopsis. With high marketing costs publishers are also disinclined to take on older new authors where future 'mileage' is limited.

## Characteristics of freelance work

The reason why a lot of practising freelancers recommend getting this kind of underpinning is not only financial. There are also psychological factors involved, especially for those who have previously worked alongside others. Freelancing is a lonely way to earn a living. With some kinds of job – writing for instance – you can spend weeks on end without seeing anyone.

It is also unpredictable. There can be long periods, particularly when you first start, when little or no work comes in and your bank balance sinks as low as your spirits. As a self-employed person, you cannot claim unemployment benefit either, even though no work is coming through. On the other hand, you still have to pay your National Insurance stamp.

> Full-time freelancers experience a continuing cycle of 'feast and famine' in their workloads.

Periods of inactivity may be broken up by spells when the workload is almost too much. Very few freelancers ever turn work away, though. Once you lose a potential customer – even though you may not need the business at that juncture – they will be very difficult to get back when circumstances change. If, however, you can't do the job because it coincides with something else, it is essential to say so rather than to make promises that cannot be kept. This applies to delivery dates as well. Full-time freelancers tend to experience a continuing cycle of 'feast or famine' in their workloads.

## Costing and pricing

Broadly, the rules set out in Chapter 15 apply, but there are additional factors to consider. As we have said, you often have to spend a considerable amount of time just looking for work; it varies, obviously, according to your status and occupation. On the other hand, whether or not you can reflect this fact in full in your scale of charges depends on our old friends – supply and demand. As against that, you have the advantage, in the case of many types of freelance work, that you are working from home. Usually your equipment costs are low too, though that would not be true of photography.

Likewise, the client, in engaging you, should consider that it is generally reckoned that the cost of having a person on the staff full time is twice their annual salary, taking into account NI contributions, holidays, pensions and so forth.

## Income tax and freelance work

Freelancers are normally taxed under Schedule D. However, as we will point out at the end of Chapter 22, HM Revenue & Customs is likely to challenge Schedule D status where most of your work is done for one particular employer, as that in effect constitutes a master-and-servant relationship. This is a particular danger when people work through an agency and are paid by the agency, not by the client.

> There is an income tax danger in being paid by the agency, not the client.

## FRANCHISING

The risky nature of freelancing might not be suitable for everyone. However, another form of self-employment that is regarded as providing reasonable security is running a franchise. The best-known UK franchises are Body Shop and McDonald's, though in fact quite a number of familiar high street shops, restaurant chains and many kinds of home and business services are operated as franchises. This means that the person operating the franchise – the franchisee – has bought from the franchisor the right to trade under an established name, rather than establishing his or her credentials from scratch.

> The person operating the franchise has bought from the franchisor the right to trade under an established name.

That in itself can be a great advantage, but taking up a franchise goes further than that. The franchisee is buying a working business blueprint that has previously been tried, tested and de-bugged by the franchise owner – the franchisor – and by other franchisees. With it is included training, start-up support, an operating manual and a helpdesk for day-to-day problems, at least in the early stages. He or she also buys the exclusive right to operate that franchise in a given territory.

> 'If you follow the format, you cannot fail because it has been tested and found to work.'

The format for operating the business is laid down very precisely, even to the stationery headings, the uniform you wear when on duty, the layout of your premises and how much you charge your customer for goods or services. The idea is that if you follow the format, you cannot fail because it has been tested and found to work. If you put in the hours, you will generate a predicted level of turnover and predictable net profit margins. These will enable you to recoup your initial investment – the start-up costs and the upfront fee you pay for the right to operate the franchise and to be trained in running it as a business – within two to three years.

The net margin is calculated to allow not only the usual overheads, but also a royalty to the franchisor. That varies between 5 and 10 per cent, depending on whether or not the franchisee involved is buying goods from the franchisor on which the franchisor makes a profit as a supplier or wholesaler.

It sounds like a wonderful idea. Where's the catch? First of all let us say that franchising has proved itself to be a very good way of starting a business of your own. Failure rates are low and because of this the banks have been more ready to lend money to franchisees than for many other forms of small business, especially in the start-up phase. In fact the franchising department of your bank is the best place to start investigating a franchise proposition, because there are quite a number of snags to watch out for.

> The banks have been more ready to lend to franchisees than many other forms of small business.

## Choosing a franchise

One unscrupulous operator confessed to me in an expansive post-lunch mood 'There's two born every minute – in case one of them dies.' There is very little legislation in the franchising field and there have been plenty of instances where franchisees have been induced into parting with their upfront fee and have seen very little in return for their money.

The bank may not say outright that this or that franchise proposition should not be touched with a bargepole, but if several banks refuse to lend you money on it, don't go further. Either you are wrong for the business or the business is wrong for you. Or it is just plain wrong, full stop, probably because the pilot stage when the format is tested has not been carried out properly, or not at all, or because the upfront fee and/or royalties are regarded as too high or because the master franchise is simply known to be badly run.

> If several banks refuse to lend money on a franchise don't go further.

There are also businesses that call themselves franchises but are really variants of pyramid selling, where you get paid for recruiting other members to a chain of people, each one selling stuff, often of very little intrinsic value, to the next link down. Strictly speaking, this form of trading is illegal, but there are ways around it which sail very close to the borders of the law without actually breaking it.

> There are franchise businesses that are really variants of pyramid selling.

Even if you don't actually need to borrow money, a check with the bank is worth making. It will cost you nothing and it could save you a great deal of money. Indeed, if the franchisor tries to pressurize you out of taking sensible precautions, walk away immediately.

In addition to the bank check, you should always ask to talk to existing franchisees, even of a reputable franchise, chosen by you

Always talk to existing franchisees chosen by you at random.

at random, not the ones nominated by the franchisor. Things can change. Ask whether they are achieving the income levels and profit margins forecast and how many hours a week it takes to do that; whether, given the chance, they would make the decision to take up that franchise again; and if there is anything they would like to change. That could be a negotiating point if and when you come to signing a contract.

A final check is to ask whether the franchisor is a member of the British Franchise Association (BFA). Not all of them are, but many of the good ones have membership. The BFA is a franchisor body but it lays down standards and conditions which also protect franchisees.

One of the problems in franchising is that not all good ideas work well everywhere. That is certainly true of franchises that have been a great success in other countries, notably the United States, but it is also true within the United Kingdom. In the 1980s there was a household-name health food franchise which did extremely well in the south-east of England, but turned out to be a terrible flop in the meat and two veg belt north of the Wash. A tremendous amount depends on the area, even within the same town.

An 'exclusive' territory does not mean all that much.

Franchisors make great play with the notion of an 'exclusive territory' but it doesn't mean all that much. There is nothing to stop a franchisee from a different franchisor opening up a similar business in your exclusive territory, or indeed a similar, non-franchised business doing this. For example, think how many fast-print shops and fast-food outlets there are around.

At the same time, there is no doubt that those who get into a good franchise at an early stage, before all the plum territories are assigned, can make a lot of money. Some of the early Body Shop franchisees are now very wealthy. It shows that franchising, although it follows a format, still calls for the exercise of some commercial judgement.

The average length of a franchise agreement is 7 to 10 years, but these days very few products or services hold their competitive advantage for as long as that. You need to be sure that the franchisor is sufficiently resourceful to keep coming up with new ideas and sufficiently resourced to develop them. In the recession of the 1990s it was noticed that some franchisees got into difficulties because the franchisors were themselves under pressure. They could not give the franchisees enough support.

Not everyone is temperamentally suited to being a franchisee. Although to a large extent it is your own business, you are still tied to the franchisor in regard to what you can and cannot do – for instance, you may be limited as to the range of services you can offer or the goods you stock. That condition may become very irksome if you think you see business opportunities that your contract prevents you from exploiting.

> Not everyone is temperamentally suited to being a franchisee.

The franchise agreement is a long and complicated document which sets out what your obligations are to the franchisor, and vice versa, during the term of the contract. Only sign it after making sure that you understand it fully and that it neither omits nor adds anything different from that which you agreed or assumed verbally. In fact, you should also show it to a lawyer who knows about franchising. That may not necessarily be your usual lawyer. If not confident of his or her knowledge in this field ask him or her, or the bank, to recommend someone who is.

> Before signing show your agreement to a lawyer who knows about franchising.

## Franchise selection

There are several agencies that can help you to identify potential franchises and put you in touch with the franchisors. They are all accessible online and provide a useful service.

You could consult the UK Franchise Directory at www. theukfranchisedirectory.org where you can enter your basic requirements in order to survey the range of opportunities that may suit you. For example, you could select the general field of business-to-business services or a specific trade such as hairdressing, specify that you want to work from home and that you are looking for a franchise where the investment is less than £10,000. Another similar service is Select Your Franchise on www.selectyourfranchise.com, where some franchises are on offer at an investment cost of less than £500 up to £100,000 or more; this website offers a free matching service.

> As a first step, visit the British Franchise Association website.

However, your first port of call should probably be The British Franchise Association at www.bfa.org, where you will find comprehensive information about franchising, what to look for in contractual arrangements and best practice as well the range of alternative product and service franchises that are available.

## MANAGEMENT BUY-OUTS

Management buy-outs (MBOs) are at the more expensive end of the spectrum of self-employment opportunities discussed in this book, but they have become more common and, at the lower end of the cost range, are comparable to setting-up costs of franchises in the medium to upper price field: £100,000 to £250,000.

> At the lower end of the cost range MBOs are comparable to setting-up costs of upper price field franchises.

The opportunity for a buy-out occurs when the owners of a business decide to dispose of all or a part of it. That may give the existing management the chance to become bidders for it themselves. Indeed, there have been cases where the entire workforce became bidders, with the existing management becoming their spearhead. A notable example some years ago was the management buy-out of the National Freight Corporation (NFC), which received a great deal of publicity when, on a subsequent flotation, large capital gains were made by those members of the workforce who had participated in the buy-out.

> More commonly, buy-out opportunities occur because the owners have specific needs.

The NFC buy-out was a large one which occurred in consequence of a privatization measure. More commonly, buy-out opportunities occur because the owners:

■ want to sell out to raise cash;
■ decide that the business is not a core activity;
■ feel the business is not sufficiently profitable;
■ feel the business needs investment which they are unable or unwilling to make.
■ see an MBO as the only alternative to administration.

In recent years, finance for buy-outs that looked as though they would stand a chance was readily available from sources of venture capital, though the bidders were expected to shoulder a

> As with other kinds of business loan, finance providers expect a detailed business plan.

considerable part of the risk. As with other kinds of business loan, the providers of finance expect to see a very detailed business plan. Among the points to be covered are:

- descriptions of the assets and liabilities of the company;
- the nature and value of work in progress;
- detailed cash-flow projections;
- the background and qualifications of the buy-out team, which must include a good finance director.

However, there is another equally important set of conditions that have to be fulfilled. By law the owners have to satisfy their shareholders that the buy-out represents the best deal for them, though that need not necessarily mean that they are the ones that have come up with the best offer financially. But if that is not the case, they do have to demonstrate that a sale to them is the best solution, either because it is the quickest or because if the buy-out participants left the company, its saleability would be diminished. The latter is often particularly true of service-based companies with few tangible assets.

## Pre-packs

A recent addition to the range of buy-out scenarios relates to companies where insolvency is imminent and the directors decide to put the company into voluntary administration or receivership. It is now legal for directors to negotiate a deal with the Receiver, even before his or her appointment, to buy back some of the assets from the company after he or she has been appointed.

Receivers/administrators are empowered to enter into such an agreement, known as a 'pre-pack', where they consider it to be in the best interests of creditors and shareholders. This may very well be the case where the value of an asset is likely to be diminished heavily or wiped out as soon as the administration/receivership is announced, eg a conference management company where attendances are part pre-paid and the conference would be cancelled.

Buy-out negotiations are complex and can be fairly protracted: four to six months is about the minimum. Good (and therefore

Buy-out negotiations can take at least four to six months.

expensive) legal and financial advice is essential and should be costed into the total financial requirements.

One question, though, is whether the owners should be approached with an offer or be asked to name a price. Some financial institutions like to have a clear idea from the start about how much money they are being asked to put up – in other words, they prefer the owners to name a price. On the other hand, a cash bid can sometimes surprise the owners into parting with the business for a modest price. This is where commercial judgement about how to structure the bid is called for.

Pricing an offer also requires a lot of preparation in assessing the value of what the buy-out team is acquiring. That should be clearly specified in the bid document; otherwise you may find that the owners are excluding a particularly promising development or valuable asset. However, the advice given by the experts is that having fixed a maximum price for the buy-out related to a sum that will enable you to repay any loans and their interest charges (and also make a living) within a reasonable period of time, you should not go beyond that figure. Plainly the choice of advisers is critical.

## Checklist: alternative self-employment opportunities

*Part-time work*

1. Have you informed your local authority if your employment creates a noise, nuisance or a smell and you intend to use your home for part-time work?

2 If you are involved in preparing food, have you informed the environmental health inspector?

3. If you are planning to work from home, have you informed your insurance company to arrange additional cover?

4. Have you assessed whether there is a market for your goods or services at a price that will bring you a worthwhile profit?

5. Have you identified your objective for working part-time, and if it is to reduce the hours worked, is the financial sacrifice worth making?

6. Are you able to fulfil the administrative demands as well as deliver your core product/service?
7. Can you hire equipment instead of buying it?
8. If you are developing a hobby as part-time work, are you able to upgrade your work, to meet professional standards and to produce it quickly and economically?

### Freelancing

1. Have you a good source of contacts? Could your current employer provide you with freelance work?
2. Are you self-motivated and have you identified further areas and media where you can investigate future freelance opportunities?
3. Are you able to work by yourself?
4. Have you identified the going rate for your work and, after taking into account periods without work, are you able to survive financially?

### Franchising

1. Have you explored the range of franchises on offer on the internet?
2. Have you approached your bank to see whether they would support your franchise application?
3. Have you talked to other franchisees to see their financial outlook and hours of work?
4. Have you contacted the British Franchise Association for guidance and advice?
5. Does your location suit the franchise product?
6. Is the franchisor well enough established to support you through economic downturns?
7. Are you prepared to follow a business structure prepared by someone else?
8. Have you asked your bank to recommend a lawyer who specializes in franchising?

### Management buy-outs

1. Have you prepared a business plan including the assets and liability of the company, the nature and value of the work in progress, forward sales and profits forecasts,

detailed cash-flow projections and the qualifications and skills of the buy-out team?

2. Have you checked the bid document to see that all important assets are included?

# Part Two

# Preparation

# 9

# Making the Most of Your Bank Accounts

The following may be stated as golden rules from the point of view of the smaller business: never borrow more than you have to; never buy until you need to. And when you need to, consider whether hire purchase or even leasing might not make more sense for you than committing cash to an outright purchase. There have been periods of recent history, such as the last few years, when the value of assets, particularly property, increased much faster than the value of the money borrowed to acquire them, but in a period when interest rates rise sharply borrowing can be so costly as to swallow up the entire profits of a business that is over-reliant on borrowed money. Conversely, when values are depreciating rapidly, the purchase of assets may be unattractive, however low interest rates may fall.

> Never buy more than you have to; never buy until you need to.

## EFFECTIVE CASH MANAGEMENT

A surprising amount of borrowing can be avoided by effective cash management. The following are the key elements of revenue and expenditure that can be managed to your advantage.

## Giving credit

Decide a credit policy. It is your choice whether to provide credit to any customer or not; however much your business needs new customers or clients, you will inevitably damage your cash flow – even your own creditworthiness – by accepting orders on credit from known late payers and companies of doubtful solvency.

> Your credit terms should reflect those of your main suppliers, but can be as much of the deal as the price.

Your credit policy should reflect the terms that you receive from your own main suppliers. By giving 30 days' credit when your suppliers give you only 15 days is certain to give you cash-flow problems. On the other hand, you have to take into account the credit terms that your competitors offer. Credit terms can be as much of the deal as the price.

Before giving credit, ask each new customer to complete a credit application and, if in any doubt, check creditworthiness by:

▪ paying a credit reference agency for an online credit rating;
▪ taking up credit references from trade suppliers;
▪ writing to the Registry of County Court Judgments at 173–175 Cleveland Street, London WIP 5PE (tel: 020 7380 0133) for details of all County Court Judgments (CCJs) registered in the last six years (the service currently costs £4.50, payable in advance, for each name at a specified address);
▪ asking for a bank reference, but be aware that these are notoriously vague and may be slow to arrive.

You might want to investigate the availability of bad debt insurance. Provided that you maintain a strict policy on opening credit accounts, there are a number of specialist insurance brokers who will provide this cover.

## Credit control

In any case, when advances or progress payments are not negotiable, always agree your credit terms at the order stage, including:

I the credit period allowed (eg 30 days from the date of invoice);
I details of any discounts or rebates you offer (eg for prompt payment or bulk purchases);
I whether your prices exclude carriage charges ('ex works');
I whether you charge interest on overdue accounts – and, if so, how much;
I a 'retention of title' clause (specifying that the goods remain your property until paid for) where appropriate.

Be sure to have these terms printed on the back of your invoices and other relevant business documents – such as credit application forms. Some customers will have standard terms of purchase that they print on the back of their orders. By law, the last terms issued in writing are the ones that apply; so you should acknowledge every piece of correspondence relating to an order and restate your terms.

> By law, the last terms issued in writing are the ones that apply.

Since November 2000 small businesses have benefited from The Late Payment Act giving them a legal right to claim interest from late-paying customers in both large and small companies at 8 per cent above the Bank of England base rate. The Act specifies a default period of 30 days where no credit period has been stated in the supplier's terms of business. If you have specified 'no credit' in the original contract, interest starts to accumulate as soon as the goods have been delivered or the service has been carried out. Full details of the Act can be found online at www.hmso.gov.uk.

## Managing debtors: progress payments

In the case of work done on contract – say, a design or consultancy job involving sizeable sums of money over a longer period of time such as three or four months – try to persuade your customer to make an advance and/or progress payments. After all, you are going to be involved in considerable expenditure of time, at least, before the final sum becomes due. Whether you can make such an approach depends, of course, on how well you know the customer and whether you think he or she needs your services as much as or

> Where work is done on extended contract, persuade your customer to make an advance and/or progress payments.

more than you need the work. In the case of assignments that run over an extended period, subject to periodic review, where the final amount of work or time charged is uncertain, your client will probably accept the case for a regular monthly or quarterly retainer to be set against the final bill.

## Facilitating prompt payment

There are a number of steps you can take to make sure that your customers/clients have no cause to delay payment and to position your invoices and statements for prompt attention:

▌ Establish how each customer pays invoices (eg payment only if there is an order number or if the invoice is passed to the accounts department by the date of each monthly cheque run).
▌ Get the order details right in written form (eg for a consultancy service, the order should specify the work to be undertaken, perhaps by referring to an agreement).
▌ Obtain proof of delivery for goods.
▌ Ensure the customer/client is satisfied. Sort out any problems immediately.
▌ Ensure that your invoices are easy to understand, with the correct order references and the agreed payment date; provide details of your address, VAT number and full bank details.
▌ Send your invoice out to the right person on the day the goods are sent or the service performed.
▌ Send statements out every month, as early as you can.
▌ Provide your bank account details on invoices and statements for direct electronic payment
▌ Start chasing for payment by telephone as soon as the account becomes overdue.

> Start chasing for payment as soon as an account is overdue.

■ Use stop lists, where appropriate, for customers to whom you do not wish to give more credit, and make sure that your staff are aware of it. Inform customers/clients that they are 'on stop' and do not supply goods or services until they have brought their account up to date.

In order to maintain an overview of your debtor situation, it is wise to maintain a debtor ageing schedule, which charts by customer the amounts owing by days outstanding under column headings, typically 'less than 30 days', '31 to 60 days', '61 to 90 days', 'more than 90 days'. Some suppliers present their monthly customer statements including this information. Amounts outstanding more than 90 days are generally considered to be 'bad or

> It is wise to maintain a debtor ageing schedule.

doubtful debts'. Most business accounting software packages, such as those offered by Sage, provide for debtor ageing analysis. Above all, if you have delegated the management of debtors to someone else in your firm, be sure that you have a clear debtor policy and that any deviation from it receives your approval.

## Managing your creditors

It is not dishonest to take the maximum period of payment allowed by your suppliers within the parameters of your agreement with them and late payment legislation. Once you have established yourself as a reliable account your suppliers may give you considerable leeway before they start pressing you for payment even on an overdue sum. Nor is it dishonest to take note that some suppliers press for payment quickly whereas others are more lax, and to pay the former first.

> Take the maximum period of payment that your suppliers allow.

In order to smooth out the demands on your cash flow, it may make sense to spread payments to certain core creditors (notably your telephone services and utilities providers who bill you quarterly) into regular monthly payments, normally by direct debit against your current account. However, be careful to ensure that the total of the direct debits you set up and their timing is covered amply by regular assured revenue. Direct debits returned unpaid will seriously damage your credit health.

## Managing your VAT payments and receipts

Assuming that you have registered your business for VAT and that your VAT quarter is January to March, you have to complete your VAT return for that quarter and submit payment of the VAT you have billed to your customers minus the VAT you have been billed by your suppliers by the end of April. Therefore, if you can send out a lot of invoices to customers on 1 January and collect the money quickly, you will have the benefit of your VAT, either in your current account or in a special deposit account, for nearly four months. Equally, if you are planning to buy a large piece of equipment on which there are many hundreds of pounds in VAT for you to claim back, juggling with the precise date on which you make the purchase, to the end of your VAT quarter, can minimize the damage to your cash flow.

> Bill as much as you can at the beginning of your VAT quarter and defer major purchases to the end of the quarter.

## OVERDRAFT VS BUSINESS LOANS

Reverting to the topics of Chapter 5, most businesses will require some form of bank finance when they are starting up, either an overdraft or a business loan. The purpose of an overdraft is to fund short-term (less than 12 months) cash-flow requirements. A business loan should be chosen when the funding is required for fixed assets (not otherwise funded), start-up capital or other longer-term requirements. A key difference between the terms of an overdraft and a term loan is that the overdraft is usually repayable to the bank on demand, whereas the loan is normally repayable only on default (if the borrower is in breach of its terms).

However, from your point of view, an overdraft may be the more acceptable alternative, assuming that both are available to you. Unless there is a commitment to reduce the overdraft incrementally, your monthly revenue is not impacted upon by repayment instalments. Moreover, you will be paying interest only on the day-to-day amount of your indebtedness in a single current account.

> With an overdraft your monthly revenue is not impacted by repayment instalments.

Some banks charge a commitment or arrangement fee for setting up a loan account, and the interest charges and repayments of principal are debited automatically to your business's current account. However, there is a marked preference by most banks for granting a business loan and sometimes insisting that you maintain your current account in credit. Fixed-rate loans have become more popular, setting the interest rate at the outset so that the cost is known when the loan is taken out. In the case of an overdraft, interest is charged on the daily balance outstanding; while this may save you money, the interest rate will fluctuate. (If you negotiated a fixed-rate loan a year or more ago, you are probably feeling disadvantaged now as interest rates have been slashed).

## ADDITIONAL BANK ACCOUNTS

Remember that you can be penalized heavily for late payments of VAT and income tax or corporation tax falling due. We have referred above to the possible opening of a separate account for VAT received and payable. Unless you are a very diligent book-keeper and cash-flow planner, you may be wise to make such a provision rather than using your VAT collections to minimize temporarily the use of the overdraft on your current account.

There are two other types of payment that you may be prudent to provide for with additional bank accounts.

## Taxation reserve account

The payment of self-assessed income tax on self-employed earnings or corporation tax in the case of companies is inescapable, even though there may be considerable time lags between the end of your accounting period and the due payment dates.

A tax reserve account is sensible once your business is established.

Accumulating your estimated taxation liabilities in a tax reserve deposit account is sensible once your business is established. In addition to smoothing your cash flow, it will have the additional value of demonstrating to your bank manager that there will be no unexpected demand for tax on your main business account.

## Payroll account

If you employ staff, probably on a monthly salaried basis, it is essential that you pay them promptly at the month end and that employer's PAYE payments are made on time. You can administer salaries most conveniently through a computerized payroll system and a separate bank account from which your bank will make direct transfers of net salaries to your employees' bank accounts on the last working day of each month, provided of course that you have previously transferred from your main account the total sum to be disbursed.

Administer salaries through a computerized payroll system and a separate bank account.

Indeed, payroll is a crucial part of your operations. You are required by law to collect tax and National Insurance (NI) under the PAYE system and penalties are imposed for failure to do so. Tax and NI contributions must be paid to HM Revenue & Customs Accounts Office by the 19th of each month. (Employers who expect to collect less than £1,500 a month in PAYE, NI and student loan repayments may pay quarterly in January, April, July and October.)

As an employer, in addition to making prompt PAYE payments you are required to:

- register with your PAYE tax office;
- keep basic payroll information for each employee;
- keep a list of all wage payments on form P11 or the equivalent;
- make additional deductions from your employees' pay (subject to the individual employees' written consent) for any contributions to occupational pension schemes, holiday pay schemes, union subscriptions, loan repayments, student loan repayments, attachment of earnings orders or corrections to previous payslips.

The new National Pensions Saving Scheme to be introduced in 2012 will impose further demands on small businesses in the management of their payroll accounts.

## MANAGING THE UNEXPECTED

In the normal course of events, unexpected crises will arise as a result of failure or success. On the one hand, your cash-flow projections may be blown apart by the sudden loss of a major customer or the decision of a regular client not to renew a long-standing contract. When that happens, it will probably not be possible to replace the business or to cut expenditure to compensate for the loss of revenue immediately. A worse case, because it would probably occur without warning, would be the sudden default of a major debtor through insolvency.

But your business can also 'suffer from the problems of success', a phrase coined by Edward Heath when he was Prime Minister to describe the dire state of the British economy in the 1970s. Many a businessperson is caught unprepared on a tide of expansion. The symptoms may emerge as problems with people, when the staff who were in at the beginning find it difficult to handle a larger-scale operation, or when mistakes are made in interviewing and selecting people for new jobs in an expanding company, or simply when the owners are stretched in too many different directions to look at individual trouble spots in sufficient detail.

Most frequently troubles turn out to be connected with finance.

Most frequently these trouble spots turn out to be connected, directly or indirectly, with finance. You are producing something for which there is a demand, the world starts beating a path to your door, you appear to be selling your product or service profitably and suddenly, in the midst of apparent plenty, you start running out of cash. What has probably happened is that you have forgotten that in general you do not get paid until you have delivered the goods or performed the service, but your suppliers and the additional staff you have taken on have to be paid out of cash flow generated by the previous and smaller scale of operation.

If your business is in manufacturing or in the wholesaling or retailing trades, a common problem arising from expansion is inadequate stock control. A better stock control system could release substantial sums of money. You should aim to maintain just enough of each type of stock to serve your customers at the required service level on an ongoing basis after taking into account seasonal fluctuations. It follows that there is an advantage in choosing suppliers who can deliver promptly, as this will help to minimize your stock levels. You should set a target stock-turn (eg six times a year) for each category of stock and monitor your performance. Sell off any old or obsolete stock, even if the best price you can get is below book value.

In manufacturing or wholesaling, set a target stock-turn and sell off any old or obsolete stock.

In Chapter 19 we address the general question of funding growth, but for now the main point is that you must find the time to check and revise your cash-flow projections, preferably weekly, on the basis of the prior month's experience and the changes that you can predict for the business. Develop red-light systems that will warn you automatically if something needs querying and, having identified any problems, take immediate action.

Above all, when the storm clouds gather, as a result of either failure or success, be sure to keep your bank manager informed. If you want to maintain the support of your bank you should always signal any unfavourable impact of the unexpected on your forward cash flow together with your plans for tackling the problem.

## Checklist: bank accounts

1. Much borrowing can be avoided by effective cash management.
2. Decide a credit policy and enforce it.
3. Beware of the unexpected problems of success as well as disasters. Develop red-light systems which will warn you automatically. Check and revise your cash-flow projections regularly, even weekly.
4. Always agree credit terms at the order stage. Have your standard credit terms printed on the back of your invoices and other business documents.
5. If you provide services, you may be able to negotiate retainers or progress payments with major clients.
6. Spread payments to your core creditors and essential suppliers on a regular monthly basis. Otherwise, take the maximum period of payment allowed by suppliers.
7. Consider opening separate bank accounts for VAT and payroll transactions and a deposit account for income or corporation tax.
8. Never borrow more than you have to. Consider using hire purchase or leasing instead of committing cash to outright purchase.
9. Always signal any unfavourable impact of the unexpected on your cash flow to your bank manager in advance, together with your plans for tackling the problem.
10. Make sure that you choose carefully between an overdraft and a loan, taking account of the length of time for which the funds will be needed and that repayment can be afforded.

# 10

# Budgeting and Cash-flow Forecasting

One principle that it is vital to grasp is the importance of liquid cash in running a business. This should not be confused with profitability. Because of the way the profit figure is arrived at on the trading account (see Chapter 13), it is perfectly possible for a business to be trading profitably and yet be quite unable to pay the tax bill or the rent because its resources are tied up in stock or, even worse, in equipment.

> Failure to understand the distinction between profit and cash flow can be disastrous.

Failure to understand the distinction between profit and cash flow is not uncommon and it can be disastrous. For example, you may be offered very persuasive financial inducements to carry or manufacture additional stock. If it is a good product and one for which there is a consistent demand, you may say to yourself that you are going to need more anyway in six months' time, so why not stock up for a whole year at a bargain price? This can be a valid argument, but before you accept it consider that when the bills come in they have to be paid with money, not with stock. Profitability means very little unless cash is there when it is needed.

This is true even for businesses that do not carry stocks, like a photographic studio producing goods only to order, or a design consultancy selling more or less intangible skills. You are still going to have outgoings on travel or materials; and even if your premises are a back room in your own house there are still bills to be met, apart from the matter of needing money to live on.

## PLANNING YOUR CASH REQUIREMENTS

Planning your cash requirements is crucial from the outset of your career as a self-employed person. It will determine much of your policy towards what kinds of work you take on. It is far better, if you are short of liquid capital, to take on a number of small jobs which will keep money coming in than one big, tempting, potentially profitable one where you might run out of cash three-quarters of the way through. For, unless you make provision to receive progress payments from your customer, backed up possibly by a bank overdraft, your suppliers are going to be pressing you for payment before you are in a position to send your bills to the customer.

Even at best, in most businesses which are not taking cash across the counter there is going to be a lag between the time you are being asked for payment and when your customer pays you.

In order to estimate what your needs for cash are going to be, you should set up and revise, at three- or six-monthly intervals, a cash-flow budget; and in order to refine it, you should also check it back against what actually happened.

> To estimate what your needs for cash will be, set up and revise a cash-flow budget at regular intervals.

The words 'cash-flow budget' sound intimidatingly technical, but mean simply that you should make a realistic forecast of money coming in and going out over the period. Again, how accurate you can be depends somewhat on the circumstances and the type of business you are in. If you have bought a going concern there may be regular contracts that you hope to maintain, or in the case of a retail business or a restaurant some kind of predictable pattern of trade which can be established from the cash book or general ledger.

If you have started a new business of your own you may not have much to go on in predicting the cash coming in. You might only have enough certain information on the next two or three months, though if you have asked yourself the questions we outlined in Chapter 2 you will have ensured, as far as possible, that there is a continuing demand for your product so that orders will go on arriving while you are completing the work you have already lined up.

But even in cases where you do not know where the penny after next is coming from, at the very least the cash-flow budget will tell you what commitments you have to meet and, therefore, what volume of sales should be your target to this end. You can include this sales target in your budget, but do not forget that, in order to achieve it, costs of materials and additional overheads will also be involved. Moreover, both in cases where income is firmly expected and where it is only a forecast of expectations, the cost of materials and wages will probably have to be met before you actually get paid.

Let us take a hypothetical case here to illustrate a cash-flow budget in operation over the first four months of the year, for a self-employed electrician. Over the three months, he has a contract to install the electrics for a local builder, J. Bodger, who is refurbishing a client's offices, another contract on two new houses in a development by Sunlight Homes and a job for Hightown District Council on an extension to the Town Hall. There is also a steady flow of small private jobs for local householders. Against this, he has to meet VAT, telephone, the running of a van, the purchase of materials, rates, electricity, and his drawings from the business and National Insurance contributions, etc.

As you will see from the forecast (see Table 10.1), the electrician budgeted for a deficit in the first two months, but he was not worried because he knew that in March and April he could expect a couple of big payments from Sunlight Homes and from the Hightown District Council. However, in order to keep solvent he had to borrow £2,000 from the bank, on which interest payments had to be paid at intervals. He also had to plan the purchase of his most costly item, electrical supplies, as close as possible to the

**Table 10.1** *An example of a cash-flow budget for a self-employed electrician*

| | January | | February | | March | | April | |
|---|---|---|---|---|---|---|---|---|
| **Income (£)** | | | | | | | | |
| From | December Statement | | January Statement | | February Statement | | March Statement | |
| | J. Bodger | 745 | J. Bodger | 1,525 | Sunlight Homes Ltd | 5,445 | Hightown District Council | 5,330 |
| Other work | | 400 | Other work | 250 | J. Bodger | 1,500 | Other work | 500 |
| | | | | | Other work | 500 | | |
| | | 1,145 | | 1,775 | | 7,445 | | 5,830 |
| **Expenditure (£)** | | | | | | | | |
| Personal drawings and National Insurance | | 835 | Personal drawings, etc | 835 | Personal drawings, etc | 835 | Personal drawings, etc | 835 |
| Telephones | | 120 | Telephones | – | Telephones | – | Telephones | 125 |
| Petrol | | 70 | Petrol | 70 | Petrol | 70 | Petrol | 70 |
| Postage | | 20 | Postage | 20 | Postage | 20 | Postage | 20 |
| Van rental | | 170 | Van rental | 170 | Van rental | 170 | Van rental | 170 |
| Electrical supplies | | 1,500 | Electrical supplies | 1,000 | Electrical supplies | 2,000 | Electrical supplies | 1,750 |
| Other materials | | 200 | Bank Interest | 60 | Utilities | 70 | Other materials | 430 |
| | | | | | VAT | 510 | | |
| | | 2,915 | | 2,155 | | 3,675 | | 3,400 |
| *Cash surplus (deficit)* | | (1,770) | | (380) | | 3,770 | | 2,430 |
| Bank opening balance | | 300 | | (1,470) | | (1,850) | | 1,920 |
| Bank closing balance | | (1,470) | | (1,850) | | 1,920 | | 4,350 |

month in which he would actually be using it for his two big jobs. There is no point in holding expensive stock which cannot be used at an early date.

In March he had to allow for two quarterly items, utilities, and VAT payment, having paid his quarterly telephone bill in January, and as the year progresses he will have to make plans to meet such major items as insurance premiums and van servicing. Note also that expenditure which is central to the activities of the business, in this case electrical supplies, has to be forecast more carefully than incidentals such as postage where a monthly average has been extended. If postage was a more crucial factor, as might be the case with a mail-order firm, this part of the cash-flow budget would have to be worked out in more detail.

Regarding the revenue part of the forecast, he had enough orders for jobbing work to budget fairly accurately for the first two months. For March and April he guessed a figure, hoping that a general upturn of business after the winter would lead to a modest growth in incoming funds after that point.

The overall March and April figures look quite rosy, but after that it was clear that he would have to turn up some more jobs like Sunlight Homes and the Hightown District Council because the overheads plus the cost of electrical supplies needed to fill forecast work were running slightly above the expected income. So even though he was running well ahead of the game at the end of April, he would be unwise to start reducing that bank overdraft just yet.

There are many other lessons to be learnt from your cash-flow budget. They vary from business to business, but the essential points are that it is an indispensable indicator in making your buying decisions both of stock and of materials, in that it helps you decide your priorities between getting work (and what sort of work) and devoting all your energies to executing it, and points to the importance of getting the maximum credit and allowing the minimum!

# 11

# Legal Basics

Going to law is a process where the cure, in money terms, is often worse than the disease – which is why so many settlements are made out of court. Even seeking legal advice is an expensive business: £100 to £200 an hour is now a normal rate, depending on where you are, and few legal bills come to less than £250, even for a short consultation. In complex disputes or where larger sums of money are involved, legal action may ultimately be the only course open. But at the more basic levels of trading law there are some straightforward principles laid down, though they are sometimes blurred by traditional tales – for instance, that a shopkeeper is obliged by law to sell anything he displays for sale. Knowing what the law actually says about this and other everyday trading transactions will help you to sort out minor disputes and, very often, save costly legal fees.

> Knowing what the law actually says will help you to sort out minor disputes and may save costly legal fees.

## THE SALE OF GOODS ACT 1979

This Act and the more recent Sale and Supply of Goods Act 1994 place some clear but not unfair obligations on you as the seller once a contract has taken place, an event which occurs when goods have been exchanged for money. Nothing needs to be written or even said to make the contract legally binding and you cannot normally override it by putting up a notice saying things like 'No Refunds' or limiting your responsibilities in some other way. This is prohibited under the Unfair Contract Terms Act of 1977.

The Sale of Goods Act has three main provisions concerning what you sell.

But what happens if you yourself have been misled by the manufacturer from whom you bought the item in question? You cannot refer the buyer back to your supplier: the Sale of Goods Act specifically places responsibility for compensating the buyer on the retailer, no matter from whom the retailer bought the goods in the first place.

1. The goods must be 'of satisfactory quality'. This means that they must be capable of doing what the buyer could reasonably expect them to do – for instance, an electric kettle should boil the water in it within a reasonable length of time.
2. The goods must be 'fit for any particular purpose' which you make known to the buyer. For instance, if you are asked whether a rucksack can carry 100 lb without the strap breaking and it fails to match up to your promise of performance, you will have broken your contract.
3. The goods must be 'as described'. If you sell a bicycle as having five speeds and it only has three, then again you are in breach of contract – as well as of the Trade Descriptions Act, if you do so knowingly.

Thus, if the goods fail on any of the three grounds shown above, you will have to take them back and issue a full refund, unless you can negotiate a partial refund, with the buyer keeping the goods about which he or she has complained. However, the buyer need not accept such an offer, nor even a credit note. Furthermore, you

Goods must be 'of satisfactory quality', 'fit for purpose' and 'as described'.

may be obliged to pay any costs the buyer incurred in returning the goods, and even to pay compensation if he or she had a justifiable reason to hire a replacement for the defective item; for instance, hiring a ladder to do an urgent DIY job because the one you supplied was faulty.

The only let-out you have under the Act – which also covers secondhand goods – is if you warned the buyer about a specific fault, or if this was so obvious that he or she should have noticed it. In the case of the bike, the buyer probably would have found it difficult to spot that a couple of the gears were not working, but could reasonably be expected to notice a missing pedal.

# THE SUPPLY OF GOODS AND SERVICES ACT 1982

This is essentially an extension of the Sale of Goods Act into the sphere of services. The point you have to watch out for is this: if you are offering a service, say, for repairs or some form of consultancy, the implied terms, which the court will read into the arrangement whether they are written down or not, are: (1) that the supplier will carry out the service with reasonable care and skill; and (2) that it will be carried out in reasonable time and at reasonable cost.

> If you are offering a service you must carry out the service with reasonable care and skill, in reasonable time and at reasonable cost.

A cautionary example of the Supply of Goods and Services Act in operation was when an architectural student carried out a small flat conversion job for a client. He neglected to obtain planning permission for some of the work and, even though he was not fully qualified at the time, it was held that, in offering his services, he should have known that this was a basic part of the service he had been offering.

Disclaiming responsibility for your actions under either of these Acts is not the answer; that would make you liable under the Unfair Terms in Consumer Contracts Regulations 1994.

# THE CONSUMER PROTECTION ACT 1987

This is essentially a health and safety measure which says that where a defective product causes damage or injury, the supplier will be held liable unless he or she can show that not enough was known about its dangers at the time of supplying it.

## OBLIGATION TO SELL

By law, all goods have to be priced but, contrary to some widely held beliefs, there is no obligation on you to sell goods on display for sale if you don't want to. For instance, an assistant in an antique shop might wrongly price a picture at £2.50 rather than £250. The intending buyer cannot force you to sell at that price, even though it is publicly displayed. However, once the goods

> There is no obligation on you to sell goods on display if you don't want to... but once a transaction has taken place it cannot be revoked.

have been sold at £2.50, even in error, a contract has taken place and cannot be revoked without the agreement of both parties.

This also applies when the buyer has paid a deposit and this has been accepted. Supposing he or she had paid £1 and offered to return with the balance, a bargain would have been made which you would be obliged to complete. It is, however, binding on both parties. If the buyer, having paid a deposit, decided to change his or her mind you would be within your rights in refusing to refund the money.

## ESTIMATES AND QUOTATIONS

Self-employed people supplying services such as repairs are often asked for a quote or an estimate. How binding is the figure you give?

This is a grey area in which even the Office of Fair Trading finds it difficult to give legal ruling. They recommend, however, that a 'quote' should be a firm commitment to produce whatever the subject of the inquiry is at the price stated, whereas an 'estimate', while it should be a close guess, allows more leeway to depart from that figure. Therefore, if you are not sure how much a job is going to cost, you should describe your price as an estimate and say it is subject to revision. This may not, of course, satisfy the customer, who may press you for a quote. If you really find it difficult to state a fixed sum because of unknown factors, you can either give some parameters (eg between £x and £y) or say that you will do £x-worth of work – which on present evidence is what you think it would take – but that you will notify the customer if that sum is likely to be exceeded to do the job properly. In general, though, an itemized firm quotation is the document that is least likely to produce disputes.

> If you are not sure how much a job is going to cost, you should describe your price as an estimate subject to revision.

## COMPLETION AND DELIVERY DATES

If you give a time for completing a job you will have to do it within that time – certainly if it is stated in writing.

In the case of delivery of goods ordered by customers the same is true. If you give a date you have to stick to it or the contract is broken and the customer can refuse the goods and even, in some cases, ask for compensation. Even if no date is given, you have to supply the article within a reasonable period of time, bearing in mind that what is reasonable in one case, such as making a dress, may not be reasonable in another – obtaining some ready-made article from a wholesaler, for example. The relevant law here is the Supply of Goods and Services Act 1982.

> If you give a delivery date you have to stick to it or the contract is broken.

# TRADING ASSOCIATIONS

In addition to legal obligations you may also belong to a trading association which imposes its own code of conduct. Such codes sometimes go beyond strict legal requirements, on the principle that 'the customer is always right'. This is not a bad principle to observe, within reason, whatever the legalities of the case. A reputation for fair dealing can be worth many times its cost in terms of advertising.

> 'The customer is always right' is not a bad principle to observe, within reason.

# THE TRADE DESCRIPTIONS ACT 1968

Another piece of legislation you need to watch out for, especially in advertisements and brochures, is the Trade Descriptions Act. This makes it a criminal offence knowingly to make false or misleading claims, verbally or in writing, about any goods or services you are offering. That includes what is known as 'passing off' – using a brand name to which you are not entitled or implying an association with some better-known product.

> Making false or misleading claims knowingly about goods or services you are offering is a criminal offence.

The notion of a trade description covers a wide range of characteristics, such as size, quantity, strength, method and place of manufacture, ingredients, testimonials from satisfied customers, and claims that the goods or service are cheaper than the same bought elsewhere.

It is possible by cunning wording to stick to the letter of the law, but not its spirit. For instance, the words 'made with' some desirable substance or other may indicate that it was made with only a minute quantity of it. But on the whole it is better to stick to the truth, since a successful claim against you could result in a compensation award – not to speak of loss of reputation.

## THE DATA PROTECTION ACT

The 1984 Act, followed by the 1998 Act that came into force in 2000, had the object of protecting individuals from unauthorized use of personal data about them; for instance, by computer bureaux selling mailing lists to direct sales organizations. Registration under the Act had to be completed by May 1986. Though failure to register is a criminal offence, the indications are that very few small businesses have actually done so, other than those which are directly affected, such as computer bureaux. In theory, though, the obligation to register is quite widespread, because anyone with a word processor that can store personal data may be liable to register at a cost of £35.

Application forms and guidance notes are available from post offices. Essentially, data users have to disclose to the Registrar what lists they hold, how and where they obtained the details on them and for what purposes they intend to use them. They must also undertake not to disclose them to any unspecified third party, or to use them for any purposes other than the declared ones. However, data used for internal administrative purposes, such as payrolls, are exempt if they are used only for that function.

> Data users have to disclose to the Registrar what lists they hold and undertake not to misuse them.

## THE PRICE MARKING ORDER 1991

This is an EC Directive. It obliges you to state the price of goods offered for sale in writing.

## Checklist: legal basics

1. Find out about legislation that applies to your area of activity, and more generally to running a business of any kind.
2. If you are selling goods, make sure that they comply with the Sale of Goods Act and that you have made appropriate checks with your supplier that the goods are of suitable standard and 'as described'.
3. Be clear about the services you are offering and that you comply with the Supply of Goods and Services Act 1982.
4. Do not commit yourself to making a quote if you are unsure. An 'estimate' should be offered first, with a quote to follow once you have assessed costs, etc.
5. Contact your trade association for codes of conduct and guidelines.
6. If you have personal data on individuals, collect forms from the post office to disclose this to the Registrar.

# 12

# Choosing Premises

The choice of premises tends to be determined by individual requirements. Over 400,000 businesses are currently home-based, accounting for over one in ten small businesses in this country. This chapter will mainly concentrate on the requirements of this group. However, for many, such as those in retailing, this simply is not an option and help is available at the end of this chapter for those who need to choose separate premises.

## WORKING FROM HOME

Research by Barclays Small Business Banking has identified the growing trend among the self-employed to work from home. Key findings include:

- Businesses operating from home are generally smaller than those with separate premises and have a quarter of the average turnover of these businesses.
- The average start-up cost for small businesses operating from home is £5,000, compared with a minimum of £13,000 for those operating from separate premises.
- Only a fifth of those business owners working from home see it as a stepping stone to operating from separate premises.

■ Business owners working from home work on average 11 hours less each week than those working from separate premises.

Commenting on this research, Mike Davis, Managing Director of Barclays Small Business Banking, identifies the reasons for the increasing number of home workers:

> The way we work is changing. Technological advances, especially in the communications field – coupled with growing frustration with time wasted travelling to and from work – has meant that more and more people are choosing to work from home.

Technological advances in communications have meant that more and more people are working from home.

Working from home needs to be given careful consideration. While start-up costs are smaller than for businesses operating from premises, you should be aware of the effects on family life and the prospect of working in isolation. Furthermore, should you need to have business visitors, a home-based office might create a bad impression of your operation unless you think carefully about presentation. You should also check whether by claiming part of the costs of running your business from home you will incur capital gains tax.

Barclays identifies two types of home worker. The first spends most of the working day at home and the second uses the home as a base but works at clients' premises. The second group is older, with over half aged over 45. Typical occupations in this group are building and gardening.

On the other hand, the group using their home as an office tend to be women, of which a sixth were formerly housewives. Indeed, in the first six months of 2006, women set up 38,100 businesses – an increase of 9 per cent on the same period in 2005. The researchers observe:

These characteristics suggest many of the owners of these businesses are trying to juggle domestic responsibilities with those of work, or have more than one job and set up in business to supplement the family income. It is more likely that they plan to maintain the size of their home-based business rather than expand it to become the main bread-winner.

> Separating work from home life is a big problem in working from home.

Indeed, the above comment points to one of the biggest problems of working from home: the difficulty in separating work from home life. Domestic distractions are one thing (the attractions of finishing off the dusting can far outweigh having to do your accounts), but if you only have one telephone for both home and business, a child acting as receptionist to potential clients will not present a professional image and might critically damage your prospects.

Setting aside a dedicated room to act as a separate office can help, if your home allows it. This will help to separate domestic and work life both physically and psychologically. Going to work in a separate space – even if it is the room next door – can help create the division. However, while there are problems in juggling domestic responsibilities and work in the same environment, one should not ignore the benefits. For example, the Barclays research found that nearly half of the women working from home stated that it was an important benefit because it allowed them to look after children and/or other dependants. Flexible working hours and practices, a reduction in travelling time and improved quality of life were also cited as benefits of home working. Table 12.1 identifies the perceived benefits of working from home:

> Flexible working hours and practices, less travelling time and improved quality of life are benefits of home working.

**Table 12.1** *Perceived benefits of working from home*

| Perceived benefit | All | Men | Women |
|---|---|---|---|
| Lower overheads | 26 | 37 | 16 |
| Allows me to look after children/dependants | 24 | 4 | 48 |
| Allows me flexible working hours/practices | 22 | 20 | 23 |
| Allows me to be my own boss | 17 | 21 | 13 |
| No need for separate premises | 16 | 20 | 12 |
| Less travelling time | 12 | 13 | 11 |
| Lower start-up costs | 8 | 10 | 6 |
| Better quality of life | 6 | 8 | 5 |
| Greater potential profits | 5 | 8 | 3 |

*Source: Barclays Bank Survey 2003*

The first two benefits are likely to be cited more frequently in 2009, particualrly in families where the number of salary/wage earners has been reduced from two to one.

## Choosing a room

What, then, should be taken into consideration when setting up an office from home? The following checklist should help:

- Noise – choose as quiet a room as possible, away from the distractions of family and other external noises.
- Position – try to think about heating and ventilation. A south-facing office might be appealing but will become a heat trap in the summer, as can uninsulated attics. Save on heating bills by purchasing a heater for your office rather than heating the whole house in winter.
- Lighting – be aware of the glare on computers and of the need for good lighting for close work such as design.
- Storage – you will never have enough space to store paperwork. However, consideration for the best use of storage facilities should be given.

■ Security – being burgled is an unpleasant experience that could be disastrous if your means of making a living are also taken. Invest in a burglar alarm, good window and door locks and mark any equipment with an identifiable label.

## Visitors

One of the main reasons cited by people who do not choose to work from home is that separate premises provide a professional image. Indeed, a visitor who has to negotiate children's toys and overeager pets might not leave with the image of the professional business that you would want. Should you expect your home business to have visitors, bear in mind the impression you are likely to give. Your office can be a comfortable environment in which to meet clients and as they know that you work from home they will not expect otherwise. However, you can also arrange to meet elsewhere, such as in a hotel or club such as the Institute of Directors, should you be a member. Furthermore, if you do not want to use your home address for business purposes, using a post office box number can help to guard privacy and, should you move, maintain continuity for your customers.

> You can arrange to meet business visitors elsewhere and using a PO box number can help to guard privacy.

## Networking

As noted previously, one of the biggest problems for people working from home is the sense of isolation. Whereas going to work in separate premises automatically introduces contact with other individuals, it is quite possible not to see another adult in your working day if you work from home.

This can impact on your work, as informal feedback from colleagues about ideas and projects is an underrated but invaluable source of advice and motivation. Daily discussion that occurs naturally in shared offices and workspaces can be helpful on a range of

> It is important to build into your work practice a way of networking with others.

issues and is often sorely missed. The lack of this informal feedback is often neglected when considering how to work from home and it is important to build into your work practice a way of networking with other people in the same occupation or in similar circumstances.

Being a member of a trade association or union can help, as regular local meetings can be attended; local Chambers of Commerce can also help you keep in contact with other businesses in your region. The internet is another way to contact people used ever more frequently through user-groups and e-mail.

However, non-professional communication is also important and building in a break to the day where contact is made with other people can also help. Peter Chatterton describes how he has overcome this problem in *Your Home Office* (Kogan Page), by forming a lunch society with other home-based workers:

> We get together on an ad-hoc basis for lunch or early evening drinks. This may sound trivial, but it is important to one's sanity in home working. But there are other benefits – our growing band of home workers have suddenly found that we can work together and give each other business. It's the start of a new wave of home business networking.

Chatterton also recommends putting adverts in local papers to make contact with other home workers and taking advantage of the flexible hours by going to a local sports club during the day when there isn't the weekend rush, adding: 'Think originally and openly – after all, you don't have the constraints of a normal job.'

## CHOOSING SEPARATE PREMISES

Working from home simply isn't an option when space needs to be found for employees, machinery, vehicles and other equipment. Indeed a sixth of small business owners cite this as the reason for working from separate premises. Research has also found that a

> 23 per cent believe that it is easier to keep business and private lives separate or that it means fewer distractions.

further 15 per cent believe that it is easier to keep business and private lives separate, while 8 per cent thought it would mean fewer distractions. However, choosing premises can be a complicated matter. It is important to consider your own specific requirements and ask some key questions before committing yourself to a lease or purchase. For example:

- Is passing trade a requirement for your business?
- Is a prestigious/prominent building important to your needs?
- What can you afford and are you going to lease or purchase?
- Do you have specific space requirements such as the need for warehousing?
- Is there sufficient utility capacity for your needs (ie gas, electricity, water, drainage, waste disposal)?
- Does the property present security risks?
- Do you need unrestricted parking for deliveries and customers?
- Will you need planning permission for your usage?
- Will it accommodate your growing business?

# LEASES

Whether you plan to trade from your home or separate premises, if the property is rented you will need to look carefully at the terms of your lease. There are likely to be restrictive covenants in the lease

> There are likely to be restrictive covenants on a leased home or commercial property.

which will prevent you from carrying on a trade in premises let to you for domestic use. This may not be an insuperable obstacle, but you would certainly have to get the owner's permission if you wanted to use your home for any purpose other than just living there.

Even when you rent commercial premises there are likely to be restrictions on the trade you carry on in them. An empty flower shop, for instance, could probably be used as a dress shop without complications, but its use as a furniture repair business might be disallowed because of the noise involved in running woodworking machinery. You and your solicitor should examine the lease closely for possible snags of this sort.

Equally important is the existence of any restrictions which would prohibit you from transferring the lease to a third party. This would mean that the purchaser would have to negotiate the lease element in the event of the sale of the business with the property owner, not with you, and this could drastically affect the value of what you have to sell. For instance, if you took a gamble on renting premises in an improving area which fulfilled your expectations by coming up in the world, you would not be able to reap the benefit of your foresight and courage if you could not transfer the unexpired portion of the lease.

> Commercial leases are usually for periods between three and seven years, with a rent review at the end.

Commercial leases, unlike most domestic ones, run for relatively short periods: usually between three and seven years, with a rent review at the end of each term or sometimes even sooner. This adds an unknown factor to the long-term future of any business in rented premises and is one you need to take into account in buying a business – again, particularly in an improving area. In Covent Garden, for instance, a number of small shops which moved in when it was a very run-down part of central London with correspondingly low rents were hit by huge increases when these rents were reviewed in the light of the improved status of the area subsequent to the redevelopment of the market building and its surroundings. The same thing is happening today in the Farringdon Road and Smithfield market. Another feature of the currently depressed commercial property market is the opportunity for short lets of a year or less on very favourable terms.

The other point to watch for in leases is whether you are responsible for dilapidation during the period of your lease. If you are, you could be in for a hefty bill at its end and for this reason it is advisable to have a survey done and its findings agreed with the owner, before you take on the lease.

## MEET YOUR OWN REQUIREMENTS

Whether working from home, or from separate premises, your environment is an important element in being able to motivate yourself and work efficiently. If you are able to discipline yourself to set hours within your home office, then this might be the answer for you. However, if being in contact with people on a daily basis is important it might be worth looking at a shared space with other like-minded self-employed individuals. Your local paper should have details of workspaces, or try your trade association or trade union for contacts. Deciding to work from separate premises will

> Disciplining yourself to set hours in your home office might be the answer.

need careful consideration. However, the Royal Institution of Chartered Surveyors publishes a book, _The Business Property Handbook_, which covers all of the main areas such as the complicated issue of signing a lease, planning permission and tax allowances. The choice of premises in relation to marketing is also discussed in this book in Chapter 16.

### Checklist: choosing premises and equipment

1. Are you able to separate domestic and work duties within your own home?
2. Are you able to work in isolation?

3. Have you identified forums for networking and are there other self-employed home workers with whom you can maintain contact?

4. Talk to your local crime prevention officer for advice on securing your office and equipment and inform your insurance company that you will be using part of your home for work.

5. Have you a room which allows adequate storage, good light, comfortable heat and ventilation and that is reasonably quiet? Check the route to your office to assess the impression a visitor might get.

6. Consider a separate telephone line for your business use and a second business line for your internet and fax connections or an ISDN line.

7. Talk to other home workers in similar businesses about their equipment before you commit yourself to buying anything. If you have low usage of a piece of equipment, such as a photocopier, assess local availability before purchasing.

8. Assess your needs when considering separate premises. If passing trade is a requirement, think about parking restrictions. Is there enough room for equipment and any future growth in staff and business?

9. Seek out legal and professional advice whether you are considering purchasing or leasing a property.

10. Check if planning permission is required before altering the premises.

# 13

# Simple Accounting Systems

Any bank manager will tell you that at least 80 per cent of all business failures are caused by inadequate record keeping. Unfortunately, this fault is by no means uncommon in small businesses because the entrepreneurial person who tends to set up on their own is often temperamentally different from the patient administrative type who enjoys paperwork and charting information in the form of business records. He or she is apt to feel that

> 80 per cent of all business failures are caused by inadequate record keeping.

what really keeps the show on the road is obtaining and doing the work, or being in the shop to look after customers. However, unless you record money coming in and going out, owed and owing, you will never have more than the haziest idea of how much to charge for your products or services, where your most profitable areas of activity are (and indeed whether you are making a profit at all), how much you can afford to pay yourself and whether there is enough coming in to cover immediate commitments in the way of wages, trade debts, tax or professional fees, rent, rates, etc.

It used to be the case that only a limited company was obliged to keep proper books of account: the definition is that they have to do so 'with respect to all receipts and expenses, sales and purchases, assets and liabilities and they must be sufficient to give a true and fair picture of the state of the company's affairs and to explain its transactions'. This provision has effectively been extended to apply to all kinds of business. You are now required to:

- Set up adequate records of all business transactions, including personal drawings and personal money put into the business. Retailers will have to keep separate records of goods taken for personal use.
- Maintain those records throughout the year and keep them up to date.
- Retain the documentation for a recommended six years.

As a rule of thumb, if your scale of operations is big enough to come within the orbit of VAT (that is, if your turnover is, or is likely to be, over £67,000 a year) we suggest you get qualified help with the bookkeeping that will be required. But first of all, let us look at the very basic records you ought to keep if you are in business for yourself at all, even as a part-time freelance.

## TWO STARTING POINTS

At the small-scale sole trader end, one reason why you need to keep records is to justify your expenditure claims to the tax inspector. For this purpose you may find that your most useful investment is a spike on which incoming receipts, invoices, statements and delivery notes can be placed. This ensures that essential documentary evidence of expenditure is retained and kept together, not used to put cups on or carried around in your wallet for making

> Carry a notebook around with you and enter any undocumented expenses.

odd notes on the back. As your business grows you may find that the spike should be supplemented by a spring-loaded box file in which all such items should be placed in date order.

However, not all expenditure can be accounted for in this way. Fares, for instance, are not generally receipted, nor is postage, or you may be buying items for personal use at the same time as others that are directly connected with your business. Thus it is a good idea to carry a notebook around with you and enter up any expenses that you have incurred that are not documented. You will find that the tax office will accept a certain level of claims of this kind provided they bear a credible relationship to the business you are in. For example, if you are earning income from travelling round the country as a management consultant, they will accept a fairly high level of claims for fares, but not if the nature of your business is carrying out a local building repair service.

For larger outlays you may find credit cards a useful record-keeping aid. Apart from the fact that when card companies render their account for payment they provide a breakdown of where, when and how items were purchased, they also, in effect, give you six weeks' credit.

## KEEPING A CASH BOOK

The next stage is to keep a cash book. It does not have to be anything elaborate. The object of the exercise is to provide a record from which an accountant or bookkeeper can write up a proper set of books and to save their time and trouble (which you have to pay for) in slogging through dozens or possibly hundreds of pieces of paper in order to do this. Since your professional adviser will have to work from your records it is a good idea to ask what is the most convenient way of setting them out. He or she may suggest that you buy one of the ready-made books of account, though such books are not suitable for every kind of self-employment. If you find it difficult to follow these instructions, or you are using a ready-made book and are having trouble with it, here is something very simple you can do (see Table 13.1).

Buy a large (A4) ruled notebook and open it up at the first double page. Allocate the left-hand page to sales and the right-hand page to expenditure. If sales and expenditure fall into further categories which you want to keep track of, say, if you want to keep travel

**Table 13.1** *Sample entries from the cash book of a cabinet-maker*

### INCOME

| Date | Invoice No | Date paid | Details | Amount (£) | VAT (£) |
|---|---|---|---|---|---|
| 2.5.03 | 8061 | | Six tables | 224.00 | 39.20 |
| 6.5.03 | cash | | Desk | 400.00 | 70.00 |
| 10.5.03 | 8062 | | Dining table | 300.00 | 52.50 |
| 12.5.03 | cash | | Repair of wooden chest | 160.00 | 28.00 |

### EXPENDITURE

| Date | Invoice No | Cheque/Credit card | Details | Amount (£) | VAT (£) |
|---|---|---|---|---|---|
| 3.5.03 | – | 911112 | Wooden Top timber yard | 850.00 | 148.75 |
| 4.5.03 | Petty cash voucher 23 | cash | Stamps | 6.00 | – |
| 5.5.03 | Petty cash voucher 24 | cash | Expenses: trip to Harwich to inspect timber | 40.00 | 7.00 |
| 13.5.03 | – | 911113 | Electricity bill | 80.00 | 14.00 |

costs separate from the cost of materials, or if you are registered for VAT, divide up the page accordingly. You should also rule up columns for the date, the invoice number and the details of the invoice. Enter up these details at the end of each day's trading and you will find that it works both as a discipline in checking that all your sales and purchases are logged and that you now have a further record in addition to the documents on your spike or in your box file.

## MORE ELABORATE SYSTEMS

This sort of record is fine as far as it goes and in a small business engaged mainly in cash transactions your accountant may not need very much more than this to produce a set of accounts. In a larger concern, or one that operates extensively on taking and giving credit, it has some obvious limitations.

For example, keeping track of when payments are made or received can become rather messy and difficult, and you will need to have a separate record, called a ledger, of the customers and suppliers with whom you do business so that you can see at a glance how much you owe or are owed in the case of individual accounts. Such details will be taken from further books – purchases and sales daybooks and a more elaborate kind of cash book than the simplified one we have described above. Though we have recommended that you leave the details of this kind of book-keeping to an experienced person, let us look briefly at what is involved:

### Definitions of books of account

1. *Cash book.* Shows all payments received and made, with separate columns for cash transactions and those made through the bank (ie payments by cheque). Amounts received from customers are credited to their account in the ledger (see below). Payments made to suppliers are debited to their account in the ledger.
2. *Petty cash book.* Shows expenditure on minor items – postage, fares, entertainment and so forth, with a column for VAT.

3. *Sales daybook*. Records invoices sent out to customers in date order, with some analysis of the goods or service supplied and a column for VAT.
4. *Purchases daybook*. Records similar information about purchases.
5. *Ledger*. Sets out details, taken from the sales and purchases daybooks, of individual customers' and suppliers' accounts and serves as a record of amounts owed and owing. Details from the analysis columns of the sales and purchases daybooks are also transcribed, usually monthly, under corresponding headings in the ledger. This enables you to see at a glance where your sales are coming from and where your money is going.
6. *Capital goods ledger*. If you own expensive capital equipment – cars, lorries, machine tools, high-class film or photographic equipment, etc – you should have separate accounts for them in the ledger because the method of accounting for them is somewhat different. Capital items depreciate over a period of time (as you will know if you have ever sold a car) and this fact must be reflected both in your balance sheet and profit and loss account, and in the way you price your goods and services.

*Note:* Writing down capital goods affects your tax liability. With some items you can write down the full advantage of this concession. How you deal with depreciation is very much an area where you are dependent on your accountant's expert advice.

## ELECTRONIC BOOKKEEPING

There are many different reasons for putting your accounts system onto a computer. Routine tasks become much quicker, statements and other regular correspondence can be mail-merged and personalized and up-to-date balances included. Correcting any mistakes can be done at the touch of a button and if your business is growing, a computerized accounting system will make life much easier when you take on new staff, increase your spending or have more invoices to chase.

Perhaps the most useful aspect of a computerized accounts system is the fact that once the information is recorded, it can be used to give you a snapshot of the business performance at any time, which is ideal when revisiting your forecasts and cash-flow projections or preparing your end-of-year accounts.

The following are a few points to bear in mind when looking to purchase a bookkeeping package.

## Criteria for purchasing bookkeeping software

■ Don't walk into a shop or dealership and buy the cheapest thing on offer. Remember, it is not the PC that does the real work, it is the software and if you buy a system that is not suited to your business it could cost you a lot of time, effort and money later on.

■ Define what it is that you need your accounting software package to do. Do you want to run your whole system on it or just do some sales invoicing? Will you need to automate just the main ledgers or would you like to put sales-order processing, purchase-order processing and stock control onto the computer? Do you have any special procedures or requirements specific to your business that you must stick to, whatever the system? It is important that you answer these questions before you start shopping around.

■ Collect some information on accounting software products and PCs and read some of the reviews published in computer magazines.

■ Talk to your accountant, who may be able to advise you about some packages. Information may also be available from authorized software dealers, large retail stores such as PC World and professional bodies such as the Institute of Chartered Accountants.

It is also worth remembering that computers do crash and if you have failed to make copies of your accounts on disk on a regular basis you could land yourself in deep water. Back-up stationery,

Computers do crash. So maintain back-up records.

such as invoices, are worth having as well in such a situation so that a technical problem shouldn't turn into an income-threatening crisis.

The better electronic accounting packages include Sage and TAS BOOKS.

## Features of good electronic accounting packages

■ manage VAT, tax and NI (many packages enable you to complete your VAT return in just a few minutes);
■ produce your annual accounts and end-of-year reports easily;
■ know which products and customers are the most (and least) profitable;
■ record and manage your stock levels;
■ keep accurate records of your customers and suppliers;
■ recover late payments and reduce the risk of bad debts;
■ run your payroll with confidence;
■ track your credit card payments and record your cash sales;
■ reconcile your books with your online bank accounts automatically.

Bookkeeping software will also help you to use your accountant more cost-effectively.

## TRADING AND PROFIT AND LOSS ACCOUNT

From the books described above, your accountant can draw together the information needed to compile the trading and profit and loss account (see Table 13.2). The function of the account is to

**Table 13.2**  *An example of a trading and profit and loss account*

*Trading and Profit and Loss Account for year ended 31.12.07*

|  | £ | £ |
|---|---|---|
| *Sales* |  | 65,000 |
| Purchases | 30,000 |  |
| Opening Stock | 5,000 |  |
|  | 35,000 |  |
| *Less* Closing Stock | 6,000 | 29,000 |
| Gross Profit |  | 36,000 |
| Rent and Rates | 3,000 |  |
| Salaries | 9,000 |  |
| Heat, Light | 600 |  |
| Phone | 350 |  |
| Travel | 800 |  |
| Repairs | 500 |  |
| Depreciation | 1,800 |  |
| Professional Advice | 450 |  |
|  |  | 16,500 |
| Net Profit |  | 19,500 |

tell you whether you have been making a gross profit and a net profit on your trading. It must be compiled annually and preferably more often than that, quarterly for instance, to enable you to measure your progress and make your VAT return.

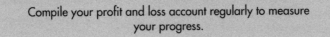

Compile your profit and loss account regularly to measure your progress.

To put together the account, your accountant begins by identifying the period you want to cover. He or she then totals up the value of all sales, whether paid for or not. Then your opening stock is added to the purchases (but not expenditure such as rent or repayment of interest on loans). From this the value of your stock is taken (based on cost or market value, whichever is lower) at the end of the period you want to cover. Deducting the value of opening stock plus purchases less closing stock from the value of sales will give your gross trading profit (or loss) over the period.

Using this information your accountant can work out the net profit and loss over the same period. The gross profit figure from your trading account appears at the top and against it is set all the items from the various expenditure accounts in the ledger. He or she also includes in this figure the depreciation on capital equipment, but not its actual cost (even if you purchased it during the period in question) because that crops up later, in the balance sheet.

Deducting these from the gross profit gives your profit over the period. If the total expenditure exceeds the gross profit you have obviously incurred a loss.

The self-employed and most partnerships, with annual turnover below £15,000, don't need to submit a profit and loss account in your tax return as this is covered in the self-assessment system.

## THE BALANCE SHEET

We have mentioned in the previous section that capital equipment does not figure in the profit and loss account, but goes into the balance sheet. The balance sheet is a picture, taken at a particular point in the year (usually at the end of a company's financial year), of what the firm *owes* and what it *owns* (see Table 13.3). (This is not the same as a profit and loss account, which covers a period of time.)

In a balance sheet the assets of the firm used to be set out on the right and the liabilities on the left, but it is modern practice to display them as in Table 13.3. However, all the assets and all the liabilities are generally not lumped together, but distinguished qualitatively by the words 'fixed' and 'current'.

> Assets and liabilities are not lumped together but classified as 'fixed' and 'current'.

'Fixed assets' are items which are permanently necessary for the business to function, such as machinery, cars, fixtures and fittings, your premises or the lease on them. 'Current assets', on the other

**Table 13.3**  *An example of a balance sheet*

Balance Sheet as at 31.12.07

| | £ | | £ | |
|---|---|---|---|---|
| *Fixed Assets* | | | | |
| Vehicles | 3,200 | | | |
| *less* depreciation | 800 | | 2,400 | |
| Fixtures and fittings | 2,000 | | | |
| *less* depreciation | 500 | | 1,500 | |
| | | | 3,900 | |
| | | | | |
| *Current Assets* | | | | |
| Stock | 6,000 | | | |
| Debtors | 1,800 | | | |
| Cash | 150 | | | |
| | | 7,950 | | |
| | | | | |
| *Less Current Liabilities* | | | | |
| Trade Creditors | | 1,590 | | |
| Net Current Assets | | | 6,360 | |
| Total Assets | | | 10,260 | |
| *Represented by* | | | | |
| | | | Authorized | Issued |
| Capital (2,000 shares at £1 each) | | | 1,000 | 1,000 |
| Loan repayable 2007 | | | | 2,000 |
| Profit | | | | 7,260 |
| | | | | 10,260 |

hand, are things from which cash will be realized in the course of your trading activities. These include the amount owed to you by your debtors (from the customers' accounts in the ledger), and the value of your stock (from the trading account). It also, of course, includes cash at the bank (from the cash book).

With liabilities, the position is reversed. 'Fixed liabilities' are those which you do not have to repay immediately, like a long-term loan from a kindly relative. What you do have to repay promptly, however, is the interest on that loan and this goes under 'current liabilities' if it is due, but has not been paid at the time the balance sheet has been prepared. The same is true of any amounts you owe to your suppliers' accounts in the ledger. Another item that goes on the 'liabilities' side is the share capital in the business and the profit from the trading account, because both these amounts are ultimately owed by the company to the shareholders. Where, on the other hand, the company has been making a loss, the amount is deducted either from profits retained from earlier periods or from the shareholders' capital.

As with the profit and loss account, limited companies are obliged to submit a balance sheet to Companies House, HM Revenue & Customs and shareholders. The self-employed and partnerships are not legally obliged to produce formal balance sheets.

## WHAT INFORMATION SHOULD YOU BE LOOKING FOR IN YOUR RECORDS?

You will want to know whether you are making or losing money, but there are many other useful bits of information to be gleaned as well. If you are making a profit, what relationship does it bear to the capital employed in the business? You can calculate this by subtracting total liabilities from total assets. If you are making less than a 15 per cent return on capital before tax, you are not, on the face of things, making much progress, though, of course, you could be paying yourself a very handsome salary before the profit figure was arrived at.

Work out your critical business ratios.

The percentage return on capital can be calculated by the following sum:

$$\frac{\text{profit}}{\text{capital employed}} \times 100$$

## Balance sheet ratios

Another thing you can work out from your balance sheet is whether you are maintaining sufficient working capital to meet your requirements for new stock or materials or to pay for wages and rent. Here you look at current assets and current liabilities. The calculation:

$$\frac{\text{current assets}}{\text{current liabilities}}$$

gives you your _current_ ratio. If you have, say, £1,000 of each you are said to have a current ratio of 1:1. Clearly, in that case you would be in trouble if a major debtor were to go bankrupt. So it may be that you should cut back on some item of expenditure you were planning on. Furthermore, the current ratio includes certain items, like stocks, which may not be immediately realizable. If your current ratio is low, and you are still in two minds whether or not to buy that new machine, you might apply what is known as the _acid test ratio_, which shows your ability to meet liabilities quickly if the need arises. Here you simply deduct stock from your figure for current assets to give you a figure for liquid assets, ie debtors and cash. If the ratio of liquid assets to current liabilities is too low, you may have more money tied up in stock than you should have.

Even the acid test ratio assumes that your debtors are going to pay you in a reasonable period of time: most likely within the terms of trade you are allowing. But is this assumption really correct? Look at the annual sum:

$$\frac{\text{debtors}}{\text{sales}} \times 365$$

If your sales are £10,000 and your debtors owe £1,000, they are near enough to meeting net monthly terms for you not to worry about it. But if your debtors, on the same sales turnover, are running to £3,000, there is something wrong with your credit control and you are probably heading for serious trouble.

## Trading account ratios

There are three commonly used ratios determined by trading results that are used in evaluating a business:

■ Gross profit margin (already defined in Chapter 2 as the percentage of gross profit to sales); in most small businesses it is difficult to trade profitably where the gross profit margin is less than 70 per cent.

■ Pre-tax net profit margin (the percentage of net profit to sales); there are plenty of businesses which survive where the net profit margin is as low as 5 per cent, but a minimum of 15 per cent should be your goal.

■ Earnings per share, calculated as the post-tax net earnings of a company divided by the number of ordinary shares in issue. This ratio is of key interest in valuing the shares of a listed or other public company, but is of little interest in the case of private limited companies. Of course, it is not applicable to self-employed businesses.

Another ratio which is certainly of interest to the manager of any business that holds trading stock is stock turn: the ratio of annual sales of product at manufactured or bought-in cost to the book value of the stock at the end of the trading period. Generally, a stock turn of seven or eight times a year is better than satisfactory. A stock turn of only four or five indicates that inventory management should be tighter.

> Your balance sheets and trading accounts are very valuable indicators of how your business is going.

There are other ratios to look out for, but we hope that you will now be clear that the balance sheet and trading and profit and loss accounts are not just a financial rigmarole you have to go through, but very valuable indicators of the way your business is going, or the financial state of some other business you are thinking of buying. They are also useful for:

1. assisting the bank manager to determine the terms of an overdraft;
2. selling your business to a proposed purchaser;
3. agreeing tax liabilities with the inspector of taxes.

## Checklist: simple accounting systems

1. Do you carry a notebook to record smaller items of business expenditure, such as taxi fares, as soon as they are incurred?
2. Have you considered using credit cards for larger outlays?
3. Do you have a system for filing incoming invoices as soon as they are received?
4. Have you asked your accountant what books and records he or she advises you to keep?
5. If you have adopted an electronic bookkeeping system, have you maintained your records on disk?
6. Do you know and understand the procedures involved? If not, have you asked your accountant to recommend someone who can help you on a regular basis – at least once a week or once a month, depending on your scale of operations?
7. Do you have any idea of the ratios current in your type of business, so that you can measure your performance against the norm?

# 14

# Invoicing and Credit Control

Time is money, as the old saying goes. It ought to be written large in the minds of anyone giving credit, that is, any business that supplies goods and services which are not on a strictly cash-on-the-nail basis, either at a physical point of sale or against orders placed online or by telephone with debit or credit card payment.

In these days of tight money there is a tendency for many customers, including large and reputable firms, to delay payment as long as possible because, as noted in Chapter 9, taking credit long – and preferably giving it short – is one way to maintain a flow of cash in the business. The supplier who does not demonstrate being in a hurry for payment, therefore, is the one who comes last in the queue. However, help to improve the payment culture came in the form of the Statutory Right to Interest (SRI), which was introduced in November 1998. Under the SRI any business with under 50 employees – including sole traders – can charge interest on late payment. While BERR hopes that the parties involved can work out a payment time between themselves, the SRI can enforce a payment schedule of 30 days, after which interest can be charged. The right was rolled out to all businesses regardless of size in the Late Payment Act of November 2000 as described in Chapter 9.

> The supplier who is not in a hurry for payment is the one who comes last in the queue.

# SENDING OUT INVOICES AND STATEMENTS

The first step towards ensuring that you are not in this position is to issue an invoice for work done or goods supplied as soon as possible after you deliver. On the invoice you should give the customer's order number. If it was a telephone order and you forgot to get an order number, you should at least give the date of the order. You should also state when you expect to receive payment. The usual period is between 7 and 30 days after delivery.

Many private individuals, in fact, pay on receipt of an invoice. Business firms, on the other hand, expect to receive a statement of their account at the end of the month, setting out invoices due or sent during this period: their dates, invoice number, the nature of the goods and the amount. You can have statement forms printed, but if you are not a limited company you can use your letterheads for this purpose, simply typing the word STATEMENT at the top.

> Send a statement to every customer who has received an invoice and not paid at the end of the month.

Every customer who has received an invoice and not paid at the end of the month when it is due should get a statement, which should repeat your payment terms.

The particulars of the invoice(s) are drawn from your customers' ledger, though it is essential to keep copies of the actual invoices as well, filed in date order. You are going to need them for VAT purposes, or to check queries. When you receive payment, check that it tallies with the amount due on the customers' ledger entry, mark off the details against each individual item as shown in the previous chapter and enter the amount in the cash book.

If the customer requires a receipt, ask him or her to return the statement (or the invoice if relevant) with remittance – otherwise you will be involved in time-consuming typing – tick off the items paid, and attach a receipt form or bang on a rubber stamp, 'Paid'. Be uniform about your systems. If you have two different ones for the same part of your operation you are going to waste a lot of time looking in the wrong place when you come to check a document.

Do not neglect the process of checking payments, because any amounts unpaid must go into next month's statement. Some invoices which have appeared on your statement will not be paid because they are not yet due for payment. For example, if your terms are 30 days and you have invoiced an item on the 20th of the month, business customers are unlikely to pay until the month following. Quite often they only activate payments at the end of the month, unless they are unusually punctilious, efficient or being offered extra discount for quick settlement.

As already mentioned, the Late Payment Act does allow interest to be charged on late payment. How many businesses are actually taking advantage of the Act and charging interest on customers' overdue balances is questionable. Any reluctance is understandable in a competitive market where customers have little difficulty in changing suppliers. At the time of its introduction back in November 1998, according to *Barclays Small Business Bulletin*, only 24 per cent of small business owners said that they were planning to use the legislation because they did not want to upset customers and create additional administration. However, there is some indication that the introduction of SRI did improve the payment culture.

## Chasing payment

Even with the additional threat of being able to add interest, there will still be times when a client can't or won't pay. What, then, happens when the payment becomes overdue? This is extremely annoying, because at best it is going to involve you in extra correspondence. You must be tactful and patient if you want more business from your clients, and remember that some large organizations are slow in paying, not by choice but because they are dictated to by their computerized accounting systems. But if your patience is exhausted, there are usually three stages in the recovery process.

> You must be tactful and patient if you want more business from your clients.

The first is a polite reminder of the amount due, how long it has been due and of your terms of supply. This should be coupled with asking the customer whether he or she has any queries on any of the invoices which might explain the delay.

If there is no reply by the end of that month, write again, referring to your first reminder and setting a deadline for payment with additional payment. A telephone call to the customer is often opportune at this stage.

If that deadline is not met, you will have to write again, referring to your previous reminders and threatening legal action unless a new and final deadline is met. (If you have a large number of credit accounts, it may save you time to have sets of blank standard letters for each stage prepared in advance.)

# LEGAL ACTION

In most cases the threat of legal action will do the trick, but how you proceed after that depends on the amount of money involved. Fortunately the Court and Legal Services Act of 1990 has simplified procedures. Debts of any amount can be recovered in the County Court, without involving solicitors – though, of course, their services may ultimately be necessary if the claim is disputed by the debtor.

> Debts of any amount can be recovered in the County Court without involving solicitors.

Then there are three important points to establish before starting legal action:

1. Can the defendant actually pay? Wringing blood from a stone is a notoriously fruitless exercise.
2. Can you prove the claim by producing documentation about what was actually agreed, such as a confirming letter? Bounced cheques, reminders to pay, etc, are also relevant.

3. Are you sure you have got hold of the right person? You may have been dealing with an individual acting on behalf of a company. In that case the claim is against the company.

The next stage is to issue a default summons in the County Court. It does not have to be in the area where the defendant lives, which could be in your favour if the case is undefended. If it is defended, the matter will automatically be heard in the defendant's County Court, though here again there is an option to full-scale proceedings. If the amount involved is less than £1,000 the matter automatically goes to arbitration. This means both parties are obliged to accept the arbitrator's judgment.

The default summons involves a certain amount of paperwork. The court officials will brief you if you choose to do this yourself rather than getting your solicitor to do so. Remember, a solicitor may charge you anything from £100 to £200 per hour, depending on how high-powered a firm you choose.

In the first place the summons is sent by post. The defendant then has 21 days in which to reply and if he or she fails to do so or to announce an intention to defend the action, then you as the plaintiff are entitled to judgment, which will include the amount claimed, plus court costs: a maximum of £70 for claims of under £5,000, plus extras which can mount up if the case drags on. The problem is not so much the court costs but the time and trouble that it all takes. However, the good news is that few defendants will let matters go as far as this and the ultimate sanction of having bailiffs called in on them, if they can pay and unless they intend to defend the case.

## BAD DEBT PRECAUTIONS

You can, of course, ask for references before giving credit, though this is a matter which has to be approached with some delicacy; but if you receive a sizeable order out of the blue from some business firm with whom you have not previously dealt, it is advisable to ask for a couple of references in acknowledging the order. Ask the referees to what amount they give credit to this particular

Ask for references if you receive a sizeable order out of the blue.

customer, how long they have been doing business with them and whether they pay promptly.

If your business consists of making or repairing goods to order – tailoring, for instance – it is not unusual to ask the customer to pay up to 50 per cent on account where an estimate of over £100 or so has been given. This helps cash flow as well as protecting you against possible default. Equally, if goods of resaleable value are left with you for repair you should display a notice reserving the right to dispose of them if the customer does not come to collect them within a reasonable time of completion of the work.

A common delaying tactic, or it may be a perfectly legitimate query, is for the customer to ask for copy invoices on receipt of your statement. Do not part with your file copy. You will have to send a photocopy if you do not keep duplicates for this purpose.

# CREDIT CARDS

For larger personal transactions and for items such as the settlement of restaurant bills, credit cards are a popular method of making payment. A business which wants to offer credit card payment facilities to its customers has to make application to the company concerned, which then sets a money limit to the transaction per customer for which the business in question can accept payment on that company's cards. Above that limit, which is based roughly on the applicant's average transaction per customer, the sale has to be referred back to the credit card company. This can be done over the telephone.

Each sale is registered electronically at the cash-out on the customer's debit or credit card and the amount is debited to the card holder's account. The advantage of credit cards from the seller's point of view is that it guarantees payment. Against this, he or she has to pay to the bank a small percentage on every

The advantage of credit cards to the seller is that he or she receives guaranteed payment.

transaction, the amount of this percentage being negotiated at the time of joining the scheme.

Most credit card companies operate on lines very similar to the scheme we have just outlined. Diner's Club vouchers, for instance, though not paid into a bank, are sent to the Club organization on certain specified dates, whereupon payment is made to the seller.

# CHECKING INCOMING INVOICES AND STATEMENTS

Unless you transact your business by paying in cash or by cheque on the spot (which is likely in only a few business spheres), you will also be at the receiving end of invoices and statements from your suppliers. The moment they come in, put them on the spike. Then, daily if possible, enter the details in the suppliers' ledger, as described in Chapter 13. File incoming invoices in date order, for you will need them for VAT purposes.

When you receive your statement, make sure it tallies with the amounts and details which you have entered in the suppliers' ledger, mark off all the items paid and write up the amount in the cash book.

> There is no need to ask for a receipt when paying by cheque since an honoured cheque is itself a receipt.

If you are paying by cheque there is no need to ask for a receipt (which only adds to the paperwork) since an honoured cheque is itself a receipt. Make sure, though, that you enter up the stubs, unless you write up the cash book at the same time as you draw the cheques.

## Checklist: invoicing and credit control

*Invoicing*
1. Are you invoicing promptly, on or with delivery?
2. Do your invoices clearly state your terms?
3. Do you ensure that the customer's name, address and order number (if any) or date are correctly stated on your invoice?
4. Are your statements sent out promptly at the end of the month? Do they state your payment terms?
5. Are they clear and easy to follow? Would they make sense to you if you were the recipient?
6. Are you checking payments received against ledger entries?

*Credit control*
1. Does every account have a credit limit?
2. Is it based on first-hand knowledge of the customer as a credit risk or personally, his or her track record as a payer with you or others in your line of business, on representatives' reports or reliable trade references, or on bankers' references, in that order of decreasing usefulness?
3. Do you exercise special vigilance on new accounts?
4. Do your statements show the age of outstanding balances and do you or your credit controller look at outgoing statements to check on customers whose payments situation seems to be deteriorating?
5. Do you have a system for dealing with customers who exceed their credit limit?
6. Do you have a sequence of reminder procedures for dealing with overdue accounts by telephone calls and/or letters?
7. Do you check orders received against a list of customers who have exceeded their credit limit or who are proving to be reluctant payers or non-payers?
8. Does the person in charge of credit control liaise with those responsible for supplying the account in question to make sure that there are no special reasons for non-payment before sharper warnings are delivered?

9. Do you regularly check on the debtor : sales ratio to make sure you are not heading for a liquidity problem by being too generous about extending credit?
10. Do you have a list of people you can contact in your principal customers' accounts departments if there are payment problems?

# 15

# Costing, Pricing and Estimating

How much should you charge your customers? Or, to put it more searchingly, on what factors should your charges be based? It is surprising that many self-employed people would be hard put to it to give a clear answer to that question. There are such things as 'going rates' and 'recommended' (or generally accepted) prices, but often these are in the nature of broad guidelines and unless you know what all your costs are, not just the cost of materials, or how long the job took you, you are sooner or later going to be in the position of either under-charging or making an actual loss.

> The scope of how much you can charge is narrow in some self-employed occupations... for some jobs there are 'going rates'.

There are some self-employed occupations where the scope for how much you can charge is either narrow or non-existent. This applies particularly to many areas of the retail trade, where goods tend to have recommended prices printed on them by the suppliers; but even there you may want to consider *reducing* some prices in order to undercut a competitor and the question arises whether you can afford to do so. This depends on your overall costs – rent, rates, power supplies and many other factors. Equally, some freelance jobs are subject to generally accepted 'going rates' and the more commonplace such jobs are (ie the smaller the degree of service or expertise that is involved) the more strictly you have to keep within that rate. But the corollary of this statement is also true: the more original your product or service, the more you can afford to charge for it.

This can apply even in the ordinary retail trade, where, on the face of things, the prospect of getting away with charging more than the competition is not promising. Recently a small supermarket opened near my house. It is open late at night, on Sundays and on public holidays and, quite rightly, it charges for that extra time. Most things cost a penny or two above what they do in the larger supermarkets, but it is offering something more than they are, and meets competition not by charging less, but by providing more – a much-needed neighbourhood service for out-of-hours shopping. More recently, several supermarket chains have begun to offer shopping online with a home delivery service, introducing a new element of competition into local food retailing.

The same principle can be applied to even rather routine freelance jobs. Provide a straightforward typing service and you will have to stick pretty much to the going rate; but offer something special, like accurately typing mathematical material or unusually high turnround speeds, and you can move into a different price bracket.

## DETERMINING YOUR COSTS

You could say to yourself: 'I'm going to charge as much as I can get away with' or 'I'm going to charge the standard rate for the job'. These are quite sensible guidelines to be going on with, but at some point you are probably going to be in the situation of wondering whether you should be charging a little more, or perhaps whether you can afford to reduce your price in order to land some work that you badly want. It is then that you have to get to grips with what your costs really are.

> If you undercharge you should be clear in your mind why you are doing so.

The most obvious one is your own time, and curiously enough it is an element that self-employed people are often confused about, because they tend to regard it as being somehow different from the time taken by employees. If a job involves your working flat out for a 100-hour week, you are underpricing the product of that work if your remuneration is less than that of an employed person doing the same kind of work at full overtime rates. There may be a reason why you *should* be undercharging: you may want a 'loss-leader' introduction to a particular customer, or to undercut a competitor, or you may simply need the money that week. But if you undercharge, you should be clear in your mind why you are doing so.

Another factor that is sometimes overlooked is that in most cases there are overhead costs incurred in running your business, irrespective of whether you have work coming in or not. We will deal with these overheads in more detail in a moment, but the point to be made here is to correct any misconception that the margin between what you charge and your basic costs in time and/or materials represents your profit. True, it is a profit of a kind – gross profit. But the real profit element in a job, the net profit, only emerges when the overhead costs have been met. So the right way to work out your price to the customer, or to determine whether a job is worth taking on, is to establish whether it will pay for materials, overheads, wages (if you employ others) and still leave you with a margin of net profit that adequately reflects the time and skill you are putting into it.

> The margin between what you charge and basic costs in time and materials represents gross profit only.

Once you have been in business for a few months you should have accumulated enough facts and figures to establish what your overhead costs are. To what extent you can control the situation beyond that depends, again, on what sort of business you are in. If you are running an ordinary retail shop, operating on margins that are more or less fixed by the supplier, there is not much you can do about pricing your goods, but at least you will know whether you can afford to spend more on extra fittings or take on more staff, or whether you should be staying open longer to attract extra trade.

But if you are manufacturing something, you can work out a rule-of-thumb method in the form of a percentage to add on to your materials costs in quoting prices or, in the case of a service an average hourly rate. It is important, though, to keep on monitoring these rule-of-thumb procedures against what actually happened, so you should keep a record detailing the specification of each job, in which actual costs can be compared against your original estimate. Over a period of time, in this way you should be able to build up a reliable set of costs which can be referred to when an assignment which sounds similar comes up. At the beginning, though, you will have very little to go on, so let us look in more detail at the factors you will have to take into account.

> Keep a record detailing the specifications of each job in which actual costs can be compared against your original estimate.

## Costs connected with your premises

Rent, heat, light, telephone, rates, insurance, finance (if you own or have bought a lease of the premises), cleaning and maintenance contracts and the uniform business rate.

## Costs of finance

Interest charged on overdrafts or loans. You should include in this calculation interest on any money you yourself have put into the business, because it should be earning a rate of return equivalent to what you could get on the open market.

## Costs of equipment

If you are renting equipment or buying it on hire purchase, this item of expenditure presents no problems. The issue is more complicated if you have bought equipment outright, because you have to figure out some way of recovering the purchase price and this is done by bringing in the concept of 'depreciation'. What this means is that you gradually write off, over a period of time based on the item's useful life, most of the amount you paid initially; not

> Depreciation is a real cost factor, not just an accounting device.

all, because it will have some resale value at the end of the depreciation period.

Supposing you bought a second-hand van for £6,000 and you think it will last you for four years, at the end of which time you could expect to get £1,000 for it. This leaves you with £5,000 to depreciate over four years – £1,250 per annum. There are also a number of other ways to calculate depreciation and your accountant will advise you on the method most advantageous to your kind of business. The important point to bear in mind, though, is that depreciation is a real cost factor, not just an accountancy device. Assets like motor cars and equipment do wear out and have to be replaced. Financial reserves should be built up to enable you to do this.

## Administrative costs

Running your business will involve general expenditure which cannot be directly related to particular assignments: stationery, publicity, travel, postage, entertainment of clients, fees to professional advisers, and so forth.

## Salaries and welfare

Salaries are best calculated at an hourly rate, based on an average working week. In the case of employees, these rates are usually determined by the market for that particular kind of employment. The problem is deciding how much you should pay to yourself. Again, this obviously varies with the kind of business you are in, but as a rough guideline you should, after meeting all your expenses, be earning at least as much as an employed person with the same degree of skill and responsibility. It is most important to cost your time properly; let us, therefore, look at a worked example of what might be involved in the case of a person in full-time self-employment.

> It is important to cost your time properly.

Supposing you were aiming to earn £20,000 a year. To start with you would want to take into account four weeks' annual paid holiday (three weeks, plus statutory holidays) and you would assume an eight-hour day and a five-day working week. However, not all your time would be directly productive: some of it would be spent travelling, on administration and on getting work. So let us say your productive time is 32 hours a week. That would give you an hourly rate based on 32 × 48 hours a year: 1,536 hours. Divided into £20,000, that means a rate of about £13.02 per hour. On top of that you have to allow for welfare items: your National Insurance stamp, possibly contributions to a retirement pension scheme and certainly insurance against sickness or death. Let us assume this comes to another £1,000 a year. Divided by 1,536 working hours, this adds another 65 pence to your hourly rate.

Similarly, when costing the time of any full-time staff working for you, it is not just a question of calculating basic rates of pay. You have to allow for holidays, the employer's contribution to National Insurance and to the graduated pension scheme. These items can add up to 35 per cent to the cost of wages.

> Holidays, employer's contribution to National Insurance and to the graduated pension scheme can add up to 35 per cent to the cost of wages.

## Variable costs

All the costs we have just described are fixed costs. You incur them whether you have work coming in or not. Variable costs are items like materials which can be attributed to specific jobs. There are circumstances in which what we have described as fixed costs can vary slightly. If you are running a lot of overtime, this will mean an increase in your fuel bills and extra payments to your staff and/or to yourself. But the benefit of achieving properly costed increases in productivity, for example in the case of a shop staying open late to attract more trade, is that, provided you are able to keep fixed overheads stable, this element will form a smaller proportion relative to your turnover, and that means a more profitable business.

# ESTABLISHING YOUR PRICES

You now have a set of basic data on costs which can be applied to your prices when you are asked to quote for a job or in making up your invoice. If you are supplying a service, the best way to do this is to take all your fixed costs, establish an hourly rate based on your usual working week and then estimate how long the job will take you. The effect of this is that if jobs do not materialize in the way the 'usual working week' concept implies, you yourself are going to be carrying the can for the fixed overheads which are being incurred during all the hours in that week when you are not working. And if you only get 20 hours' work during a week in which you had budgeted for 40, loading your charges to the customer to make up for the shortfall could mean that you will come up with an unacceptable quotation or a price that will discourage your customer in the future.

The other lesson to be learnt is that fixed overheads should be kept as low as possible. For instance, if you are planning a freelance design service to earn extra money in the evenings, you should be chary of acquiring expensive equipment. In the limited hours of work which a part-time freelance operation implies, you may never be able to charge enough money to do more than pay the overheads. As far as possible, keep your costs in the variable category by hiring or renting equipment only when and for as long as you need it.

> Keep your costs in the variable category by hiring equipment or people only when and for as long as needed.

This is also true of businesses that produce manufactured articles (and activities which operate on lines similar to manufacturing, such as a restaurant, where the product is created in the form of a meal), though in these cases some machinery and equipment are usually essential. The price here will be based on a unit per item rather than on an hourly rate, but the principle is the same. Instead of fixing an hourly rate based on an expected working week, calculations should be made on total projected costs spread over the number of units sold. Thus, if you aimed to sell in a week 20 chairs which cost you £15 each in materials, your variable costs would be £300. If your fixed overheads, including your own remuneration, came to £500 a week, you would have to charge £40 per chair just to break even. And do not forget that even if your object is only to make a living wage out of your business, you should still be putting aside reserves to replace equipment as it wears out, and that the cost of doing so will, in periods of inflation, be a great deal higher than its original cost.

## MARGINAL PRICING

Marginal pricing can be defined as the pricing of a product or service at more than the unit direct/variable cost but less than would be necessary to break even at normal trading levels. In other words, sales at marginal prices will make a contribution only to overheads. Marginal pricing is used most normally by manufacturers and retailers to offer product promotions at discounted prices in order to increase sales.

Marginal pricing can be a very effective tool to increase sales (and absolute profits) but it is also a dangerous device when sales are below break-even level and additional promotional sales are gained at the expense of sales at full prices. In the two examples given for break-even analysis in Chapter 3, price-cutting would not help Fred's contract gardening business (Example 2) because he needs to sell his capacity at full price in order to draw the income that he needs. In the case of Angela's boutique (Example 1), marginal pricing on additional products or discounting the prices of more expensive garments that are slow sellers could add both volume and profits when the shop is already close to break-even. Equally, the pricing of excess and slow-moving stock at only slender margins above book value should generate additional profitable sales turnover and will certainly improve stock turn.

## PREPARING QUOTATIONS

With many jobs, whether they are a service or a commission to manufacture something, you will be asked to supply a quotation before a firm order is placed. Once that quotation has been accepted it is legally binding on both parties, so it is important not only to get your sums right but to make it clear in the wording attached to them what exactly you are providing for the money. In the case of a decorating job, for example, you should specify who is providing the materials and, if you are, to what standards they are going to be. Consider also whether any out-of-pocket expenses will be involved (travel, subsistence) and whether these are to be met by your customer or whether they have been allowed for in your quotation.

> Since a quotation is legally binding once accepted, you must be clear in the wording exactly what you are providing.

Apart from variable factors such as these, every quotation should set out the conditions of sale under which it is being offered. Different businesses will involve different kinds of conditions, but here are some basic points to bear in mind:

1. In particular, you should make it clear that the prices quoted are current ones and may have to go up if costs rise during the course of the job.
2. Terms of payment should be set out, for example 30 days net.
3. You will have to cover the not uncommon situation of the customer changing his or her mind about the way the job is done subsequent to accepting your quotation. You should leave yourself free to charge extra in such circumstances.
4. If you have agreed to complete a job within a certain length of time, set out the factors beyond your control which would prevent you from meeting the agreed date.
5. You should make it clear what circumstances of error, loss or damage will be your responsibility and what would fall outside it.
6. You should stipulate that once the quotation is accepted, the order cannot be cancelled except by mutual consent and that the customer will be liable for all charges up to that point.

7. You should mention that the total is subject to VAT at the rate ruling at the date of invoice. This is particularly important when the customer is a private person who is unable to claim back VAT inputs. (See Chapter 20 for details of VAT.)

Having gone to all the trouble to set out the quotation and conditions of sale, you should not neglect to check, before you start work, that the customer has actually accepted it in writing! It is all too easy to forget this or to imagine that an amicable verbal OK is sufficient. If a dispute arises, however, you will be very thankful to have carried out all the formal steps of documentation.

Every few months sit back for half an hour and consider your pricing policy. If you have set up as a consulting engineer and have no wish to get involved with renting offices and employing others, your workload capacity is limited to the number of hours you put in. To start with, you will probably be glad of work at any price, but as your business builds up to the point where you are working all hours, the only way you will be able to increase your real income is to increase your prices. So if you have a reliable supply of work coming in which is giving you a reasonable income, do not be afraid to put in some highish quotes for new work. It is not always the case that the lowest tender wins the job, particularly in the field of consultancy.

> Before you start work, check that the customer has actually accepted your quotation and conditions of sale.

## Checklist: costing, pricing and estimating

1. How original is your product or service? If it is not particularly uncommon, how can you make it more so?
2. How essential is it to the customer?
3. What is the competition charging for the same or a similar product or service?
4. How badly do you need the job or order?
5. Is your customer likely to come back for more if the price is right, or is it a one-off?
6. Will doing business with this customer enable you to break into a wider market, and thus enable you to reduce your unit costs?
7. What is the element of risk involved (ie is the customer, to your knowledge, a quick and certain payer)?
8. Do you have any idea how long the job will take you?
9. Can you relate the time element to your fixed costs?
10. Have you made a full assessment of all your fixed costs?
11. Do you have any idea what your materials are going to cost you?
12. Have you costed your own time properly?
13. Will the job leave you a margin of net profit? Or should you forgo this in the interest of meeting fixed costs?
14. Should you adopt marginal pricing?
15. Have you prepared a quote, specifying exactly what you are going to provide or do, including terms of payment?
16. Has the customer accepted your quotation?
17. Are you keeping records of what the job cost you so that you can adjust your prices or quote more accurately next time?

# Part Three

# Building Your Business

# Effective Marketing

Good ideas, it is sometimes dismissively said, are ten a penny, the implication being that the really difficult part is putting them into effect. Apart from the obvious virtues of persistence, hard work and technical know-how, this also requires a modicum of marketing skill. In other words, you will have to know whether there is a big enough demand for your product or service at the price you need to charge to make a living and how to identify and reach your potential customers.

## MANUFACTURERS

You may be the world's most skilful maker of hand-carved model sailing ships, but unless enough people want them you are going to have a hard time trying to make a living out of producing them commercially. It is worth doing some research before you start in business and the following methods should help you direct your products more effectively:

■ Look around. Go to gift shops, luxury stores or wherever it is that the kind of item you are aiming to produce is being sold and find out about prices, quality standards and the extent of the demand. Shop managers might help advise you on any modifications required to your idea.

■ Consider whether there is a long-term future for your product. Are you able to keep ahead by being in a position to meet the next craze before the big manufacturers become aware of it?

■ Keep an eye on competitors of your own size to ensure your own commercial viability and to see if there is a gap in the market for your product.

But no matter how good or original your product may be, the ultimate key to success lies in effective sales and distribution. At the smallest level you might be selling direct to the public through your own shop, as is the case with many craft goods, but you have to bear in mind that you need to achieve a considerable turnover for a shop in a good location to be viable. This is difficult if the range of specialization is very narrow, and many small-scale manufacturers, therefore, combine having their own shop with direct mail and mail order (which we shall come to in a moment) and with marketing to other retail outlets. Shop and workshop premises can be combined in the same floor area, so that you can switch readily from the sales counter to the workbench when the shop is empty. This requires permission from the local planning authority if a 'change of use' of what were originally shop premises is involved.

> However good or original the product, the ultimate key to success lies in effective sales and distribution.

Starting-up costs will eat deeply into your capital, so unless you have enough experience of the marketing (as opposed to the manufacturing) end of your speciality to be absolutely convinced that you can sell it, it is a good idea to begin by making a few prototypes of the product and its packaging and by trying to get orders from retailers. Though your friends and family may think your idea is wonderful, the acid test is whether it will survive in the marketplace. In the course of investigating this, the natural conservatism of most branches of the retail trade may at times depress or irritate you, but it is worth listening to what people who are involved in it have to say. If the same criticisms keep on cropping up, you should think seriously of modifying your prototype to take them into account.

Distribution can be another big headache and your premises should be big enough to enable you to hold roughly as many days' or weeks' supply of stock as it takes to replace it at its rate of demand. If a business is selling 10 chairs a week and it takes two weeks to get that number of replacements, there should, ideally, be space for something like 20 chairs. A customer might be prepared to wait a week before delivery, but is unlikely to wait a month.

Accessibility of non-selling areas is important too. Adequate entry for goods and materials at the rear or side of the premises is often essential and will always save time and energy.

# DEALING WITH LARGE COMPANIES

Winning an order from a large company can put a small business on its feet at a stroke, not only directly but in terms of gaining credibility with other customers. But pursuing orders of that kind is not without its perils. For one thing, large firms are not necessarily rapid payers; nor, as some bankruptcies have shown, is a household name inevitably a sign of financial soundness. Careful checks with your bank are essential.

The implications of a big order also need to be thought out very fully in cash-flow terms, and if progress payments are not offered, other forms of finance will have to be found. A further point to consider is that it is highly likely that a major customer will seek to impose conditions not only of price, but of quality and delivery. Fair enough; but in combination these three can make what seems like a high-value order look much less tempting on the bottom line of profitability.

> If progress payments are not offered with big orders, other forms of finance will have to be found.

The whole thing becomes even more complicated if you find you have to subcontract part of the job, as is often the case when a small business lands in the big time. Unless you can control the subcontractor's work very tightly by writing and being in a position to enforce a very clear set of specifications, you can land yourself in the position one small book publisher got into once. It won an order from a major chain of multiples for many tens of thousands of copies of a number of titles. For cost reasons these had to be printed in the Far East and when they were delivered they did not match up to the very strict merchandising standards that had been stipulated. What had looked like a wonderful stroke of good fortune turned into a horrifying, litigation-laden loss.

> Large companies seldom deal with small businesses whose approach is less than 100 per cent professional.

Of course, large companies are anxious to avoid this sort of thing, so they seldom deal with small businesses whose approach is less than 100 per cent professional. A lot of them, by all accounts, fall down at this first hurdle. However good your idea or product, it will never even come up for discussion unless your letter is clearly and neatly presented, reasonably well written and, above all, sent to the right person. Firms are full of stories of letters being sent to executives who had long left the company and whose names had been gleaned from some out-of-date directory. One phone call would have done the trick.

The lesson that small things make big impressions is also worth remembering when the big customer you have been courting finally sends his or her inspection team or purchasing officer round. Nothing looks worse than a scruffy reception area or sounds worse than badly briefed staff. Indeed, you yourself should make sure that you can answer convincingly all the questions you are likely to be asked on such things as capacity, delivery, the quality of your workforce and whatever is connected with the business you are trying to win.

## SHOPS AND SERVICE INDUSTRIES

The first large shopping centre built in Britain many decades ago was a flop because, among other disadvantages, it had no parking facilities and was situated in a working-class area a few minutes' walk away from a large, long-established and very popular street market. The developers, for all their vast financial resources, had ignored hotel magnate Conrad Hilton's three factors in siting a business serving the public: location, location and location. If you are thinking of setting up a shop, restaurant or some other service outlet, find out as much as possible about the area and ask:

- Who lives there?
- Is the area declining economically or is it on the up and up?
- What is the range of competitors and how well are they doing?
- If you are thinking of opening a high-class restaurant and there are nothing but fish and chip establishments in the neighbourhood, does this mean that there is no demand for a good restaurant or a crying need for one?

Take the case of a bookshop. You would want to conduct some rule-of-thumb market research about the area before going any further. For example, you would want to know whether there were enough people in the area to support such a venture, whether they were the sort of people who regularly bought books, how good the local library was and how strong the competition was from national multiples. You would also want to know what impact the result of your market investigations might have on your trading policies. Thus, if there were a lot of families with young children around, you should be considering getting to know, and stocking, children's books; or, if there were a lot of students in the neighbourhood, it would be worth your while finding out what textbooks were being used in local educational institutions. Alternatively, if your bookshop is highly specialized – medicine, academic history, chess, or some other specific activity – an expensive high street location is likely to be wholly inappropriate. You

Do not overlook basic market research just because you are buying a 'going concern'.

will want to be near the centre of that activity, or, more likely, will want to sell to your well-defined audience through direct mail.

The same broad principles apply to almost every kind of retail or service outlet and you will have to conduct this kind of research, which is really just plain common sense, whatever your venture. Do not be tempted to overlook it just because you are buying what is supposed to be a 'going concern'. One reason why it is up for sale may be that, despite the owner's or agent's protestations to the contrary, it was doing badly. If that was because the previous owner was a poor manager or stocked the wrong kind of goods for the neighbourhood you might be able to turn the business around, but if there was simply too much competition in the area from similar shops and there is no chance of trading viably in something else from the same address, you would be well advised to forget about those premises, however good a buy they may seem from a purely cost point of view. You will also be able to check on the vendor's assertions by looking, preferably with your accountant, at his profit and loss accounts, not just for the past year but the previous three to five years, to get a picture of the general trend of things. On the whole, buying a going concern has to be approached with great caution, particularly by the inexperienced, because of the difficulties of valuing stock and goodwill with any accuracy. See Chapter 8 for more detailed treatment of these points.

## FREELANCE SERVICES

Most freelancers agree that the way you get work is by knowing people who are in a position to give it to you. That sounds rather like a chicken-and-egg situation and, to begin with, so it is. You would be ill-advised to launch into freelance work, certainly on a full-time basis, until you have built up a range of contacts who can provide you with enough work to produce some sort of living for at least the first few months. Often these are people whom you have got to know in the course of a full-time job, or while doing temporary work. Many advertising agencies, for instance, have

> To start with you get work by knowing people who are in a position to give it to you.

been started by a breakaway group taking a batch of clients with them when they start up.[1] And it may even be that your employer, having been compelled to make you redundant, will still be willing to put work out to you on a freelance basis.

Once you have got going and established a reputation for doing good, reliable work, things get much easier. For one thing, word-of-mouth recommendations have a strong effect in the freelance world. Moreover, you will be able to produce examples of work sold, or be able to refer prospects to other clients who have engaged you successfully. Evidence, for instance, that your fashion photographs have actually been used by national magazines is generally more impressive than a folder of prints, no matter how good they are. In freelance work, as in other spheres, nothing succeeds like success.

> Word-of-mouth recommendations have a strong effect in the freelance world.

One problem with freelance work, though, is that clients often want something done in a hurry – over a weekend or even overnight. This can be highly inconvenient at times, but it is generally a bad idea to turn work down simply for this reason. If you have to be selective, turn away the smaller, less remunerative jobs or commissions from people who are slow to pay their bills. One thing you should never do is to let a client down. If you cannot, or do not want to, take on an assignment, say so immediately.

## PRESS ADVERTISING

Advertising is a marketing tool and like any other tool you have to use it in the right place, at the right time and for the right job if it is going to be of any use to you. If you are a local building contractor, there is no point in advertising in national newspapers, because most of the circulation, which is what you are paying for in the rates charged, will be outside the geographical area you are

---

[1] To combat this trend many firms now include clauses in their employment contract expressly stating that it is not permissible to work for a client of the employer for two years after leaving that employer.

Use advertising in the right place, at the right time, for the right job.

working in. On the other hand, if you are making a product to sell by mail order, the bigger the circulation the better. There are, however, still provisos; there is, for example, no point in advertising a product aimed at 'top people' in a mass-circulation tabloid.

When considering advertising think about:

- The right medium for the product or service you have to sell.
- The quality of the circulation rather than the figures. A small specialist or local paper might provide as good a return as a mass circulation publication.
- A regular 'classified' insertion will remind readers of your services and will be relatively inexpensive.
- Display advertising can be placed in eye-catching positions. These are more expensive than classified adverts and will need to be designed by a graphic designer (look in *Yellow Pages* or the *Thomson Local* directory) but you can control where they are placed.
- Experiment with different days for your advert to appear as some days can produce a better response than others.
- Experiment with wording, but do not use too many words. Be specific about how goods and services can be obtained. Your address and availability times should be prominent.
- Include an order coupon stating price *and* postage. This will also provide information on where your sales come from and will help future marketing efforts.

## PUBLIC RELATIONS

It may be possible, particularly if you have a specialist line of business, to obtain free coverage in trade journals and local newspapers by sending them press releases to mark events such as the opening of an extension or the provision of some unique service. You simply type the information on a slip marked PRESS RELEASE; 'embargo' it – ie prohibit its use – until a date that suits you, and send it to newspapers and magazines you choose as the likeliest to use it. Be sure to include your full contact details. Newspapers and other news media – don't forget about local radio and even local TV – are, however, only interested in _news_ and the mere fact that you have opened a business may not interest them much. Try to find a news angle; for instance, that you have obtained a large export order, or are reviving a local craft or are giving employment to school-leavers. If you have any friends who are journalists, ask their advice on the sort of information that is likely to get the attention of editors. Better still, ask them if they will draft your press release for you.

> Try to find a news angle that is likely to get the attention of editors.

There are many other PR activities – sponsorship, stunts, celebrity appearances at your premises, public speaking, and so on. All are designed to publicize who you are and what you do, and suggest to the public that you provide a worthwhile and reliable service. PR for the small business is covered thoroughly in Michael Bland's _Be Your Own PR Man_ (published by Kogan Page).

## DIRECT MAIL AND DIRECT RESPONSE PROMOTION

Direct mail selling is a considerable subject in its own right. It differs from mail order in that the latter consists of mailing goods direct to the customer from orders engendered by general press advertising, whereas in the case of direct mail selling the advertising is a brochure or sales letter specifically directed at the

> Unless you are very skilful at writing sales literature, get an expert to do this.

customer. Direct response promotion consists of an ad plus coupon placed in a newspaper or journal, to be posted to the manufacturer as an order. If you use these methods, remember to allow for postage in your pricing, and since the response to direct mail averages around 2 per cent, the postage cost per sale is quite a considerable factor. It can, however, be a very effective way of selling specialized, high-priced items (£25 is around the viable minimum these days) or of identifying people who are likely to buy from you regularly if you are selling variations on the same product. Unless you are very skilful at writing brochures or sales letters, you should get this done for you by an expert. Such people are employed by mailing list brokers (you will find those in the *Yellow Pages*), who will often provide a complete package: they will sell to you, or compile for you, specialized lists, address and stuff envelopes, and produce sales literature.

> Before you plunge into a direct mail campaign, test the market with a sample mailing.

Their services are not cheap and before you plunge into a direct mail campaign there are relatively inexpensive ways of testing the market for yourself. Pick 100 specialist addresses of the type you want to reach on a bigger scale – again, you may find them in the *Yellow Pages*. A small 'wanted' ad in one of the advertising industry's trade papers will soon raise the services of freelance copywriters and designers if you need such help. From the percentage reply to the sample mailing, you will be able to gauge whether a bigger campaign is worth mounting and you will also get some idea of how to price the product to take into account the likely mailing costs per sale. It is generally essential, by the way, with direct mail advertising, to include a reply-paid card or envelope with your sales literature. Details of how to apply for reply-paid and Freepost facilities are available from the Post Office.

## Mail Order Protection Schemes

Before you can start selling by direct response advertising in a newspaper or periodical, you will have to get permission to do so from its mail order protection scheme (MOPS). These schemes have been set up under the auspices of the Office of Fair Trading to protect consumers from fraudulent advertisers. Essentially, the various media act as insurers and undertake to refund readers' money if the advertiser absconds or fails to deliver for some reason or other. Before accepting the insurance risk, papers and periodicals will therefore try to satisfy themselves that the advertiser is above board. In the case of national media their requirements will be quite searching; they may want to see accounts, take up credit and other references and even look over your premises. Applications for MOPS clearing at this end of the advertising market have to be accompanied by a fee which can go well into four figures and which has to be renewed every year. Requirements in local and trade media are less exacting, but you still need clearance before they will take your advertisement.

## MARKETING ON THE INTERNET

The first question is to decide whether or not you need a website in order to promote your business. Why would any potential customer want to visit your website? Of course, they will only come if they know it exists or they stumble upon it while browsing the internet.

Having found your website, potential customers will only stay if it is interesting and only purchase your product online if the purchasing routines are straightforward and convenient. Plainly, if you are offering a local service, such as contract gardening or a taxi service, potential customers are unlikely to search for your service online, and are more likely to do so in the _Yellow Pages_. Therefore, for service providers that are not national firms, setting up your own website is not likely to do more than increase costs. Even for businesses with products that are eminently saleable over the internet, setting up a website creates a fresh problem because you will have to make an additional marketing effort to promote the website in order to attract visitors. Do not underestimate either the cost or effort of continually updating the website and installing and operating an efficient ordering and fulfilment system.

## Attracting visitors

The first step is to register your website on one or more search engines, such as Google, that display a list of sites of interest if a visitor types in a topic. In order to do this you will need to send a summary to the search engine editors and probably pay a fee, as well as including keywords on your website.

You could also promote your website by establishing links with other websites where there could be a reference (your website address, logo or words) which once clicked will direct visitors to your website. Of course, most websites would only agree to a link if there is a perceived opportunity of attracting traffic from your site through to theirs by means of a reciprocal link. Therefore, reciprocal links are most effective when the products or services of the collaborators are complementary. If you market your products or services locally, you might be able to negotiate a link on the website of your local authority or tourist office.

Another alternative is to advertise your products or services on someone else's websites, but don't expect too much. Many browsers of the Internet are irritated by advertisements and you should not be too impressed by the number of daily or monthly 'hits' claimed for any website when buying space.

The cheapest way to promote your website is to put your website address on all your firm's literature, including letterheads, catalogues, flyers and order forms. Some of your customers may prefer to access information about your firm and its products on the web before talking to you.

## Designing your website

Having taken the decision to proceed, keep the following points in mind when designing your website:

- Allow easy entry to your website. Don't put visitors off by requiring them to register first.
- Encourage visitors to register later by offering benefits, such as a newsletter or priority access to special offers. What you are after is their e-mail addresses, which you can use for direct mail campaigns.

▎ Focus your site on being a rapid source of information rather than over-elaborate. Too many illustrations and graphics simply slow the process down.

▎ Offer real service and real value to potential customers.

▎ Think carefully about how to receive payments from orders placed online. You can use specialists to design secure links for you to accept payments direct. Alternatively, linking up with reputable parties to whom you can subcontract payment collection and receipt could relieve you of an administrative burden.

▎ Budget for the overall website development in your business plan.

Online for Business is a public–private partnership run by BERR that provides hands-on information and communications technology experience for businesses. For more information and advice, telephone 08457 152000 or visit its website www.ukonlineforbusiness.gov.uk. For a full account of internet marketing, see _Doing Business on the Internet_ by Simon Collin (Kogan Page).

## Checklist: marketing your work

_Manufacturers_

1. Have you tested your idea by discussing your proposed product with potential customers? Or, better still, by showing it to them?
2. Is the market for it big enough? How accessible is it?
3. Can the customers you have in mind afford a price that will produce a profit for you?
4. Have you studied the competition from the point of view of price, design quality, reliability, delivery dates, etc?
5. Should you modify your product so as to get the edge on the competition? What will this do to your costs?
6. Is there a long-term future for your product? If not, do you have any ideas for a follow-up?
7. Can you handle distribution? Do you have access to a van if the market is local? Do you have adequate parking facilities if it requires dispatching?

8. Have you taken dispatching costs into account in working out how much the product will cost the customer?
9. Do you have adequate space to hold stock, taking into account production time?
10. Do you have someone who can deal with customer queries and complaints? Or have you allowed for the fact that you will have to take time out yourself to deal with them?

*Shops and service industries*
1. How much do you know about the area?
2. Is the location good from the point of view of attracting the kind of trade you are looking for?
3. What competitors do you have?
4. How are they doing?
5. Based on your study of the area, and the people who live in it, how does this affect the type of goods or the nature of the service you are going to offer?
6. If you are buying a going concern, have you checked it out thoroughly with your professional advisers?

*Freelance services*
1. Do you have any contacts who can give you work?
2. Have you made a realistic appraisal of how much you can expect to earn over the first six months?
3. Have you allowed for the fact that you will need spare time to go around looking for more business?
4. What evidence can you produce of your competence to do freelance work in your proposed field?
5. Have you shown that evidence to the sort of person who might be a customer to get his or her reaction on whether it is likely to impress?
6. Who are your competitors, what do they charge and what can you offer that is superior to their services?

*Advertising and promotion*
1. Have you chosen the right medium to promote your product or service?

2. Do you have any idea of the circulation and how this is broken down, geographically or by type of reader?

3. Have you worked out any way of monitoring results, for instance by including a coupon?

4. Have you included the cost of advertising and promotion in your cash-flow budget and in costing your product?

5. How many orders do you need to get from your advertising/promotion campaign to show a profit?

6. In the case of a display advertisement, have you specified a position in which it is to appear?

7. Again, in the case of a display ad or a brochure, have you had it properly designed?

8. Does your advertising/promotion material state where your product or service can be obtained and the price?

9. Is the wording compelling? Does it clearly describe the product or service and does it motivate the customer? Would you buy it, if you were a customer?

10. In the case of a classified advertisement, have you specified under which classification it is to appear?

11. Are all the statements and claims you are making about your product or service true to the best of your knowledge and belief, bearing in mind that untruths can leave you open to prosecution under the Trade Descriptions Acts?

12. Have you looked at other companies' websites to see what works for users before designing your own?

13. Is your website attractive to customers and easy to use? Do you update it regularly?

14. Have you registered with search engines?

15. Can you build a database for direct e-mailing?

# 17

# Using IT to Run Your Office

Advances in technology over the past decade have made information technology (IT) an essential tool for even the smallest office and everyone in business. Whereas 10 years ago a personal computer, fax and answerphone were probably all the equipment that start-up businesses needed, the phenomenal growth of e-commerce has caused most individuals and all businesses to consider how best to harness information and communication technologies (ICT) for their use.

For small businesses the ready accessibility and affordability of ICTs, and in particular the internet, have had a threefold impact. They have:

1. made working from home easier;
2. given credibility to the smallest businesses, whatever their physical location;
3. provided access to a global market.

> ICT gives credibility to the smallest business.

However, there are several downsides to e-trading. First, there are serious concerns over the ability of the internet to be secure and to maintain confidentiality of customer data. Data security is a matter of public concern, particularly in light of major lapses that have emerged on the part of government departments over the past few years in relation to personal records.

Second, and of relevance to both small businesses that grow fast and larger businesses that sell their products online, the risks of over-trading are enhanced as a result of e-trading. Websites may boost sales to such an extent that businesses are unable to service orders properly because their distribution and warehousing facilities are inadequate. Taking orders that cannot be serviced within the stated time span is a certain recipe for losing customer goodwill and damaging a supplier's reputation. Even Amazon.com suffers from this problem, particularly in the case of books that are unexpected bestsellers.

Of course, experience will iron out some of these problems and the benefits of e-commerce for small businesses greatly outweigh the risks. In today's climate, most small businesses, particularly those providing intangible services, that fail to adopt ICT systems and e-commerce into their work practices cannot expect to remain competitive.

> Adopt ICT systems into your work practices or risk being uncompetitive.

Be sure to take advantage of the internet and your ICT connections to manage your bank account online, to make payments and to receive payments from customers by direct electronic transfer.

# DEVELOPING YOUR IT SYSTEM

If you have no prior experience of building an IT system, start by assessing your business needs, and choose solutions that address them now while allowing for adaptation and extension in the future as you business grows and changes. The aim is to get the most you can from IT in your business and it is easy to over-sophisticate at the outset.

## The basic components

There is a strong argument for deciding what software you need before selecting and buying the hardware on which it will operate.

The temptation to buy expensive state-of-the-art hardware which may have inadequate capacity (memory and hardcore) to satisfy your requirements or with more capacity than you can use in the short-term should be avoided.

Focus first on selecting the software to run your business and then develop a specification of the appropriate hardware capability in terms of processing and memory (MHz and RAM) that will provide the technical criteria for your choice of hardware. These days all standard hardware packages include a range of software, but not necessarily the standard software that you need for your business. For example, a laptop PC or desktop configuration may be on offer at an attractive price with Microsoft Vista Home Premium software when what you need is Microsoft Windows XP Professional. You can buy the XP Professional software separately and install it, but that may blunt the edge of your perceived bargain.

> Focus first on identifying the software that suits your business requirements best.

As a first step in the selection process, you should visit the Business Link website: www.businesslink.gov.uk, where you will find two informative guides, 'Computer software: the basics' and 'Computer hardware: the basics'. You are unlikely to want payroll software when starting to work for yourself, but a computerized accountancy system is worth considering and there are a number, such as Sage, on the market. There is another useful guide on the Business Link website, 'Accounting software', that you can consult.

> It is cheaper to adapt your business processes to standard software than have a special program written.

You should avoid committing yourself to software that requires 'bending' (adapting) to your particular application. This may well be possible but it is extremely expensive and it will almost certainly be cheaper to change your operating procedures or business processes rather than commission a special bespoke program to be written for you.

When starting up your business, you are well advised to use IT systems from the outset. Converting from paper-based systems to electronic processes is a tedious and time-consuming chore.

Having defined the capability specification, your first decision in selecting from the appropriate hardware available will be between a laptop PC and a desktop with peripherals. Desktops are considerably cheaper than laptops, but if you are on the move a lot it may make more sense to buy a laptop with the complete wired and wireless connectivity that enables you to access the internet and send and receive e-mails remotely. The current generation of laptops have impressive specifications and match desktops in terms of GHz and RAM. Nearly all desktops and laptops include a modem and fax facility.

> Laptops match desktops in terms of processing speed and basic memory.

If you like to work with a large screen, although 17" screens are now commonplace on laptops, you can enhance the screen image when you are at your home base by plugging in a larger screen monitor.

# MORE EFFECTIVE COMMUNICATION USING IT

The rationale for most IT and e-commerce systems is to make communication between buyers and sellers or between clients and service providers both faster and more reliable.

## Telephone systems

The choice of telephone lines and tariffs for your telephone and internet connections used to be a simple matter, but there are now a variety of alternatives ranging from broadband to an Integrated Services Digital Network (ISDN) line. When starting your business you will probably find the first or second level of broadband more than adequate. The availability of broadband in all but the most remote areas provides an attractive low-cost alternative for faster communications to which most business users have now been converted. The top level of broadband is significantly faster in transmitting and receiving data but also considerably more expensive and its capability is more than most small businesses need.

> Most small businesses starting up will find the second level of broadband adequate for their needs.

ISDN is a high-speed digital equivalent to a normal telephone line and is recommended if you want to link several users to the internet. It is estimated to be as much as four times as fast as most modems and can connect you to your internet service provider (ISP) almost instantly. Therefore, if there are three or four people working with you in your office the ISDN alternative merits serious consideration.

## Mobile telephony

Mobile telephones seem to have become a lifestyle essential. For businesspeople on the move they are almost indispensable. The newest versions offer internet access, fax, e-mail and texting functions. Some also have entertainment functions with integrated music, DVD and photographic facilities that are less relevant to business, although perhaps offering comfort to those away from home. In choosing your mobile telephone you should include it in your overall integrated ICT strategy.

## Internet service provider

You will need to sign up with an Internet Service Provider (ISP) to access the internet and to send and receive e-mails. ISP monthly

> Be careful to choose an ISP that is compatible with the leading international ISPs.

fees vary widely, typically £23 to £29 per month. There are many cheaper providers, some with 'free' introductory offers, but opting for one of these may be a false economy since technical support services may be an additional cost. You should also consider whether the ISP you choose provides a compatible connection to all the better-known international ISPs. For example, some of the smaller UK-based ISPs have difficulty in transmitting e-mails or their attachments to AOL, one of the foremost global service providers.

## Networks

Local networks are used by companies to link their employees either within a single building, or to teleworkers based in various locations. If your business relies on knowledge outworkers, a Local Area Network (LAN) might be useful, allowing files and resources to be shared. Access to the internet can also be provided by connection to an ISP via an ISDN or leased telephone line.

## Electronic data interchange (EDI)

EDI facilitates the exchange of business documents between the computers of trading partners. It allows purchasers and suppliers to handle transactions down telephone lines by sending purchase orders and invoices in an electronic form. For small and start-up businesses where the number of transactions is relatively small, EDI is unlikely to be cost-effective, and using e-mail with attachments will be more appropriate.

# DAY-TO-DAY MANAGEMENT ISSUES

There are simple best practice procedures and routines that you should observe, if you don't have technological expertise, to manage your day-to-day IT operations. The various guides to be found on the Business Link website: www.businesslink.gov.uk will provide you with a basic briefing.

## ICT checklist

- Choose your computer software with extreme care to suit your business. Develop the software specification first before shopping for hardware and peripherals.
- Install maintenance routines, back-ups and a disaster recovery plan. (At the least, copy the important files on your computer onto CDs frequently and store the CDs in a different location).
- Consider outsourcing the regular maintenance of your IT system.
- Make sure that your system can communicate with others, both inside and outside your business as necessary. Use your ICT system to manage your banking online.
- If you have a website or run an e-commerce site, ensure that the site content is accurate and updated regularly.
- Secure your systems by making the small investment required in a firewall and anti-virus software.
- Find out how to protect yourself against online threats caused by hackers or denial-of-service attacks.

# 18

# Is Foreign Trade Fun?

'Exporting is fun' said Harold Macmillan when he was prime minister more than 50 years ago, though it may perhaps be doubted whether he knew much about filling in bills of lading in sextuplicate or waiting for an onward flight in a corrugated iron shed in Burkina Faso. At any rate, it took a long time for the export message to sink in with British firms and even now many small companies put exporting fairly low on their list of priorities. But while it is true that it is usually essential to get one's place established in the domestic market, there are many attractions to exporting.

## Benefits of exporting

- It increases sales and therefore lowers unit costs.
- It decreases dependence on the UK market.
- It can produce increased profits in countries where you can charge higher prices or where sterling has a poor exchange rate.
- It broadens one's awareness of other markets and sometimes gives warning of competing products being developed or on sale elsewhere.
- It gives you a chance to see the world 'on the company'.

Even if you find none of these reasons compelling enough to make you want to leave your home patch, there are circumstances under which you can become an exporter without really wishing to. If you have a good product, it is very possible that someone abroad will get to hear of it and want to buy it. This is more likely today than ever before if your business has is own website. Indeed, that is how many small companies first become involved, having made the wise decision that business should never be turned away.

> If you have a good product, someone abroad will get to hear of it and want to buy.

If, however, you decide to play a more active role as an exporter than just meeting the demand as it occurs, what special factors should a small business look at? Actually, in many respects they are not very different from those that apply domestically: that the product has to be competitive in price and quality or that it has a unique feature which places it in a class of its own, but for which there is also a viable demand at a price you are reasonably sure the market will pay. Where export does raise special problems is that you also have to make sure that the product meets local specification in terms of technical requirements and consumer laws; that it can thrive under what may be quite different environmental and climatic conditions; that manuals and user instructions are intelligible, either in English or in translations; and that it does not breach any cultural taboos. The last named is often more important and wide ranging than people realize. One Australian meat company nearly lost a huge Middle East order because their house symbol was stamped on their cheques. It was a pig, an unclean animal in Muslim countries.

> Exporting raises special problems in terms of technical requirements, consumer laws and climatic conditions.

Indeed, all markets have their peculiarities and the advice generally given to exporters is first to visit one country or region and get to know it rather than trying to sell to the world. For example, exporters to the US market often fail to realize that the United States is such a huge country that the characteristics of the Midwest are different from those of California and that both are different from the South or New York City. Freight is a factor there too – freight costs can eat deeply into margins and you have to consider that the price of your goods to the customer has to include the cost of physically getting them delivered.

Similar lessons can be drawn from Africa with its widely different climatic conditions and its heavy ingredient of political risk, from Asia and Australia where sheer distance from the United Kingdom means that it can take weeks to get the goods there and further weeks to get payment, and even from the EU. Generally, exporting to the more sophisticated markets of Asia, where there is a demand for your products, is a more fruitful and less trying experience.

# WHERE TO GET HELP

Fortunately, there are quite a few sources of help and advice for those who want to become exporters. Addresses and websites can be found at the back of this book.

▪ Local Chambers of Commerce are often well informed about major markets.
▪ Many of Britain's major trading partners maintain trade associations in London (eg the German-British Chamber of Industry and Commerce, the Arab-British Chamber of Commerce) and though some of them are more concerned with exporting to this country than importing into their own, they do also know what the requirements are in the latter case.
▪ The customer service division of the overseas departments of the big four banks.
▪ BERR. They produce basic information online on all the major countries which do business with British firms and you can also get special reports on particular countries, which cost somewhat more. They can also tell you about buying missions from overseas buying organizations established in this country by major foreign department stores, for instance.

Equally usefully, departments of BERR organize trade missions through local Chambers of Commerce or trade associations. These enable you to visit major markets as part of a group with a substantial government subsidy. Since contacts can be arranged in advance, this is a considerable saving in time as well as money. Usually, if you go on your own to another country, it takes days simply to find your bearings and set up meetings.

▌ UK Trade and Investment, with its own informative website. When contacting UK Trade and Investment, ask to be put through to the country desk dealing with the country you are planning to export to. The website address is www. uktradeinvest.gov.uk.

▌ Through its trade division, BERR also organizes local seminars for small exporters – call 020 7215 8000 for details.

## SETTING UP SALES ARRANGEMENTS

Few firms will want to move so far, so fast, though. Usually it is a question of setting up some kind of sales operation by appointing a local agent; you may already have been approached by one keen to handle your business. Flattering though such interest is, and though it certainly helps to start out with someone who feels optimistic about your prospects, agents do have to be checked out. Bad ones may not only hinder your progress, but may cost you a lot of money by alienating dealers or by taking commission on business which you would have got anyway and which they have

Be sure to check out agents thoroughly before engaging them.

made little effort to expand.

The best plan is undoubtedly to go out to the territory and meet the prospective agent personally. Apart from any impressions you form of the agent and his or her office – you should certainly see the latter – you should find out who else he or she is working for and preferably get a statement of that in writing. You will be known in that territory by the company you keep. Quite apart from the fact that the agent's other clients should be appropriate to your business – there is no point in having someone handling medical supplies when all their other agencies are office equipment – they should also be reputable. Preferably, the principals in some cases should be known to you so that you can make further inquiries back in the United Kingdom.

Once you have satisfied yourself of the agent's bona fides, there should be a written agreement.

## Basic agency agreement terms

- The territory.
- The period of time the agreement is to run for.
- Payment terms.
- Whether the agency is exclusive or not; and, if customers are still free to buy direct from you, whether the agent gets commission on such business.
- Whether or not he or she is to be a stockist, and if so, on what terms he or she has the right to return unsold goods.
- What you undertake to provide, free or otherwise, in the way of promotional back-up.

Once you have appointed an agent it is equally important to keep taking an interest in activities. If he or she never hears from you, the agent will assume that you have forgotten his or her existence. A word of praise, or even complaint, never comes amiss.

Keep taking an interest in your appointed agent's activities.

Remember the US saying, 'The wheel that squeaks loudest gets the most oil'.

## DOCUMENTATION

What chiefly deters small businesses – and some larger ones – from actively pursuing export sales is the documentation it involves. This is particularly true in countries with a strong bureaucracy or where the purchasing is done by the State. Invoices have to be correct in every detail and to conform exactly to quotes or other documents to which they relate; otherwise the goods may not be collected or, worse, not paid for. There are also problems in some countries with certificates of origin of the goods, usually because of political considerations. Quite a number of countries, for instance, do not buy – or at any rate profess not to buy – goods from countries of which they disapprove politically, and demand certified invoices attested by a Chamber of Commerce in multiple copies. In some cases, it must be said, the documentation is literally not worth the trouble it costs – it has to be a matter of judgement related to the value of the goods being supplied or the importance of the customer otherwise.

> As an exporter, you will have to become familiar with export documentation.

As an exporter you will also have to familiarize yourself with the arcane vocabulary of export documentation – phrases like CIF, CIP, FOB, FRC and so forth. An excellent account of this and other matters is given in *Getting Started in Export* by Roger Bennett, published by Kogan Page. For more detailed instruction on the export order process and export finance, readers are referred to *The Handbook of International Trade* by Jim Sherlock and Jonathan Reuvid, published by GMB Publishing in association with the Institute of Export.

Fortunately, freight forwarders – a list of them can be obtained from the British International Freight Association – will handle the documentation for you, for a fee, which is quite modest considering the hassles involved: about 5 per cent of the total freight costs. Some freight forwarders are less than competent, though. Ask your colleagues in other firms for their recommendations and the name of the person they deal with. Good service quite often depends on one particular individual who is well worth rewarding with some good Scotch at Christmas time.

Sales to VAT registered customers in other EU countries are zero rated. You must show their VAT number (with their country code prefix) on the invoice and the goods must be sent to a destination

> Select your freight forwarders carefully.

outside the United Kingdom. You cannot, for instance, zero rate goods which are being sent to a customer's hotel in the United Kingdom and which will be taken with him or her on the journey home. The prefix GB has to be shown on your own VAT number, so if you do a lot of exporting it may be worthwhile using it for all your invoices. In that case, however, you will also have to make a further quarterly return to HM Revenue & Customs, the so-called EU Sales List (ESL). This is a record of all the sales you have made to customers within the EU.

You can also claim refunds of VAT incurred while doing business in other EU countries, but the documentation involved is very cumbersome. The matter may not be worth pursuing unless very substantial sums are involved.

## GETTING PAID

One thing freight forwarders cannot do for you is to collect payments, and the mechanics of this are a great deal more complicated than in the United Kingdom. The reason for this is largely that invoices, which trigger the payment process, also have to serve as a Customs clearance document and must therefore have all kinds of data on them which are not required in the United Kingdom: weight, value, origin of the goods and so forth. The requirements vary from country to country and are set out in a book called _Croner's Reference Book for Exporters_. Your bank should be able to help you with them. They should also be able to advise you on the best method of getting paid once the invoice has been presented. Generally, it involves some method of transferring money from the customer's bank to yours, so you need feel no hesitation in calling on your bank for assistance.

> Payment routines are complicated. Your bank will advise you on the best way of getting paid.

If you just receive the occasional order from abroad and don't want to get involved in extended payment procedures, the best plan is to send a _pro forma_ invoice. This still has to have details which are shown on the commercial invoice, but it means the customer has to pay in advance if he or she wants the goods. However, you should wait to clear the cheque before dispatching them unless payment is made by some form of mail transfer, again through the bank.

The devaluation of sterling on 'black Wednesday' in 1992 brought handsome profits for those who had quoted prices in one of the currencies that appreciated against the pound. However, sterling rose by a good 10 per cent against some of these currencies during 1993, so those who went on quoting in them lost some of the money they had gained earlier. Again, businesses which had quoted in local currencies lost out badly when sterling soared in 1997/98. Most exporters agree that the safest bet is to quote in your own currency. You won't make any windfall profits that way, but at least you know you will be able to pay your UK suppliers in the currency at which you have bought from them, namely pounds sterling.

> Most exporters agree that the safest bet is to quote in your own currency.

## PURCHASING FROM ABROAD

Although this chapter is mainly about exporting you may also want to source supplies from abroad. For example, if Christmas decorations and novelties are part of your product range and you want to buy at the lowest prices, you will inevitably find yourself ordering from China. You must expect that your suppliers will be as careful in selling goods to you as you are in exporting abroad. Until you have established yourself as a reliable customer they will probably ask for letters of credit with your orders, which is a safe form of trading for both vendors and customers. If your purchases from abroad are regular it will be a good idea to ask your bank for a separate facility from your overdraft, which will allow you to

> For regular purchases from abroad ask your bank for a separate letters of credit (l/c) account.

issue letters of credit up to an agreed limit that may be presented to your bank with the formal documentation. The facility may take the form of a 'revolving credit' so that as you sell on the imported goods to your customers and the proceeds are credited to your account you may raise further letters of credit up to the limit available.

It goes almost without saying that if you have someone whose judgement you trust who can visit suppliers before you finally select them, at an acceptable cost, you would be wise to use that person. Better still, visit your main suppliers yourself, unless they can visit you.

---

Have someone you trust visit your main suppliers, or visit yourself.

---

## THE SINGLE EUROPEAN CURRENCY

The single European currency was introduced by 11 European states on 1 January 1999, and there are now 15 members of the Eurozone. Although Britain is unlikely to adopt the single currency in the foreseeable future (if at all), businesses are advised to prepare for its introduction now. The 'euro' was introduced as hard currency on 1 January 2002. Many larger international firms had already switched all accounting across Europe – including the United Kingdom – to euros. Any British business trading with large European companies or exporting to Europe has come under pressure to adopt the euro for electronic payments and invoicing. The advantage of the euro – if the United Kingdom joins – will be an end to currency fluctuations. However, until we join, sterling could be in for a bumpy ride, so make sure you prepare for this when trading with the Continent. HM Treasury, BERR, UK Trade and Investment and the British Chambers of Commerce have combined to offer a new information service, The Euro – Now In Business, tel 08456 010199, and at www.euro.gov.uk. Factsheets and short case studies of firms in a variety of industries are available on request.

## Checklist: exporting

1. Have you considered local conditions and regulations to ensure your product is suitable for the market?
2. Seek out help from UK Trade and Investment, your local Chamber of Commerce or your bank.
3. Have you researched the territory you are planning to export to and checked up on the local agent through the UK Trade and Investment status report for the area?
4. Make sure a written agreement specifies issues such as territory and the period of time the agreement will run for.
5. Contact the British International Freight Association for a list of freight forwarders and ask colleagues for recommendations.
6. Consider setting up a euro account if you are trading with EU members and ask your bank about the best way to receive foreign payments.

# 19

# Planning for Growth

This chapter is intended for those who have suffered the birth pangs of starting a business, are working successfully for themselves and have achieved the objectives of their original business plans. Where do you stand and where do you go from here?

It is time for a strategic rethink. Having surmounted the initial hurdles to working for yourself, there are three main issues affecting the future of your new business that should be addressed sooner rather than later:

- sustainability;
- growth;
- personal goals.

These three issues are interrelated.

## SUSTAINABILITY

Will your business continue to prosper as it is? If you are a self-employed consultant or freelance operator, will your original clients or customers continue to support you? As you will have discovered, one of the problems of working for yourself – by

The flow of business is uneven and the peaks and troughs of revenue and cash flow are a 'feast or famine' syndrome.

yourself – is that the flow of business activity is uneven. Either your time is fully occupied in servicing the business that you have gained – so that there is little or no opportunity to prospect and gain new business – or all your assignments come to a close and there is a lapse in revenue while you focus on gaining new clients and contracts.

The peaks and troughs in revenue and, therefore, cash flow are a 'feast or famine' syndrome from which it is difficult to escape. Hopefully you have provided for this imbalance in your cash-flow projections, but this kind of one-person business is hard to sustain unless you are able to generate a proportion of long-term contracts or a high level of repeat business.

The same problem arises in the case of partnerships providing services, unless the partners are able to phase their activities so that there is an appropriate proportion of partners' collective time always available for sales development.

> The only way forward may be to expand sales turnover requiring additional funding.

Small companies in retailing, distribution and manufacturing face a different set of problems. First, they are vulnerable to changes in market conditions; when recession strikes, new entrants to a market are usually the first to feel the pinch. Second, after an initial period of success in a slow-growing market, they may become the target of backlash from competitors anxious to recapture the business they have lost. Most likely, the pressure will take the form of price undercutting, which an established company can maintain on a small proportion of a wider customer base. For your company, retaliation in the form of matching price cuts or offering added benefits is likely to result in an erosion of profit margins across a high proportion of your sales turnover. As a small company, you may find it impossible to counteract the loss of margin by a reduction in fixed costs (other than a reduction in your own salary). The only way forward may be to expand sales turnover, and that is sure to demand additional funding.

It is an often repeated maxim that 'in business you cannot stand still'. If you try to maintain your current level of activity and no more, the business inevitably declines.

The corollary is that growth is an essential ingredient of sustainability.

# GROWTH

Financial analysts will tell you that there are two forms of corporate growth: organic growth and M&A (merger and acquisition). They are not necessarily mutually exclusive, but for the young, thriving business it is wise to examine the organic growth opportunities first.

## Organic growth

Put simply, organic growth means expansion of the original business based on its core resources, broadening the range and depth of business activities but not straying too far from its original character. Thus, organic growth encompasses additions to the range of products or services, broadening the customer base, adding distribution channels, expanding territorially with new offices or outlets, licensing or franchising your branded products or service, appointing export agents or distributors.

> Organic growth means expansion of the original business based on its core resources.

Moving into a new kind of business involving different skills and expertise with a different market does not qualify as organic growth, even if there is an overlap in the target customer base and shared overheads. Returning to the garden centre Business A example of Chapter 12, taking the decision to grow your own stock or open a second outlet would be an organic growth activity. Adding a restaurant or a Christmas decorations department in season might just qualify; opening a ladies' hairdressing salon on the same premises would not.

> Diversification involves different skills and expertise.

Most kinds of organic growth involve additional funding. Even the appointment of a franchisee or an export agent will add cost in the form of management time expended and, possibly, working capital for additional stock and debtors. The real impact is likely to be on the burden of fixed cost until such time as the add-on activity has taken off and is contributing gross profit (revenue less direct cost) to cover incremental overheads.

At its simplest, suppose you decide to expand your consultancy business by taking on a second consultant to support your work on assignments and to free up some of your time for business development. The additional fixed cost is £5,000 per month (salary, pension, National Insurance, other benefits, non-recoverable office and travel expenses). Let us say that all direct costs are chargeable to the client, so that revenue and gross profit are the same. Therefore, until you have generated an additional revenue of £5,000 per month in cash received, there is an unfavourable impact on your bottom line and, of more immediate concern, on your cash flow.

In more complex businesses organic growth may involve more than additional working capital. For example, expansion of the chauffeur-driven limousine service used as an example in Chapter 3 would require the addition of at least one more quality car, so that there is either a substantial capital investment to be made or a significant addition to monthly overheads in leasing or hire purchase charges, in addition to the cost of another driver. At this stage you would need to reconsider carefully the different sources of capital surveyed in Chapter 3. Indeed, the whole process is reiterative as you would need to prepare an updated business plan and possibly carry out further research to prove that there is a market demand for the extension of services or new products which you are planning to introduce.

> You would need to prepare an updated business plan.

## Extension of premises

At some stage during periods of organic growth the issue of extending existing premises or moving into larger ones will arise. If growth involves increasing your staff, other than engaging home workers, and, in particular, if you started up your business with an office at home, you will need to face up to this problem sooner rather than later.

## Buying

Buying a freehold or longer leasehold property is a major financial commitment and you will require faith in the long-term future of your business before making such an investment. The following are some of the key considerations:

- Can you afford an investment in premises that will tie up so much cash?
- Property is an investment for your business that may give a good return, but do you understand the commercial property market?
- The long-term cost of buying premises is generally less than the rent you would pay. (The overall cost of buying is usually higher for the first five years, equal for the second five years and cheaper after that.)
- You may gain operational flexibility by owning your own premises; there may for instance be opportunities to let part of the premises, or remortgage or arrange a sale and leaseback deal.
- In the case of an industrial building, you may be able to claim capital allowances on plant.

## Leasing

By comparison, renting premises through a lease or licence is flexible and ties up a minimal amount of capital. However, property law is a minefield and verbal agreements do not count. All arrangements must be in writing and you are strongly advised to engage a solicitor with expertise in 'conveyancing' property.

Particular issues to watch out for in a lease are:

- How long is the period of the lease and, if more than a few years, is there a break clause for you and/or the landlord to terminate the lease early?
- Do you have the right to sub-let or assign the lease, and if so, what are the conditions? For example, is there a requirement to guarantee the next tenant's payments?
- When are the rent review dates? Is the rent review based on open market rent or changes in the Retail Price Index, and what happens if you cannot agree?
- What are the tenant's liabilities for repairs and maintenance, and what happens when the lease expires?
- What service charges are there and how are they calculated?

For businesses in the start-up and early stages where the future is uncertain it may be prudent to enter into an 'easy in, easy out' licence instead of a lease, as this will provide you with maximum flexibility. The particular features of a licence are as follows:

- Licences normally cover a period up to two years. You and your landlord usually have the right to give one month's notice of termination.
- Many licensed business premises provide support services, such as staffed reception and building security.
- The licence agreement should be short and simple in plain English.
- Your payment liabilities should be limited to payments for the licence fee (rent), rates and any extra services.

Avoid licences with complex terms or a long fixed licence period without the right to terminate, which are more like leases.

## Diversification

Business growth can also take the form of diversification into unrelated businesses where any commonality may be restricted to shared overheads, distribution channels or an overlap of the

> When diversifying you are advised to treat it as a separate business for funding purposes.

customer base. Instead of trying to justify the new business as an extension of the original, you are better advised to treat it as a separate business for funding purposes, with an additional business plan and a separate bank account. Unless the expertise which you have deployed in starting the first business is directly relevant to the second, you are engaging in a different kind of entrepreneurial venture in which you will be more dependent on the knowledge and experience of others. If your people judgement proves poor, you want to insulate the first, successful business from the harmful side-effects of a less successful venture or even a failure.

## Expansion and alliances

While you need to be achieving organic growth with your original business for sustainability, you may aspire to own and manage a larger business and you will get there faster through merger or acquisition than by organic growth alone over a number of years. So, start thinking about possible acquisitions at an early stage. Alternatively, you can build alliances with companies that you might subsequently acquire. You might be able to gain greater geographical reach by aligning yourself with a similar business in a different location; similarly, you could form an alliance with a company offering something slightly different with opportunities to cross-sell to each other's customer base. On the whole you should avoid an alliance with a business that has a very different offering to your own, or with companies up- or downstream from you in the process or supply chain. M&A professional advisers will tell you that such mergers and acquisitions seldom work well.

> You will get there faster through merger or acquisition.

Before embarking on a merger or acquisition adventure it is important to analyse your strengths and weaknesses as well as the opportunities and threats that the deal represents; in other words, make a complete SWOT analysis. The following are just a few of the questions that you should consider.

## Another SWOT analysis

■ What are your strengths, and would the deal complement them or risk diluting them?
■ How good are your product, your market position and your market share?
■ Are you financially strong?
■ Do you have advantages in technology or intellectual property?
■ Are your overheads taking too high a proportion of your income?
■ Do you have significant management weaknesses?

Buying a company or merging with another company larger than your own will probably involve you in negotiating capital investment from a venture capitalist or business angel, as outlined in Chapter 5, if you want to remain the controlling shareholder in the enlarged enterprise. This is the point where you move beyond dependence on your bank alone and a whole new set of considerations apply.

Remember that venture capitalists have an exit strategy of three to five years maximum.

The capital funding you will need will almost certainly be a mixture of loan capital and equity, as described in Chapter 5. Remember that venture capitalists are looking for a return on their investment within an exit strategy of three to five years maximum; but before you address venture capitalists' needs, take time out to identify and articulate your own goals.

# PERSONAL GOALS

What are your longer-term objectives? Do you want to go on running and building up your business for the foreseeable future, simply maintaining a livelihood up to pensionable retirement age? Or is your aim to build the business to a size where it can be sold for a substantial capital sum so that you will then have the option of living on the unearned income or even reinvesting in another business and starting again?

> Never fall in love with the business you own.

There is another well-worn investment maxim that says that you should 'never fall in love with the business you own'. Without a personal exit strategy there is a very real risk that you will soldier on in an increasingly blinkered and self-indulgent manner and fail to maximize the business potential. If you were enough of an entrepreneur to start working for yourself, you will almost certainly want to maximize the value of your endeavour.

These are the reasons why you may choose the M&A route to growth and will need to become skilled in negotiating and operating the more sophisticated funding arrangements and in working with the investment community. But that, as they say, is another story and the subject matter for another book.

## Checklist: planning for growth

1. Having started your business successfully, address the three main issues for the future: sustainability, growth and personal goals.
2. Plan how to smooth out the peaks and troughs of your cash-flow cycle.
3. Learn how to reduce your vulnerability to changes in market conditions and to counter aggressive competition.

4. Examine organic growth opportunities first before considering mergers and acquisitions.
5. Most kinds of organic growth involve additional funding. Calculate the effects on cash flow before you embark on expansion.
6. Organic growth may cause you to consider extending or moving your business premises.
7. Take expert legal advice on all leases and licences. For businesses in the start-up and early stages it may be prudent to enter into an 'easy in, easy out' licence.
8. If you diversify into an unrelated business, run it as a separate business and insulate your first business from any harmful effects if the second venture fails.
9. M&A may be a faster route to growth than organic development, but before embarking on a deal carry out a thorough SWOT analysis of your own business.
10. What are your long-term objectives? Develop your personal exit strategy.

**Part Four**

# Necessary Administration

# 20

# VAT

If the taxable outputs of your business, which for practical purposes means what you charge your customers for any goods or services that are not specifically 'exempt', exceed, or are likely to exceed, £61,000 in a year, you will have to register with HM Revenue & Customs (HMRC) as a taxable trader for VAT purposes. This means that you will have to remit to HMRC either monthly or quarterly, 15.0 per cent of the ex-VAT price you charge on your 'outputs', this being the temporary standard rate of VAT, until the government reverts to the normal standard rate of 17.5 per cent. However, you will be able to deduct from these remittances most VAT which you yourself have been charged by your suppliers – your 'inputs'. This item covers not only VAT on materials used in producing the goods or services you supply to your customers, but everything which you have to buy to run your business, including such things as telephone charges. VAT also extends to goods purchased from outside the EU.

Not all goods and services carry 15 per cent VAT. A 'reduced rate' of VAT at 5 per cent is applied to supplies of fuel and power used in the home and by charities. Some items are 'zero rated' – basic foodstuffs, books, newspapers, young children's clothing and exported goods being notable examples. Full details are contained in VAT Notices 700 and 701, issued by HMRC (available from the HMRC website: http://customs.hmrc.gov.uk) and you should obtain from them these Notices together with any others about VAT which are relevant to your trade or profession. You will find your local office listed in the phone book. The significance of zero rating is that even though you do not charge VAT on goods of this nature that you supply, you can still claim back VAT on all your inputs, excluding the purchase of cars and business entertainment of domestic customers.

Zero rating is not, however, the same as 'exemption'. Zero rating carries a theoretical rate of VAT, which is 0 per cent. Exemption means that no rate of VAT applies at all and examples of exempt suppliers are bookmakers, persons selling or renting land and buildings, and various types of medical services. The exempt status is not particularly desirable, because if you are exempt you still have to pay VAT on all your inputs but have no outputs to set the tax off against.[1]

In this sense exempt traders are like private individuals, and the question, therefore, arises as to whether you should, as you are entitled to do, ask to be registered as a taxable trader even though your outputs are less than the mandatory £67,000 a year level. HMRC might, of course, refuse to register you on the grounds that your outputs are too low, though no hard-and-fast minimum figure for this has been fixed. Your accountant should be able to advise you on this point, but the main consideration would be the level of your taxable inputs. Thus if you are a part-time cabinet-maker you would be buying a lot of materials which carry VAT. But, if you were doing something like picture restoration, the VAT inputs might be quite low and the administrative work involved in being a taxable trader might not be justified by the amount of VAT you could claim back against your outputs.

The point to be realized is that if you register as a taxable trader, voluntarily or otherwise, you are going to be involved in a fair bit of extra administration. At the end of each VAT accounting period (quarterly or monthly, the latter being more usual with traders in zero-rated goods), you will have to make a return of all your outputs, showing their total value and the amount of VAT charged. Against this you set the total of your inputs and the amount of VAT you have paid. The difference between the VAT on your outputs and that on your inputs is the sum payable to HMRC. This obviously causes problems for retailers making a great many small

---

[1] The distinction between zero-rated goods and exempt goods is important in determining whether you should be registered for VAT. Exempt goods do not count towards total 'turnover' for this purpose, but zero-rated goods do. Thus, if your turnover is over £67,000 including exempt goods but under that figure without them, you are not liable to pay VAT.

sales and particularly for those supplying a mixture of zero-rated and standard-rated goods (eg a shop supplying sweets, which are taxable, and other items of foods, which are mostly zero rated). It also underlines the vital importance of keeping proper records and retaining copy invoices of all sales and purchases, because although your VAT return need only show totals, HMRC inspectors are empowered to check the documents on which your return is based and require you to keep these records for six years. There is obviously, therefore, a link between the records you have to maintain for ordinary accounting purposes and those that are needed to back up your VAT return.

There is also a close connection between VAT and the problem of cash flow. When you receive an invoice bearing VAT, the input element can be set off against the VAT output on your next return, irrespective of whether you yourself have paid the supplier. Therefore, if you are buying an expensive piece of capital equipment it will make sense for you to arrange to be invoiced just before your next return to HMRC is due.

The boot is on the other foot, though, when you yourself are extending credit to a customer. The sale is reckoned to have taken place when the invoice has been rendered, not when you have received payment. Therefore you may be paying VAT on your output before you have actually received the cash covering it from your customer. However, VAT can be reclaimed on bad debts, which in this case means amounts overdue by six months.

However, as a concession to small businesses with a taxable turnover (exclusive of VAT) of under £67,000, HMRC will allow you to operate what is known as cash accounting. This enables small firms to account for tax when cash is paid and received rather than on presentation of an invoice.

It is also worth noting that if you are liable for VAT, inputs can be claimed on goods purchased for the business before it opens which are in place at the time of opening. VAT can also be claimed back on services such as professional advisers' fees supplied within six months of starting to trade.

Once you have registered for VAT, you will receive, at the end of each quarter, a form on which to make your return to HMRC. It is very important to do this within the time stated (one calendar month for quarterly returns), because there are financial penalties for making late returns, which can go as high as 15 per cent for repeated defaults.

There are also penalties for 'serious misdeclarations'. If you find, however, that you have accidentally underdeclared any of your taxable outputs, you can apply to HMRC to make a 'voluntary disclosure for accidental underpayment'. This would not make you liable to a penalty.

Before making a quarterly return, it is a good idea to check your own figures. Dividing the VAT total by the net total should show that the VAT is 15.0 per cent of the net, or at least very close to it. HMRC will accept a tolerance like 0.25 per cent. But anything more than that suggests a mistake in your arithmetic somewhere. Better to pick it up yourself than to invite a visit from the VAT inspector.

As from 1 April 2008, you can apply to deregister from VAT if your taxable outputs have fallen below £65,000 and are likely to remain at a lower level.

# 21

# Employing People

A fairly common observation about employing people has been to say that this is when your troubles begin. Apart from the difficulty of finding Mr or Ms Right – a task that even experienced personnel people admit, in their more candid moments, is something of a lottery – employers also have to comply with various articles of employment legislation. Whole books could be and have been written about the legal technicalities involved, but all we can do in this chapter is to draw your attention to some of the major pitfalls you should look out for when you start employing people.

The most obvious question to ask yourself is whether you really do need to take someone on permanently at all. The principle we have put forward for the purchase of equipment – never buy anything outright unless you are sure you have a continuing use for it and that it will pay for itself over a reasonable interval of time – also applies to personnel. The legal constraints that cover part-time or full-time employees do not extend to genuine freelancers, personnel from agencies or outside work done on contract, and this could well be the best way of tackling a particular problem such as an upward bump in demand until you are sure that it is going to last.[1]

---

[1] However, in some cases freelancers have successfully argued retrospectively that, since they were subject to the same conditions as the ordinary employees of a firm, they were covered by employment law. It is not enough to say that A is a freelance and B is not. There must be recognizable differences in the way they work. The freelance must not be under your direct supervision and control, or he or she will be likely to be classified (for the purposes of redundancy pay, etc) as an employee.

It is worth remembering, too, that when you take on staff you take on a good many payroll and administrative overheads in addition to their salary. These can add quite significantly to your costs. The introduction of the minimum wage in April 1999 should also have made you consider the costs of recruitment. The standard rate is currently £5.73 an hour for those aged 22 and above, having risen to £5.73 in October 2008, and for those aged 18 to 21 it is now £4.80 an hour. Exemptions include 16- and 17-year-olds and apprentices between the ages of 18 and 26 who are in the first year of their apprenticeship for whom the hourly minimum rate is £3.55 from October 2008.

However, increased need for staff is one of the first signs of a successful and expanding business. The first issue to consider is how best to address this business need. As stated, there are various options available to a business. Which option is most suitable will depend on the resources of the business and the likely duration of the staffing need.

By way of summary, consideration could be given to:

▍ Employing individuals on an independent contractor basis to undertake limited one-off tasks.

▍ Engagement of staff through a third party employment agency. Though pay rates may be marginally higher for such agency staff, your business will be freed from the hassle of recruitment and payroll administration and in most cases will not have the standard obligations of the employer. Staff can also be utilized as and when there is a business need rather than their use being dictated by the terms of a contract of employment.

▍ If employing staff is the preferred or most suitable option, then consideration could be given to employing such individuals on fixed-term contracts or part-time contracts with the option of extending such fixed-term periods or providing paid overtime. This again allows staffing resources to remain adaptable.

If employing staff is the preferred or most suitable option for your business, it is important to ensure that you are aware of your obligations and liabilities to staff whom you employ.

In view of the scope and complexity of current UK employment legislation, this chapter can only set out a summary of the key issues and cannot be a substitute for taking proper legal advice.

When considering the business's relationship with the staff it employs it is often helpful to consider the relationship in three stages:

▌ recruitment;
▌ performance management;
▌ termination.

# RECRUITMENT

Proper recruitment procedures are probably the most commonly overlooked in the United Kingdom, with regard to employment of staff. The reasons are probably historical as until October 1998 staff had to be continuously employed by a business for two years before they gained protection for standard unfair dismissal claims. Therefore employers could take greater risk in employing staff as they had a two-year 'loyalty period' during which to assess the suitability of any individual employees.

However, such a loyalty period was reduced to one year in October 1998, and the numbers of Exceptional Statutory Claims that require no minimum period of employment have also increased.

These changes to the legal landscape mean that proper recruitment procedures are more important than ever. If one considers our European counterparts, where the concept of 'loyalty periods' are alien or apply in much more limited circumstances, such countries have a far greater emphasis on recruitment procedures in avoiding poor employment candidates.

The cost of discharging staff, for whatever reason, makes it imperative that you should make the right decisions in recruiting people to work for you in the first place. We have heard it said that the sphere of personnel selection is something of a lottery. It need not be.

A good recruitment procedure will involve:

▌ considered wording and placement of an advertisement externally and if applicable internally within the business;
▌ thorough vetting of job applications received and applicants' CVs;

■ provision of the job description to applicants called to interviews;

■ comprehensive interviews and, when dealing with senior individuals, the procedure should at a minimum be a two-stage interview process;

■ obtaining of proper references – a minimum of two references should be obtained and should not be from friends or family of the applicant;

■ making an initial offer of employment conditional.

## Considered wording and placement of an advertisement

Ensure that you advertise the post as widely as possible and to the most tailored market possible for the role you are seeking to fill. Ensure that the advertisement makes clear the ambit of the role and the type of organization the employee would be joining. If such wording is sufficiently thought out you will avoid misunderstanding and ideally attract only suitable candidates who will meet the demands of the business.

Both in framing your recruitment advertisements and in interviewing, take care not to offend against provisions of the Sex Discrimination Act 1975 and 1986, the Race Relations Act 1976, the Disability Discrimination Act 1995 and more recently the Employment Equality (Sexual Orientation) Regulations 2003, The Employment Equality (Religion or Belief) Regulations 2003 and the Employment Equality (Age) Regulations 2006, which came into force on 1 October 2006.

## Thorough vetting of job applications received and applicants' CVs

Again it is important that you assess such details objectively. Issues to look out for are an excessive number of previous employers for the applicant's age, any unexplained career gaps and that the applicant has appropriate qualifications/experience for the role.

## Provision of the job description to applicants called for interview

This will generally make the interview more constructive and the applicants may be able to relate any existing experience they have to the proposed role. It will also ensure that applicants are not under any misunderstanding of what the role requires.

## Comprehensive interviews

Interviews are the best opportunity for assessing the suitability of an applicant. It is often commented that interviewers make their minds up about an applicant in the first 60 seconds. This should be resisted as it is too subjective a basis for making a sound and reliable decision. Though 'gut feel' is important, it should be supported by objective factors.

An objective structure for the interview should be prepared for all candidates, and thorough notes should be taken of the interview. This will prevent a decision being made too prematurely and will also provide a helpful and objective measure for comparing various candidates.

The more senior the role that is being filled, the greater the number of interview stages that should be included in the interview process. Also, it is always helpful to involve others in the selection process, again to prevent subjective influences dominating the selection process.

Some helpful questions to consider including could relate to:

▌ How many previous employers have applicants had? Has their progress been up, down or steady? Is this move part of the overall employment pattern?

▌ If they are willing to take a large drop in salary, find out why – there could be a perfectly good reason, but it is worth being cautious.

▌ Test candidates' reactions to your request to telephone their employer for a reference.

▌ If you are interviewing sales representatives, as well as asking them how long they have been in the business, try to find out which buyers they know and how well they know them.

Be careful that the job specification stays within the growing range of employment protection legislation. Many employment agencies will advise you on the dos and don'ts of these contentious areas before you start interviewing candidates.

Finally, you should ensure that selection or non-selection of candidates has not been contrary to the candidates' rights under the Sex Discrimination Acts 1975 and 1986, the Race Relations Act 1976, the Disability Discrimination Act 1995 or the more recent Employment Equality (Sexual Orientation) Regulations 2003, Employment Equality (Religion or Belief) Regulations 2003. You should also remember that as from 1 October 2006 age discrimination regulations came into force within the United Kingdom.

## Obtaining of proper references

Ensure that a minimum of two references are obtained from parties who are not friends or family of the applicant.

Hard copy references addressed 'To whom it may concern', are often agreed as part of an acrimonious termination of employment and so should be more carefully considered or questioned.

Ensure that all references are obtained. Often employers do not chase an errant reference when one favourable reference has been received. If a referee fails to respond to a request, this in itself may be a point of concern. In such circumstances enquire of the employee why the reference has not been forthcoming and request details of an alternative referee.

Ensure that all referees are also contacted by phone to confirm and elaborate the details of the reference. This will prevent issues of fraud regarding the reference but also the referee may be prepared to be more truthful about the employee in an 'off-the-record' telephone discussion.

## Making an initial offer of employment conditional

You may want to consider making the initial offer of employment conditional on:

▌ provision of satisfactory references;
▌ a probationary period of employment;

■ satisfactory completion of induction procedures;
■ medical fitness to work.[2]

# PERFORMANCE MANAGEMENT

## The terms of employment

The terms of an employment statement, which has to be issued in writing to every employee who is going to work for you within two months of joining, is in fact not a pitfall, but a rather sensible document that clarifies right from the outset what the terms of employment are.

Employment lawyers will testify that more disputes arise from circumstances where there are no written documents governing the employment relationship than where the parties have agreed clear written terms. There are always more likely to be contentious disputes where employment terms are uncertain or ambiguous.

From the employer's point of view, the necessity of drafting a terms-of-employment statement should concentrate the mind wonderfully on issues about which it is all too easy to be sloppy at the expense of subsequent aggravation, such as hours of work, holidays and, above all, exactly what it is the employee is supposed to be doing. The following points have to be covered in the contract, and you must say if you have not covered one or other of them:

■ the names of the employer and employee;
■ the date when the employment began; and
■ the date on which the employee's period of continuous employment began (taking into account any period with a previous employer that counts towards that period).

Additionally the statement must also contain particulars (as at a specified date not more than seven days before the statement) of:

---

[2] Where the applicant is a disabled person within the meaning of the Disability Discrimination Act 1995, consideration would have to be given to reasonable adjustments to enable the applicant to undertake the role.

▋ the scale or rate of remuneration or the method of calculating it;

▋ any terms and conditions relating to hours at work;

▋ any terms and conditions relating to:
  - entitlement to holidays (including public holidays) and holiday pay (the particulars being sufficient to enable the employee to calculate precisely his or her entitlement, including to accrued holiday pay on the termination of employment);
  - incapacity for work due to sickness or injury including any provision for sick pay; and
  - pensions and pension schemes;

▋ the notice the employee is required to give and entitled to receive;

▋ the employee's job title or a brief description of the work he or she is employed to undertake;

▋ if the employment is not permanent, the period for which it is expected to continue or, if a fixed term, the date on which it is to end;

▋ the employee's place of work or if the employee is required or permitted to work at various locations an indication of that and the address of the employer;

▋ any collective agreements that directly affect the termination of employment;

▋ where the employee is required to work outside the United Kingdom for more than one month, the period for which he or she is to work outside the UK, the currency in which the remuneration will be payable, any additional remuneration payable to him or her and any benefits provided by reason of his or her being required to work outside the UK and any terms and conditions relating to his or her return to the UK.

A further requirement is that employers must issue on or before each payday and for each employee an itemized statement showing:

▋ gross wages/salary;

▋ net wages/salary;

▋ deductions and the reasons for them (unless these are a standard amount, in which case the reasons need only be repeated every 12 months);

- details of part-payments, eg special overtime rates;
- the rate of pay and how it is calculated;
- whether it is paid weekly or monthly;
- the period of employment, if it is temporary.

## Working time

Since 1 October 1998, The Working Time Regulations have given a wide range of rights to employees and other workers, including, for the first time, a statutory right to paid leave. This right arises and accrues immediately following the employee commencing employment. The minimum annual paid leave is four weeks (20 days). The right to four weeks (20 days) relates to full-time employees and must be prorated in respect of part-time employees.

Working time must be recorded including overtime and must not exceed an average of 48 hours (averaged over a period that is usually 17 weeks) unless there is a written agreement between the employer and employees opting out of this restriction. In such regard it is important to appreciate that under the regulations the employee is at liberty to opt into the regulations on notice and must not suffer a detriment for doing so.

Night workers also have restrictions on hours worked and have the right to free health assessments. The regulations also give workers rights to rest breaks and daily and weekly rest periods.

## Conditions of work

Numerous regulations affect working conditions and you should be conversant with those relevant to your area, particularly if it is a potentially dangerous trade. Length of hours, minimum wages, employment of young persons, etc, will tend to apply to all businesses, and though you may escape prosecution for a while, to fall foul of the law is likely to be embarrassing and expensive.

# TERMINATIONS: UNFAIR DISMISSAL

Probably the area of legislation that it is easiest and most common to fall foul of is that relating to wrongful and unfair dismissal. Wrongful dismissal relates to the termination of employment in breach of the employee's contract of employment, most typically in regard to breach of notice provisions. Unfair dismissal relates to the statutory claim pursuant to the Employment Rights Act 1996.

In this connection it is important to be aware of the concept of 'constructive dismissal'. Constructive dismissal is not a claim in itself but a way of turning a resignation in law into a dismissal so that the employee is then eligible to bring dismissal-related claims such as unfair dismissal. An example is an employer changing the terms of employment by action such as substantively lengthening hours, reducing pay or benefits or even adversely changing the status of an employee, which can be tantamount to unfair dismissal. Employees are now normally required to lodge a grievance with their employer and allow the employer to try to resolve the complaint within 28 days before being in a position to resign and present a valid complaint of constructive dismissal.

Every employee who has more than one year's continuity of service, including part-timers, must be given a written statement of the employer's reason or reasons for termination of employment if the employer wants to dismiss him or her. Such reasons must be given to the employee in writing within 14 days of the request being made by the employee.[3]

In circumstances other than proven gross misconduct you must also give employees one week's notice if they have been with you continuously for four weeks or more and, after two years, one week's notice for every year of continuous employment up to a maximum of 12 weeks' notice. You can also pay in lieu of such notice, if there is such a right under the contract of employment.

Employees who have over a year's service can be dismissed only for one of the five fair reasons for dismissal allowed under the Employment Rights Act 1996.

Fair enough, you might say, particularly as, on the face of things, what the law regards as fair grounds for dismissal is perfectly reasonable:

---

[3] Section 92 of the Employment Rights Act 1996.

1. Dismissal for incapability or poor performance, eg incompetence.
2. Dismissal for misconduct.
3. Dismissal for statutory restriction reasons. This is where the law dictates an individual cannot continue his or her employment, a crude example being a taxi driver losing his or her driving licence.
4. Dismissal for genuine redundancy.
5. Finally, the catch-all dismissal for 'some other substantial reason'.

The problem is that the employee is at liberty to disagree with you on the fairness issue and to take the case to an employment tribunal, which stipulates that the employer's grounds for dismissal must be reasonable.

In addition an employer must show not only that the reason for dismissal was one of the allowed five fair reasons but also that the dismissal was fair in all the circumstances. Therefore fairness has a dual test of being substantively (for a genuinely fair reason) and procedurally (carried out as part of a fair procedure) fair.

All employees with more than one year's continuity of service must be dismissed in accordance with the minimum statutory disciplinary procedures.

All employees subjected to a disciplinary process, regardless of length of service, have the statutory right to be accompanied at such meetings by a colleague or trade union representative.

Redundancy is a ripe and common area for misunderstanding. Redundancy occurs when a role disappears or diminishes or a place of work disappears through closure. An example is a firm ceasing to trade or having to cut down on staff.

One 'acid test' to determine the genuineness of redundancy is whether the employer's organization has reduced by the number being made redundant.

It does not have the same restrictions as dismissal, but nevertheless does involve some financial penalties for employers if the employee has been continuously employed by the firm concerned for one year or more. In that case he or she will be entitled to redundancy pay on a formula based on length of service and rate of pay.[4]

The principal obligations of a fair redundancy procedure involve:

■ Notifying affected staff of the risk of future redundancies as early as is practical.

■ *Before* a decision is reached to make staff redundant, to consult with affected staff to examine ways to avoid or minimize the proposed redundancy. Consultation is the cornerstone to a fair redundancy procedure.

■ Where more employees undertake a role than are to be made redundant it is important that the employer applies objectively fair selection criteria to determine which employees are retained and which are made redundant.

■ When a decision has been fairly reached to make staff redundant, the employer is under an obligation to give consideration to offering existing suitable alternative employment. The employer is not under a duty to create a role for redundant staff.

If you intend to make 19 or more staff redundant there are additional statutory obligations. Specialist advice should be sought in such cases about advance warning to the relevant unions if any of their members are to be made redundant, consulting with the workforce representatives about proposed redundancies and notifying the Department for Business, Enterprise and Regulatory Reform.

What happens if you buy a business, lock, stock and barrel, together with the staff? You may find that you do not like some of the people the previous owner took on, or that you want to change or drop some of the things that were being done, with the result that staff will be made redundant. Irrespective of the fact that you did not hire the people concerned, you are still stuck with the responsibility towards them as their current employer, so that being the proverbial new broom can be a very costly exercise. Before buying a business, therefore, it is very important to look at the staff and at the extent of any redundancy payments or dismissals situations you could get involved in. You must also seek advice regarding the implications of the Transfer of Undertakings (Protection of Employment) Regulations 1981 regarding any purchase of a business, which protects the rights of transferred staff on the sale of a business.

---

[4] An employee needs two continuous years' employment to be entitled to a statutory redundancy payment.

It is important to note that there are certain unfair dismissal claims that do not require a year's service but can be brought from day one of an employee's employment, most typically:

■ Dismissal or detrimental treatment for discriminatory reasons: sex, gender reassignment, race, disability, sexual orientation, religious/philosophical belief. Age discrimination became unlawful in October 2006.
■ Dismissal for asserting a statutory right.
■ Dismissal for 'whistleblowing' – making a protected disclosure under the Public Interest Disclosure Act 1998.
■ Dismissal for trade union activities.
■ Dismissal for raising health and safety complaints.

There are four areas of employment law of particular relevance to small businesses employing staff:

1. The qualifying period for alleged unfair dismissal is one year (or one month in some medical cases or some disputes over statutory rights).
2. Employment tribunals are directed to take account of the size and resources of the employer. For example, where an employee proves unsatisfactory in one job, a large employer might be able to offer him or her another position, but a small employer would find this more difficult in most cases.
3. Post-maternity reinstatement is waived for firms of fewer than five employees, if reinstatement is not practicable.
4. Frivolous or misconceived claims presented to the Employment Tribunal are to be deterred by a liability to costs.

If the employee has been guilty of gross misconduct, such as persistent lateness, you will probably win your case, provided you warned the employee in writing to mend his or her ways well before you dismissed him or her. The point here is that, not only must you have good reasons for dismissing the employee, but also you must have acted reasonably in the dismissal procedure. This means that you have got to follow a proper sequence of written warnings – not fewer than three is the number generally recommended – stating the employee's inadequacies, telling the employee what he or she has to do to put them right and spelling out the consequences if he or she fails to do so.

When it comes to matters of competence, though, things are rather less clear cut, particularly if the task involved is not one where performance can be readily quantified or where there are many imponderables. It would be relatively easy to argue a case against a machine operator who was consistently turning out less work than colleagues on similar machines, but far more difficult in the case of a sales rep who could plead that a poor call-rate was the result of difficulties in finding car parking or inefficient back-up from the office.

The fact is that in all matters affecting competence you really have to do your homework very carefully before dismissing someone. The inexperienced employer may unwittingly contribute to an adverse judgment by the tribunal by such steps as including the person concerned in a general salary rise not long before informing the person that he or she is not up to the job.

There may be cases where you, as the employer, are satisfied that dismissal is fair, but where the law does not agree with you. One where you have to be very careful is dismissal on medical grounds. No reasonable employer would dismiss anyone in such circumstances if they could help it, but if you get stuck with someone who is persistently off sick and is able to provide satisfactory medical evidence, you would have to show proof that the absences were of such a nature as to cause disruption to your business before you could discharge him or her. Even more tricky is the case of employees who are engaged in public duties, such as being on the local council. You have to give them reasonable time off to attend to those duties, though not necessarily with pay.

The matter has been further complicated by the introduction of the Disability Discrimination Act 1995. Where employees have to be dismissed on medical capabilities grounds it is likely that they will have protection under the Disability Discrimination Act, which places additional obligations upon an employer before being in a position to consider a 'fair dismissal'. For such reasons it is now essential for an employer to seek appropriate advice before dismissing employees on medical capability grounds regardless of their length of service.

The Sex Discrimination Act and the Equal Pay Act mean that women have in all respects to be treated on an equal footing with men, though since 1982 firms with fewer than five employees have been exempt from the former provisions. There are also occupations where discrimination is legal because of the nature of the work.

There is also now the right to take parental leave for a child born after 15 December 1999. Before the child reaches the age of five, parents are allowed 13 weeks in periods of not less than one week and up to a maximum of four weeks per year. Even male employees after 26 weeks' employment are entitled to Statutory Paternity Pay (SPP) for two weeks' leave.

Nor does it end there. You will have to maintain all benefits other than remuneration – and if you bring in a replacement for the employee, or any other employee who is off for any longer period of time, be very careful. The employee's replacement could sue you for unlawful dismissal unless you notify him or her in writing that the appointment is a temporary one and give notice when it is coming to an end.

The penalties for losing an unfair dismissal case can be ruinous for a small firm. A standard claim for unfair dismissal is subject to a statutory cap of £58,400 from February 2006, although this excludes the Basic Award, calculated along the same lines as Statutory Redundancy Pay. However, figures for 2004 indicated an average award of £7,000–£8,000. The extent of compensa- tion is determined by the level of the employee's pay and how quickly the employee mitigates his or her loss by finding new employment.

Because of the potential levels of compensation liabilities, if you are in any doubt at all about a dismissal you should consult a solicitor who is versed in this aspect of the law. Having regard to the increased risk of employee claims for discrimination and unfair dismissal, as well as the pensions minefield, owners of small businesses should think even more carefully than hitherto before taking on employees.

# STATUTORY SICK PAY

Finally, under the Social Security Contributions and Benefits Act

1992, employers are responsible for paying Statutory Sick Pay (SSP) of £75.40 a week (in the tax year 2008/09) to virtually all employees earning £90.00 or more a week, for up to 28 weeks' sickness in the year; and note that there is no longer a minimum number of weeks for which an employee has to have worked before being able to claim sick pay. The obligation begins after the employee has been off work sick for more than three consecutive days. These need not be working days, though. They could include the weekend, or days when the employee would not normally be working. SSP is treated as earnings, so you should deduct PAYE and pay the employer's National Insurance contribution on it.

After these three days, and once the employee starts qualifying for SSP, it is only payable for the days when the employee would have been working. This means that when you employ part-timers – a growing part of the workforce – you would be well advised to specify their working days in the terms of employment, rather than having a loose 'as and when needed' arrangement.

Good paperwork in SSP situations is all the more important because you can claim back the payments you have made provided they exceed 13 per cent of your gross National Insurance contribution for the month (that is, NIC for employer and employee). The excess is deducted from the employer's National Insurance contribution.

The employee can offer self-certification for up to seven days. After that the employer should ask for a doctor's certificate. Careful records have to be kept of SSP payments and retained for three years. When you start employing people, you should get guidance from the DSS on how they require this to be done.

# GUIDANCE LEAFLETS ON EMPLOYMENT

A great many leaflets giving guidance on employment matters are available free from the Department for Work and Pensions. For an up-to-date list, write to the General Office, Information 4, Department of Employment, Caxton House, Tothill Street, London SW1H 9NF.

In the same context, another Act of Parliament you should keep an eye open for when buying a business is the Health and Safety at

Work Act, which lays down standards to which working premises have to conform. Before putting down your money you should check with the inspectors of the Health and Safety Executive that any premises you are buying or leasing as part of the deal meet those standards.

Further guidance can also be found online at:

- http://www.dti.gov.uk/er/index.htm;
- http://www.acas.org.uk/;
- http://www.lawsociety.org.uk/choosingandusing/findasolicitor/view=solsearch.law;
- http://www.ksblaw.co.uk/.

## Checklist: employing people

1. Do you really need to take on staff? Will there be enough to keep them busy a year from now?
2. Plan your recruitment procedure carefully. With employment issues, prevention really is better than cure.
3. Have you worked out a job description that sets out the purpose of the job, the duties involved and who the person appointed will report to?
4. Have you decided how much you can afford to pay?
5. Does your advertisement or approach to a recruiting agency spell out the job description, the salary and an indication of the experience you are looking for?
6. Does it in any way contravene the various discrimination Acts?
7. Have you prepared a series of questions that will throw some light on the interviewee's competence, personality and previous record of employment?
8. Have you taken up and checked references?
9. Are you satisfied, before making the appointment, that you have seen enough applicants to give you an idea of the quality of staff available for this particular job?
10. Do you have a procedure for reviewing the employee's progress before the expiry of the probationary period

after which he or she can claim unfair dismissal if you decide he or she is not suitable?

11. Do you make a practice of putting matters in writing to the employees concerned?

# 22

# Other Taxation

How you are affected by taxation depends on the nature of the commercial activity in which you are engaged. Virtually everyone pays tax on income from some source, whether this be from full-time employment, from dividends or interest, or from self-employment, or from a combination of several of these elements. The various kinds of income are assessed under several headings or schedules and the ones we will be particularly concerned with are:

1. Schedule D Case I and Case II: Income from trades, professions or vocations. (In the interests of simplicity we will refer to this as Schedule D, though there are four other 'Cases' of Schedule D income.)
2. Schedule E: Wages and salaries from employment.

There are also other ways in which you may be involved in tax matters. You may be paying capital gains tax on the disposal of capital assets. If you are employing people full time, you will be responsible for administering their PAYE payments; also, in certain circumstances, your own PAYE. If you are a shareholder in a limited company, it will be paying corporation tax on its profits. Lastly, you may – and if your turnover exceeds £67,000 a year, you must – for the supply of certain goods and services collect VAT from your customers and pay it over to HM Revenue & Customs (HMRC) less any VAT on goods and services supplied to you in the course of business (as discussed in Chapter 20). Essentially, if you are running your own business you will either run it directly yourself (as a 'sole trader'), or you will run it through the medium of a limited company.

Let us look in broad outline at some of its principal implications. There are certain income tax advantages in working for yourself, or even in earning a supplementary income from part-time self-employment. For example, you may be able to offset certain expenses (eg travelling expenses) against taxable income in a way that an ordinary employee cannot.

If you carry on business via a limited company, the company will generally pay you a salary which will be liable to employee and employer National Insurance contributions in the normal way. However, if you carry on the business as a sole trader or a partnership, you will be subject to the specific National Insurance regime applicable to the self-employed. Essentially this consists of two parts: Class 4 National Insurance contributions, and flat-rate Class 2 contributions. The amount of contribution is subject to a certain amount of annual tinkering. Class 4 National Insurance is payable by men under 65 and women under 60 and it currently stands as a levy of 8 per cent of business profits between £5,435 and £40,000 in 2008/2009 and 1 per cent over £40,000. It used to be the case that the self-employed could deduct 50 per cent of the Class 4 National Insurance contributions from their income for tax purposes, but this was abolished a few years back. Class 4 contributions are collected by HMRC. Contributions are payable if your profits exceed the threshold of £5,435 even if you work full time or part time in addition to being self-employed. However, there is a maximum amount of contributions that you have to pay in a year, so those who are employees and self-employed may be exempt from paying some or all of their Class 4 contributions. See below for details.

In addition, the self-employed must also pay a flat-rate weekly Class 2 National Insurance contribution if their profits are more than £5,435 a year. Those earning less than this can apply to be exempt. Ask for leaflet CA02 'National Insurance contributions for self-employed people with small earnings' from your local Contributions Agency (see your telephone directory) and fill in the exemption form CF10. The standard flat rate Class 2 contribution for 2008/2009 is £2.30 per week payable to the Department of Social Security. Most people pay this contribution by direct debit from their bank but alternatively you can be sent a quarterly bill.

As with Class 4 contributions, there is an overall maximum of Class 2 contributions payable in any tax year if you are self-employed and an employee. If you have earnings as an employee taxed under PAYE you will pay Class 1 National Insurance contributions if you earn more than £100 a week in the 2007/2008 tax year at 11 per cent.

If you earn £770 or more a week from employment (the so-called 'upper earnings limit' for 2008/2009, further employee Class 1 National Insurance contributions are payable at 1 per cent above that figure.)

In general terms, and in terms of maximizing your entitlement to the state retirement pension, any Class 2 contributions for any one tax year count as a contribution year in terms of building up your entitlement to the state retirement pension in exactly the same way that employee National Insurance contributions build up the entitlement of an employee to the state retirement pension.

If you are self-employed, but you are not liable for Class 4 or Class 2 contributions as a result of having insufficient income, you can make a voluntary contribution in order to 'buy' the relevant year's contribution history to your state retirement pension entitlement.

As with income from employment, the profits of the self-employed are subject to an ascending rate of tax, with income falling into different tax bands. If you have income from employment and self-employment, this is added together when calculating how much income falls into each tax band.

All income up to the basic Personal Allowance of £5,435 for the 2008/2009 tax year is tax free. For those aged 65–74 the personal allowance is increased to £9,030 and for those aged 75 and over to £9,180. If you are both an employee and self-employed, remember that you can have only one allowance which is offset against your total income. Income above this tax threshold then falls into two tax bands starting with income (above your personal tax allowances) up to £36,000 which is taxed at 10 per cent. Any income above £36,000 is taxed at 40 per cent. The total amount of income that will be taxed will also depend on any tax reliefs due – for example, personal pension contribution tax relief. For savings income and dividends, the basic rate of tax is 10 per cent up to £36,000, rising to 32.5 per cent thereafter.

As discussed, the main difference between taxation of employees and taxation of the self-employed is that the self-employed can deduct a vast array of costs and expenses when calculating their taxable profits. The self-employed can deduct any expenditure 'wholly and exclusively incurred' in carrying on a trade or profession. It is essential that you are aware of what you can – or cannot – deduct as it will enable you to reduce the amount of your taxable profits and therefore the amount of tax you will have to pay.

## THE MAIN ALLOWABLE BUSINESS EXPENSES

You can deduct 100 per cent of the cost of buying the following items unless they are purchased for part business and part private use, in which case only the business proportion may be deducted:

1. *The cost of goods bought for resale and materials bought in manufacturing.* This does not include capital expenditure on items such as cars, machinery or computers, although you can deduct some of the cost of buying these via a 'capital allowance claim' (see page 262). However, small items of expenditure such as filing trays, software or small tools can be deducted.
2. *The running costs of the business or practice.* Under this heading come heating, lighting, rent, rates, telephone, postage, advertising, cleaning, repairs (but not improvements of a capital nature), insurance and the use of special clothing. If you are using your home as an office, you can claim up to two-thirds of the running costs of the premises as a business expense – provided you can convince the tax office that you are indeed using as high a proportion of your house as this exclusively for business purposes. Some people have been advised not to make this type of claim at all, because of the probability that, on selling, they might have to pay capital gains tax on the 'business' part of the sale, thus outweighing any income tax advantage. One way round this is to use a room mainly for business rather than exclusively. You will generally need to agree with your tax office what proportion of costs you can deduct. If you have one or more separate business telephone lines, their total cost is allowable.

3. _Carriage, packing and delivery costs._
4. _Wages and salaries._ Any sums paid to full-time or part-time employees. In circumstances where you carry on the business as a sole trader or partnership, however, you cannot count any salary you or your partners are taking from the business, but you can pay your spouse a salary (provided he or she is actually doing a reasonably convincing amount of work for you). This is an advantage if his or her income from other sources is less than £5,435 a year, because that first slice of earnings is free of tax.
5. _Travel._ Hotel and travelling expenses on business trips and in connection with soliciting business. You are not, however, allowed the cost of travel between home and office, if you have a regular place of work. In addition to these expenses you can claim for the running costs of your car (including petrol) in proportion to the extent to which you use it for business purposes. WARNING: you cannot deduct the cost of entertaining as this is a disallowable expense.
6. _Interest._ Interest on loans and overdrafts incurred wholly in connection with your business. This does not include interest on any money you or your partners have lent to the business.
7. _Hire and hire purchase._ Hiring and leasing charges and interest element in hire-purchase agreement (not the actual cost, because this is a capital expense).
8. _Insurance._ Every kind of business insurance, including that taken out on behalf of employees, but excluding your own National Insurance contributions and premiums paid on your personal life insurance. You cannot deduct personal pension contributions as such when calculating your business profits, but when calculating your tax these contributions – which qualify for tax relief at your highest rate of tax – can be used to reduce the amount of tax you will have to pay.
9. _The VAT element in allowable business expenses (unless you are a taxable trader for VAT purposes)._ This would include, for instance, VAT on petrol for your car. The VAT on the purchase of a motor car is allowable (for the purposes of a capital allowances claim – see below) in all cases, since such VAT cannot be reclaimed in your VAT return.
10. _Certain legal and other professional fees._ You are allowed to claim for things like audit fees or court actions in connection with

business, but not for penalties for breaking the law (eg parking fines!).

11. *Subscriptions to professional or trade bodies.*

12. *Bad debts.* These are bad debts actually incurred, though provision is generally allowed against tax in the case of specific customers whom you can show are unlikely to meet their obligations; for instance, if their account is overdue and they are failing to respond to reminders. A general provision for a percentage of unspecified bad debts is not allowable against tax, however sensible it may be to make such provision in your accounts.

    Trade debts owing to you count as income even if they have not been paid at the end of the accounting period. Likewise, debts owed by you count as costs, even if you are not going to pay them until the next accounting period.

13. *Gifts.* Business gifts costing up to £10 per recipient per year, provided they are marked with the firm's name (but excluding food, drink and tobacco). All gifts to employees are allowable, but generous employers should remember that the employees may have to declare them on their tax return and you will normally have to declare them on form P11D.

## Capital allowances

Generally you are allowed to write off against taxable profits 20 per cent of the cost of capital equipment on a reducing balance basis after the first year. For instance, in the year of purchase, if you buy a piece of equipment for £1,000, you will be granted £500 first-year allowance. For the following year, the writing-down allowance will be 20 per cent of £500 (£1,000 – £500 = £500) giving an allowance of £100.00 and so forth. Small businesses can claim first-year allowances of 50 per cent for most plant and machinery (except for cars, assets you leave out and some 'long-life' assets with a life of more than 25 years).

In addition, you can claim 100 per cent first-year allowances on designated energy-saving and water-efficient investments.

The writing-down allowance of 20 per cent per annum also extends to cars used for business, up to a maximum of £3,000 per annum. Equipment bought on hire purchase is eligible for the writing-down allowance in respect of the capital element. The interest charges inherent in the hire purchase agreement themselves can be claimed as business expenses, spread over the period of the agreement.

In calculating your writing-down allowances you will have to take into account whether or not you are a taxable trader for VAT purposes. Capital allowances will be calculated on the net amount excluding VAT (except in the case of motor cars in respect of which, as explained in Chapter 20, the input VAT is never reclaimable on your VAT return).

Major changes to the capital allowance regime from 2008/2009 were announced in the March 2008 Budget. All businesses will have an Annual Investment Allowance on the first £50,000 of expenditure on plant and machinery.

## STOCK VALUATION

If you are in a business which involves holding stock (which may be either finished goods for resale, work in progress or materials for manufacture), it must be valued at each accounting date. The difference in value between opening stock and closing stock, when added to the value of purchases during the year, represents the cost of sales. Obviously, therefore, if you value your closing stock on a different basis from the opening stock, this will affect the profit you show. If you value the same kind of items more highly, it will depress the cost of sales and increase the apparent profit. If you value them on a lower basis, the cost of sales will be increased and the profit decreased.

Plainly, then, it does not make sense for you to up-value your closing stock in order to show a paper profit. Equally, you are not allowed to depress it artificially to achieve the reverse effect. However, if you can make a genuine case that some stock will have to be sold at a lower margin than the one you normally work to in order to be able to sell it within a reasonable time, a valuation in the light of this fact will generally be accepted by the tax office. Table 23.1 provides two examples of profit arising on stock valuation.

**Table 23.1** *An example of stock valuation (assuming no purchases)*

| Example A | | | Example B | | |
|---|---|---|---|---|---|
| Sales | | £150 | Sales | | £150 |
| *Opening Stock* 100 Rose bushes @ £1.00: | £100 | | *Opening Stock* 100 Rose bushes @ £1.00: | £100 | |
| *Closing Stock* 50 Rose bushes @ £1.50: | £75 | | *Closing Stock* 50 Rose bushes @ 60p: | £30 | |
| Cost of Sales | | £25 | Cost of Sales | | £70 |
| Profit | | £125 | Profit | | £80 |

# COMPUTING TAXABLE PROFIT

Normally, unless you choose to complete your own self-employed accounts and tax return yourself, your accountant will prepare a set of accounts for you for each year you are in business. Your accounting date need not coincide with the tax year (ending 5 April). The profits shown in these accounts will be the basis of your assessment.

As stated earlier, certain costs which are genuine enough from the point of view of your profit and loss account are nevertheless not allowable for tax purposes: for example, entertaining customers. You are also not allowed to charge depreciation against your profit (though remember that when claiming capital allowances you will receive a writing-down allowance which, in the end, has a similar effect). These and other non-allowable expenses must be added back to the profits.

Equally, certain profits which you have made are to be deducted for the purposes of Schedule D assessment because they are taxed on a different basis and are subject to a return under another heading. Examples are gains from the disposal of capital assets, income from sub-letting part of your premises, and interest paid to you by the bank on money being held in a deposit account.

In recent years some new kinds of business spending have come in for tax relief, notably incidental costs of raising loan finance and start-up costs incurred before you begin trading.

# LOSSES

If your business or professional occupation has made a loss in its accounting year (and remember that from the tax point of view non-allowable expenses are added back to profits and you will have to do the same in terms of computing any loss for tax purposes), you can have the loss set off against your other income for the tax year in which the loss was incurred and for the previous year. It is also possible for a trading loss to be offset against capital gains if you have no other income to offset it against.

If your income for the year in which you made the loss and that of the previous year still does not exceed that loss, you can set off the balance against future profits. There are special rules regarding losses incurred in the start-up years of the business. In the case of traders and partnerships, losses incurred in the first four years of business can be carried back against income from other sources, including salary, in the three years before commencing business as a self-employed person or partner. However, it should be noted that this does not apply to losses incurred by a limited company of which you are a shareholder – such losses can only be set off against profits chargeable in the form of corporation tax. However, if you carry on your business by a limited company, and you subscribe for new shares in it, and the company then goes bust, you would normally be able to offset the loss you make on the shares against your taxable income.

# SELF-ASSESSMENT

Since 1997 the taxation of the self-employed has been radically changed. The main effect on the self-employed was that instead of being taxed on profits in their accounting year ending in the preceding tax year, they are now taxed on what is known as a 'current year basis'. This means that if, for example, your accounting year ends on 31 March 2008, you will be assessed for tax on those profits at the rates applying to the 6 April 2007 to 5 April 2008 tax year. Under the old regime you would not have been assessed until the following tax year. So, in effect the self-employed must pay tax on profits more quickly than they did under the old regime.

The self-employed pay tax on three different dates – two advance or 'interim' payments made by 31 January within the year of assessment and by 31 July following the end of the tax year of assessment, and the third payment, the final balancing payment, by the following 31 January. To go back to the example above, a business with an accounting year to 31 March 2009, the first payment – usually half the tax on trading profits paid in respect of the previous tax year – will be payable on 31 January 2009, the second payment on 31 July 2009 and a final balancing payment (if any further tax is due) on 31 January 2010. If your profits are likely to be much lower than in the previous year you can apply to have your interim payments – also known as 'payments on account' – reduced. On the other hand, if your accounting year ends on 30 April, you will be paying tax in 2009 on your profits for the year ended 30 April 2007 and not paying tax on your profits for the year ending 30 April 2008 until the tax year 2009/2010.

The other change introduced by self-assessment is that you can calculate your own tax should you want to. However, this is not mandatory. If you want HMRC to calculate your tax liability you must complete and submit your tax return by 30 September following the end of the tax year on 5 April. However, dates for the submission of self-assessment tax returns are to be advanced for the year ending 5 April 2009.

If you – or your accountant – wish to calculate the tax owed, the tax return does not have to be submitted until 31 January (see Table 23.2). If you miss this deadline, you will be fined (see Table 23.3).

Self-assessment also requires taxpayers to keep and retain records to support information on their tax return. The self-employed must keep records for five years after the 31 January following the end of the tax year of assessment concerned.

The amount of information you need to give on your tax return will depend on your turnover. For the year ended 5 April 2008, those with a turnover of less than £15,000 a year needed only to submit three-line accounts – turnover, expenses and profit/loss.

Note: For tax returns issued on or after 6 April 2008 relating to the 2007/2008 tax year and later years, the deadline for filing paper returns was brought forward to 31 October following the end of the relevant tax year, whether or not the taxpayer calculates the tax.

**Table 23.2** *Key dates to remember during the 2009/2010 tax year*

| | |
|---|---|
| 31 July 2009 | Second interim payment on account for the 2008/2009 tax year now due |
| 30 September 2009 | Final deadline for 2008/2009 tax return to be submitted by those wanting HMRC to calculate their tax bill |
| 5 October 2009 | Deadline for those who need to inform HMRC of new sources of income in 2008/2009 tax year |
| 31 January 2010 | Final deadline to send back completed 2008 online tax return sent out following the end of the tax year on 5 April 2009 |
| | First payment on account for the 2009/2010 tax year now due |
| | Final balancing payment for the 2008/2009 tax year now due |

Other sole traders and partners have to produce more information, including a detailed breakdown of expenses claimed. As accountancy fees are tax deductible by the self-employed, you are strongly advised to use an accountant to help you – at least in your early years – to ensure that you claim all that you can to reduce your taxable profits and to ensure you are not fined by HMRC.

**Table 23.3** *HM Revenue & Customs fines and penalties re 2008/2009 tax return*

| | |
|---|---|
| Failure to submit tax return by 31 January 2010 | £100 |
| Failure to pay tax due on 31 January 2010 | 6% interest |
| Failure to pay tax by 28 February 2010 | 5% surcharge plus interest |
| Failure to submit 2008/2009 tax return by 31 July 2009 | a further £100 |
| Failure to pay tax by 31 July 2010 | second 5% surcharge plus interest |
| Returns still not submitted after this date | up to £60 a day |
| Failure to keep accurate records | up to £3,000 |

# SPARE-TIME WORK

Even though you have a full-time job which is being taxed under Schedule E and thus being taken care of under your employer's PAYE scheme, you may also have earnings from part-time employment in the evenings and weekends which you have to declare. Your employer need not know about this second income because you can establish with your tax inspector that the tax code which fixes the amount of PAYE you pay (see below) only relates to the income you receive from your employer.

Your spare-time income is also eligible for the allowances on expenses 'wholly and exclusively incurred' for business purposes. This means that it is most important that you should keep a proper record of incomings and outgoings. If your spare-time activities are on a small scale, you will not need to keep the kind of detailed books of account described in Chapter 13; but you should certainly maintain a simple cash book, from which at the end of the year you or your accountant can prepare a statement to append to your Income Tax Return.

Tax on spare-time work is payable in the same way as described earlier in this chapter.

Probably the largest item you will be able to set off against spare-time income is any sums you can pay your spouse for assistance up to the level of their tax-free allowance of £5,435, provided they are not earning as much as this from another source.

# PARTNERSHIPS

Partners pay tax on their share of the partnership profits in the same ratio as that in which they have agreed to split profits. Until the introduction of self-assessment in respect of tax year 1996/1997 *et seq.*, the partnership was taxed as a single entity with tax collected from the partnership as a whole, not the individual partners. However, the new rules stipulate that each partner is liable for his or her own tax. Most of the other tax rules relating to partners are the same as for the self-employed, so that means that salaries cannot be deducted when calculating profits and any interest on money put into the business by partners is considered as part of the partnership profits. Partners are deemed to start in business when they join the partnership and cease in business when they leave.

# CORPORATION TAX

Corporation tax is payable by limited companies. Its provisions are somewhat complicated and it must be assumed, for the purposes of this brief chapter on taxation, that readers who are intending to set up businesses in this form will seek professional advice on tax aspects. However, the salient points are as follows:

1. The standard rate of corporation tax is 30 per cent, but decreased to 28 per cent from 6 April 2008. There is a reduced small companies rate of 19 per cent on all profits up to £300,000 for the financial year from 1 April 2007. However, the small companies rate increased, to 21 per cent from 1 April 2008 and to 22 per cent from 1 April 2009. The previous concession, applicable for the year 2005/06, of zero corporation tax on the first £10,000 of profits has been withdrawn.
2. Unlike Schedule D income tax, corporation tax is normally payable nine months from the end of each accounting period, except for large companies where it is payable by instalments.
3. If you are a director of a limited company, any salary paid to you by the company will be subject to income tax under PAYE and to National Insurance contributions (see later in this chapter for a description of PAYE).

# INHERITANCE TAX

This tax is in some ways similar to the older concept of death duties in that a charge is made on transfers of assets at death, up to a maximum of 40 per cent on amounts over £312,000 after 1 April 2008. If you make an outright gift more than seven years before death, no inheritance tax will be paid on this. Tax can become due on gifts made within seven years of death, although in certain cases such tax may be at a reduced rate. Such outright gifts are known as 'potentially exempt transfers'. In his March 2006 Budget, the

Chancellor also ruled that money held in pensions by investors aged 75 and over would now be subject to inheritance tax at 40 per cent when the investor dies.

Business assets of those who have an interest in a small business or a farm qualify for substantial concessions which can reduce or eliminate the tax. You are advised to seek professional advice. However, generally, business relief means there is no inheritance tax to pay on business assets such as goodwill, land, buildings, plant, stock or patents (reduced by debts incurred in the business). What are regarded as private and business assets at death are, however, bound to be a subject of potential dispute with HMRC, so it is vital to seek professional advice on the implications of this tax when making a will.

# CAPITAL GAINS TAX

If you sell or give away assets – usually cash, shares, property or other valuables – you are liable to capital gains tax on the gain made. This gain is generally calculated as the price you sell the asset for (or its market value) *less* the cost of purchasing the asset (or its value on 31 March 1982 if it was bought before then) and any costs incurred in buying, selling or improving the asset. However, you do not pay tax on gains to the extent that they do not exceed your annual exemption for capital gains purposes (£9,600 in the 2008/09 tax year). If you are liable for capital gains tax it will be at your top rate of tax. So higher-rate taxpayers will pay it at 40 per cent.

The March 1998 Budget made significant changes to capital gains tax – with many of these new rules having a major impact on those running small businesses. Until the Budget, those selling assets could deduct the effects of inflation when calculating their gains. However, inflation will only be deductible if the asset was bought before 1 April 1998 and then the effects of inflation can only be deducted until April 1998. For small businesses a major concession, retirement relief given to those selling their business after age 50 or retiring earlier due to ill-health, was phased out over five years until the tax year 2002/03. In the past this relief meant that the self-employed paid no capital gains tax (CGT) if they owned the business for 10 years before the sale and sold it for less than £250,000. Tax on gains between £250,000 and £1 million was halved. This relief was replaced by a new tapering system of relief which reduced the amount of tax paid the longer the asset was held.

However, after much controversy the taper relief regime was abandoned in the March 2008 Budget with immediate effect. There is now a single rate of CGT at 18 per cent, subject to the tax-free annual exempt amount (currently £9,200). There is relief on gains made in the disposal of all or part of a business up to a lifetime total of £1 million, on which an effective CGT rate of 10 per cent is charged.

One area where those running a business can be caught out is if they run a business from home. Profits made on the sale of your main residence are generally exempt from tax. However, if you use your home for business and have been claiming part of the costs of running the business including a share of heating, lighting, rates and your mortgage or rent, you could have to pay capital gains tax. The easiest way to get round this is to not use a room 'exclusively' for business but only 'mainly'. So if you have three rooms in your home (other than bathrooms and kitchens) and use one for business, instead of claiming a third of the running costs of your home, claim slightly less than this. Always agree the business proportion of these costs with your Tax Office.

# APPEALS

All taxpayers, be they an individual or a corporation, have the right to appeal against their tax assessment, if they have grounds for believing they are being asked to pay too much. Such appeals have to be made in writing to the Inspector of Taxes within 30 days of receiving an assessment. They are usually settled by more or less amicable correspondence, but ultimately can be taken to a hearing by the General or, in more complex cases, Special Commissioners.

# PAY AS YOU EARN (PAYE)

If you employ staff you will be responsible for deducting PAYE from their wages. The same applies to your own salary from a limited company. The sums have to be paid monthly to HMRC by the employer.

You will receive from the tax office a tax deduction card for each employee, with spaces for each week or month (depending on how they are paid) for the year ending 5 April. On these cards, weekly or monthly as the case may be, you will have to enter under a number of headings, details of tax, pay for each period and for the year to date. You will know how much tax to deduct by reading off the employee's tax code number, which has been allotted to him or her by the tax office, against a set of tables with which you will also be issued. Without going into technicalities, the way the tables work is to provide a mechanism, self-correcting for possible fluctuations of earnings, of assessing the amount of tax due on any particular wage or salary at any given point of the year.

At the end of the tax year you will have to make out two forms:

1. Form P14 for each employee for whom a deductions working sheet has been used in the year just ended. Two copies are sent to the tax office. The third copy is called Form P60, and is issued to each employee. This gives details of pay and tax deducted during the year.

2. Form P35 for HMRC. This is a summary of tax and graduated National Insurance contributions for all employees during the year. It is a covering certificate sent with the Forms P14.

Both of the above have to be submitted to HMRC by 19 May following the tax year ended on the previous 5 April.

When an employee leaves, you should complete another form, P45, for the employee. Part of this form, showing his or her code number, pay and tax deducted for the year to date, is sent to the tax office. The other parts are to be handed by the employee to the new employer so that they can pick up the PAYE system where you left off.

Employers are also responsible for deducting Class 1 National Insurance contributions from their employees and will have to pay these along with their own employer's contributions (which are also based on a percentage of each employee's pay) at the same time as making PAYE tax payments. If you are using a computerized payroll service, the process will be eased greatly.

# THE BLACK ECONOMY

One cannot these days write about taxation without some reference to the 'black economy'. There is a good deal of evidence to suggest that the response to the way rising wages and salaries are pulling an increasing number of people into higher tax brackets has been tax evasion on a large scale by a variety of means, such as straight-forward non-declaration of earnings, making or receiving payments in cash, arranging remuneration in kind or, simply, barter deals. Some of these methods are easier for the tax inspectors to spot than others, but this is not the place to give advice on a highly contentious topic, except to say that all forms of tax evasion are illegal. In fact, there are enough loopholes and 'perks' available to self-employed people with a good tax consultant at their elbow to render law-breaking an unacceptable and unnecessary risk.

# THE CHALLENGE TO SELF-EMPLOYED STATUS

In recent years there has been an increasing tendency for HMRC to challenge taxpayers' claims to be assessed under Schedule D and to try to bring them within the PAYE scheme. The challenge hinges round the nature of the relationship between the provider of work and the performer of it. If the provider of work is in a position to tell the performer the exact place, time and manner in which the job is to be done, then the relationship between them is, to use an old-fashioned phrase, a master-and-servant one and clearly does not qualify for Schedule D taxation. On the other hand, if the performer of the work is merely given a job to do and is absolutely free as to how it is done, except in so far as it has to be completed within certain specifications of time, quality and price, then the performer can be regarded as self-employed. There are, however, some potential grey areas here; for instance, a freelance working mostly for one client may be straying into a master-and-servant situation. HMRC is also now treating any income derived under a contract of service as liable to PAYE – even if it is only for one or two days a month. This means that formal contractual arrangements should be avoided when worthwhile payments are involved. A guidance note has been issued (IR56) under the title *Tax – Employed or Self-Employed*, but the Inspector of Taxes is still entitled to take his or her own view of your situation.

By 6 July following the end of the tax year to 5 April the employer has to prepare:

▌ a form P9D in respect of each employee earning less than £8,500, covering expenses and benefits provided to the employee in the tax year concerned;

▌ a form P11D in respect of employees earning more than £8,500 per annum, again setting out information regarding expenses and benefits provided to the employee in the tax year concerned.

The above have to be submitted to HMRC by 6 July, with a copy to the employee in each case. You will need to follow the complex guidance notes which will be given to you by HMRC and again you will be well advised to take professional advice where appropriate.

There has been much discussion in the media over recent years regarding the dreaded 'IR35', which came into effect on 6 April 2000. IR35 only affects people who carry on a business via a limited company. Essentially, IR35 allows HMRC to treat the income of your company as that of you personally, in circumstances where the relationships between the company and its customers are similar to the relationships which you would have had as an employee of the respective customers concerned. This is a complex area, and if you believe you might fall within IR35 you would be well advised to take professional advice, as indeed you should also do in circumstances where HMRC threaten to invoke IR35 on you.

HMRC has a degree of autonomy which is not generally realized by the general public. It is not, for instance, answerable to Parliament except in the widest political sense; so it is no use writing to your MP, no matter how unjustified you may feel a tax decision is. Your only recourse is to take the matter to an Independent Appeals Tribunal, but unless a large sum of money is involved it is probably not worth the trouble – though self-employed people who are members of a professional association may find it willing to take up on their behalf something that looks like a test case.

# Complaints

If you have a complaint about the way your affairs have been dealt with by HMRC there is a leaflet about complaints procedures relating to VAT: *Complaints Against Customs & Excise*, available from any local VAT office.

Beyond that, there is a complaints supremo, who deals with income tax and benefits as well as VAT matters: The Adjudicator's Office (see Appendix 2).

### Checklist: taxation

1. Inform the Department of Social Security if you have recently become full-time or self-employed.
2. Collect receipts for allowable business expenses. Check with your accountant if you are not sure what is permissible.
3. Become acquainted with the important dates related to self-assessment and make sure that you do not miss the deadlines.
4. Contact your tax inspector if you have a second, self-employed, job and establish that your tax code fixes the amount of PAYE you pay only for the income you receive from your employer.
5. Be aware that you might be liable to pay Capital Gains Tax on the sale of your home if you claim tax relief on using part of it as a business premises.
6. If you are likely to exceed £64,000 a year taxable outputs, register with HMRC for VAT and consult your accountant.

# 23

# Pensions and Health Insurance

Until two or three years ago, it was scarcely possible to open the financial pages of any newspaper without seeing at least one advertisement for self-employed pensions. It is also a fair bet that these are studied more closely by financial advisers than by the self-employed at whom they are aimed, unless of course the latter are nearing the age at which pensions begin to become of immediate interest – by which time it may be too late to do anything about it. The trouble is that the self-employed, by temperament, are more attuned to risk than security and tend to place provisions for retirement rather low on their scale of priorities.

However, there are compelling reasons why you should take self-employed pensions seriously and find out what they involve, an outline of which is the object of this chapter. In urging you to read it, we promise to avoid the mind-boggling pension jargon that generally sends readers of newspaper articles on the subject straight to the less demanding pastures of the sports or fashion pages.

For the moment, pension plan salespeople and investment fund managers are under the microscope of public scrutiny. With the collapse of stock exchange equity values, pension fund assets have dwindled in all developed countries.

In the United Kingdom, pension fund assets fell to $934 billion in 2002 from $1,400 billion in 1999 and have fallen even more dramatically since the start of the credit crunch. No reliable quantification is yet available. Well-known life assurance companies, which have been household names in the pensions industry for decades, have had to declare severely reduced pension benefits and pay-outs. A host of well-known companies, such as Marks & Spencer, British Airways, Abbey, Dixons and WH Smith, have closed their traditional defined-benefit final salary schemes to new entrants. Indeed, defined benefit schemes are nearing extinction. Worse still, the employees of some companies that have gone into receivership, such as MG Rover, have found that their pensions are at risk. The government has set up a compensation fund for those whose occupational pensions have been damaged but the fund has been insufficient to provide for the number of cases that have come forward.

The Financial Services Authority (FSA) and the Association of British Insurers offer an online pensions calculator to encourage individuals to start saving earlier for retirement. The calculator, which is intended for those in the stakeholder salary range of £10,000 to £20,000 who have no retirement savings, may be found on www.pensioncalculator.org.uk. Age, gender and planned retirement age are the key determinants together with either the weekly retirement income required or the amount to be saved monthly. The model also provides for users to specify an amount of tax-free cash on maturity up to 25 per cent of the fund's value.

# STATE SCHEMES

Everyone in the United Kingdom is entitled to the basic state pension provided they have built up a record of National Insurance contributions for a quarter of their working life (from age 16 through to state pension age). Contrary to popular belief, not everyone qualifies for the full state pension – only those with a record of contributions for nine-tenths of their working life. The self-employed should take particular care to ensure that they build up adequate contributions as they generally do not have a company pension to rely on when they retire. However, the primary state pension is very basic: just £90.70 a week for a single pensioner from April 2008.

The second state pension was the top-up scheme known as SERPS – the state earnings related pension scheme – but this was replaced by an equally complicated scheme called the State Second Pension (SSP) from April 2002. The self-employed are not members of this scheme as the contributions to it are made from Class 1 National Insurance contributions paid by employees (however, if you were an employee in the past you may have built up some SERPS entitlement). Only a quarter of working people are members of SERPS; the rest have opted out (known as contracting out) through either a personal pension plan or their company pension scheme. If you have past SERPS entitlement check how much pension this will provide. If you also have earnings from employment and are under age 45 and a man, or under 40 and a woman, and earn at least £10,000–£12,000 a year, you should consider contracting out of SERPS and investing rebates in a personal pension plan (provided you are not a member of a company pension scheme).

A new National Pensions Savings Scheme (NPSS) was announced in December 2006, which the government is to introduce in 2012. Under the changes:

▌ All companies must offer their employees auto-enrolment in the scheme, unless they offer auto-enrolment in their own occupational pensions scheme, which must meet certain minimum standards.

▌ Companies will have to make a compulsory contribution of 3 per cent of salary to the NPSS, with employees paying 4 per cent and the government 1 per cent via basic rate tax relief.

▌ Self-employed individuals will be able to join the scheme on their own account.

# STAKEHOLDER PENSIONS

Stakeholder pension schemes offer a low-cost option for people who do not currently have the right pensions provision, particularly those who cannot join an occupational pension scheme. They are a good option for people earning less than around £10,000 a year, but the maximum contribution allowable before tax is only £3,600 per annum. The schemes are offered by commercial companies and are registered with HMRC and the Occupational Pensions Regulatory Authority (OPRA). The rules are designed to ensure that schemes offer value for money and flexibility. For example:

▌ A stakeholder pensions scheme cannot charge more than 1 per cent a year on the value of each member's funds.

▮ Members must be able to transfer into or out of a stakeholder pension, or stop paying for a time, without facing any extra charge.

▮ All stakeholder pensions schemes must accept contributions of £20 or more, though some may accept lower payments.

Advice is available from the Department for Work and Pensions (the successor to the DSS) website, www.pensionguide.gov.uk, or their Pensions Info-Line on: 0845 7 31 32 33. OPRA keeps a register of approved schemes, and can be contacted at http://www.opra. gov.uk.

As an employer, you may have to provide access to a stakeholder pension scheme for any employees over the age of 18 who earn more than the National Insurance lower earnings limit. This is the case if you have five or more employees (of any age or wage level) and do not already offer specific pension plans. Eligible employees can join the scheme if they so choose, though they do not have to do so. You do not necessarily have to make contributions as an employer. You do not yourself run the scheme, and are not responsible for its performance, although if you are dissatisfied you can change to a different scheme.

Similarly, if you take on a fifth employee, you must provide access to a scheme for all eligible employees within three months. To do this, you must:

▮ choose a registered stakeholder pension scheme or schemes from the OPRA list;

▮ discuss your choice of scheme with employees who qualify for access;

▮ designate (formally choose) the stakeholder pension scheme and give your employees its name and address;

▮ arrange to deduct contributions from employees' pay for those who wish to join (how much they pay is their decision), and inform them in writing of the arrangements;

▮ send your employee contributions (and any employer contributions) to the stakeholder pension scheme provider within the given time limits; schemes must accept payments of £20 or over, and some schemes accept lower amounts;

▮ record the payments you make to the stakeholder pension scheme provider.

New employees who already have a stakeholder scheme can continue to pay directly to that scheme, or elect to join your designated scheme and have deductions made through the payroll.

During this process, you should offer help and information but must not advise employees that they should or must join this (or any other) scheme; the FSA has strict rules on who is entitled to give advice. Guidance on stakeholder pensions is available from HMRC's Employer's Helpline, 08457 143143 (textphone 08456 021380), and the Occupational Pensions Regulatory Authority, 01273 627600.

# TAX BENEFITS

Not being eligible for earnings-related benefit is in itself a reason why you should make additional arrangements as soon as you possibly can, but for the self-employed there is another compelling incentive. Investing in a pension scheme is probably the most tax-beneficial saving and investment vehicle available to you at this time. Here are some of its key features:

1. Tax relief is given on your contributions at your top rate of tax on earned income. This means that if you are paying tax at the top rate of 40 per cent you can get £1,000 worth of contributions to your pension for an outlay of only £600.

2. Pension funds are in themselves tax exempt – unlike any company in whose shares you might invest. Thus your capital builds up considerably more quickly than it would in stocks and shares.

3. When you finally come to take your benefits – and you can take part of them as a lump sum and part as a regular pension payment (of which more later) – the lump sum will not be liable to capital gains tax and the pension will be treated as earned income from a tax point of view, as distinct from investment income, which is regarded as 'unearned' and taxed much more severely.

The advantage of all this over various DIY efforts to build up a portfolio of stocks and shares – even if you are more knowledgeable about the stock market than most – should be obvious; you are contributing in that case out of taxed income, the resultant investment income is taxed at unearned rates and capital gains tax is payable on the profits you make from selling your holdings.

The advocates of the DIY road may at this point say: 'Ah, but under my own provisions I can contribute as, when and how much I can afford and I am not obliged to make regular payments to a pension plan when it might be highly inconvenient for me to do so.' Pensions, however, are not like life insurance, though misguided or less scrupulous sales reps sometimes try to make out that they are. You need not contribute a regular amount at all. You can pay a lump sum or a regular amount. In fact, you need not make a payment every year. There are even a number of plans now available under which you are entitled to borrow from your pension plan.

The only current restriction that is put on you is imposed by the government and relates to tax benefits. In order for self-employed pensions not to become a vehicle for tax avoidance, the amount you can contribute each year is limited.

There are also further concessions for older people making their own pension plans. Since an increasing number of self-employed people – and their financial advisers – have come to recognize the merits of these schemes, a great many companies have moved into the market for self-employed pensions. Under a fair amount of jargon and often confused lineage of print, the plans they offer boil down to the following options:

1. _Pension policy with profits._ In essence this is a method of investing in a life assurance company, which then uses your money to invest in stocks, shares, government securities or whatever. As we said earlier, the advantage from your point of view is that pension funds are tax exempt, so the profits from their investments build up more quickly. These profits are used to build up, in turn, the pension fund you stand to get at the end of the period over which you can contribute. There is no time limit on this period, though obviously the more you do contribute the greater your benefits will be and vice versa; also, you can elect to retire any time between 50 and 75. The downside, of course, is what happens when equity values fall,

as they have in the recent past. 'Profits' have been wiped out and retirement expectations have been destroyed. As a result of the financial collapse of certain well-known life assurance companies that were underfunded to meet their policy commitments, with-profits policies are today viewed with disfavour.

At retirement you can choose to have part of your pension paid as a lump sum and use it to buy an annuity. This could in some circumstances have a tax advantage over an ordinary pension, but the situation on it is quite complicated and you should seek professional advice in making your decision. What happens with an annuity, however, is that you can use it to buy an additional pension, the provider of which takes the risk of being out of pocket if you live to a ripe old age. Equally, you might die within six months, in which case the reverse would be true. The statistical probabilities of either of these extremes have been calculated by actuaries and the annuities on offer are based on their conclusions.

One important point about a conventional with-profits pension that often confuses people is that it is not really a form of life insurance. If you die before pensionable age, your dependants and your estate will not usually get back more than the value of the premiums you have paid, plus interest. The best way of insuring your life is through term assurance, of which more later.

2. *Unit-linked pensions.* Unit linked policies are a variant of unit trust investment, where you make a regular monthly payment (or one outright purchase) to buy stocks and shares across a variety of investments through a fund, the managers of which are supposed to have a special skill in investing in the stock market.

Combining investment with a pension plan sounds extremely attractive and much more exciting than a conventional with-profits policy, and it is true that in some instances unit-linked policies have shown a better return than their more staid rivals. However, as unit trust managers are at pains to warn you (usually in the small print), units can go down as well as up and if you get into one of the less successful unit trust funds – and there are quite wide variances in their performance – you may do less well than with a conventional policy.

Although the 2008/2009 period of stock market depreciation has  affected the value of holdings adversely, over a
period of time these fluctuations should even themselves out
– you can get more units for your money when the market is
down, and fewer when share prices are high. The only
problem is that, if your policy terminates at a time when share
prices are low, you will do worse than if you cash in on a
boom. However, there is nothing to compel you to sell your
holdings when they mature. Unless you desperately need the
money you can keep it invested until times are better.
Remember, though, since this policy is for your pension, you
may not be able to delay using the funds for too long.

Most unit trust companies run a number of funds, invested
in different types of shares and in different markets: for instance, there are funds that are invested in the United States,
Australia, Japan or China, or in specialist sectors such as
mining or energy. If you find that the trust you are in is not
performing as well as you had hoped (prices are quoted daily
in the press), most trusts will allow you to switch from one
fund to another at quite a modest administration charge.

3. *Unitized with profits.* This is a newer type of pension, which
   combines elements of with-profits and unit-linked pensions.
   Your investment is given in terms of units (as with unit-linked
   policies) but you also earn bonuses, which, once added to
   your pension fund every year, cannot be taken away or fall in
   value should the stock market perform badly (these bonuses
   are added to with-profits policies each year and on retirement).

4. *Term assurance.* While this is not a form of pension at all, it may
   be attractive to add term assurance to your pension policy for
   tax purposes. Term assurance is a way of insuring your life for
   a given period by paying an annual premium. The more you
   pay, the more you (or rather your dependants) get. If you do
   not die before the end of the fixed term (eg 20 years) nothing
   is paid out. As with any other form of insurance, your
   premiums are simply, if you like, a bet against some untoward
   event occurring.

5. *Pension contribution limits.* Until the tax year beginning 5 April
   2006, there were limits to the amounts of annual payments
   that contributors could make to personal pensions and retirement annuities.

The one thing that all types of pension scheme have in common is that their sales forces are all eagerly competing for the self-employed person's notional dollar. They will be anxious to extol the virtues of their own schemes, to withhold any unfavourable information about them and to make no comparisons, which could be odious, with other schemes. Although the Financial Services Authority (FSA) has clamped down on misleading information and selling practices, your best plan in making your selection is to work through a broker registered with the FSA and to let him or her make the recommendation, though that does not mean that you can abdicate responsibility altogether. For one thing, in order for a broker to make the right selection of pension plans appropriate to your circumstances, you have to describe what your needs and constraints are:

1. Can you afford to make regular payments?
2. Does the irregular nature of your earnings mean that the occasional lump sum payment would be better?
3. Do you have any existing pension arrangements – eg from previous employment?
4. When do you want to retire?
5. What provision do you want to make for dependants?

Under the new pension regime effective from 5 April 2006, described on page 285–86, you are able to contribute what you want, when you want, to a registered pension scheme and get tax relief on those contributions up to 100 per cent of your relevant earnings. If you have no earnings in any year, or earn less than £3,600, you will be able to pay contributions with relief up to that amount.

This new regime is particularly helpful if your level of income fluctuates from year to year and you never know the amount until the end of the tax year. The old carry-back provision for pension contributions no longer applies from 5 April 2006.

# USING A BROKER

Very likely the broker will come up with a mix of solutions – for instance, a small regular payment to a pension scheme, topped up by single premium payments. The suggestion may also be made that you should split your arrangements between a conventional with-profits policy and some sort of unit-linked scheme; certainly you will be recommended to review your arrangements periodically to take care of inflation and possible changes in your circumstances.

Brokers have to be registered nowadays, so it is unlikely that you will be unlucky enough to land up with someone dishonest. Check that the person you are dealing with really is a registered broker – not a consultant, because anyone can call him- or herself that. However, whoever you deal with, there are, as in other things in life, differences in the quality of what you get, which in this case is advice. It is as well to have a few checks at your elbow that will enable you to assess the value of the advice you are being given. For instance, national quality newspapers such as _The Times_, the _Financial Times_, the _Daily Telegraph_, the _Guardian_ and the _Independent_, as well as some specialist publications such as _The Economist_ and _Investors Chronicle_, publish occasional surveys of the pension business that include performance charts of the various unit funds, showing those at the top and bottom of the league table over 1-, 5- and 10-year periods. There are also tables of benefits offered by the various life companies showing what happens in each case if, for instance, you invest £500 a year over 10 years. There are quite considerable differences between what you get for your money from the most to the least generous firms. If your broker is advising you to put your money in a scheme that appears to give you less than the best deal going, you should not commit yourself to it without talking to your accountant. In selecting brokers, as with many other professional advisers, the best recommendation is word of mouth from someone you can trust who can vouch for the ability of the person in question.

## THE NEW PENSIONS REGIME

If life wasn't complicated enough already, a new pensions regime came into force on 5 April 2006 (known as 'A-Day'). The main effects for the self-employed appear to be:

▮ From April 2005 you have been able to put off receiving your state pension indefinitely and earn an increase in the pension for each year that it is deferred. Alternatively, you will be able to convert the increase into a cash sum.

▮ The earliest age from which an occupational or personal pension may be taken will increase from 50 to 55 by 2010.

▮ From April 2006 the limits on annual contributions and retirement benefits were replaced by a single lifetime limit on the amount of pensions savings built up that qualify for tax relief. The lifetime limit started at £1.5 million in 2006 and will increase each year up to £1.8 million in 2010. Any assets in your pension fund that exceed the lifetime limit at retirement will be taxed at 55 per cent.

▮ If you are fortunate enough already to have a pension fund with an asset value estimated to exceed £1.5 million at April 2006, you could register your funds on A-Day or for three years thereafter to protect them from the tax charge.

▮ There is an annual limit on how much your pension fund can increase in value. The limit started at £215,000 in 2006 and will be increased each year in line with inflation. For 2007/2008 the limit is raised to £225,000. Defined benefits are valued using a multiple of 10, and if individual and company contributions exceed this, the individual is liable to 40 per cent tax on the excess.

You should certainly review these changes and their implications for you personally before entering into any new pension commitments or altering your current arrangements.

When you start self-employment it is also a good time to review the advantages of setting up a self-invested personal pension (SIPP). Most personal pension plans restrict your investment choice to just a few funds. A SIPP allows you to take responsibility and decide where to invest your money: in funds from top managers, or individual stocks and shares.

There are big tax advantages which make SIPPs possibly the most tax-efficient way to save for your retirement, whenever that will be. For example (depending on your circumstances), if you contribute £7,800 as a basic rate tax payer, the government will make your investment up to £10,000. If you are a higher-rate taxpayer, you can claim up to an additional £1,800 back via your tax return.

Originally, the new pensions regime introduced on A-Day allowed people to place a very wide range of assets in their SIPPs, but the Chancellor subsequently narrowed the field. You should definitely take professional advice before making any commitments.

# HEALTH INSURANCE

Running your own business requires stamina and good health. If you are unlucky enough to become ill it will be a priority to get back on your feet as quickly as possible. Private health insurance has become increasingly popular among the self-employed for this reason. There are four types of health insurance currently available on the market, as defined by the most recent Office of Fair Trading report:

- **Private medical insurance.** This insures against the cost of short-term acute conditions in a private hospital or as a private patient in an NHS ward.
- **Permanent health insurance.** Replaces some or all of the income lost when a person becomes sick or disabled and unable to work and is normally paid to retirement age.
- **Critical illness insurance.** Provides a lump sum in the event of a serious illness.
- **Long-term care insurance.** Covers the cost of long-term care for those who become unable to look after themselves.

However, an Office of Fair Trading report has criticized the insurance industry for its lack of standardized products and complicated jargon. Indeed, it might well be worth getting independent advice before you commit yourself to purchasing a policy. It is also worth keeping an eye out for products specifically geared towards the self-employed, as there has recently been the launch of a combined health insurance policy that caters more closely to the needs of individuals working for themselves.

# Checklist: pensions and health insurance

1. Review your current pension arrangements and assess whether or not they are adequate for your retirement needs.

2. Discuss with your accountant the most tax-efficient way to invest in a pension scheme and with your broker about what kind of scheme is most appropriate in light of the new pensions regime effective from 5 April 2006.

3. Consider whether regular payment and/or one-off lump sum investments are best suited to your financial arrangements.

4. Take account of the government's revisions to state pension schemes when published.

5. Check that you are receiving independent advice from a registered broker.

6. Examine surveys of pensions within the national press to ensure that you are receiving adequate advice from your broker.

7. Identify if it is speed, location or choice that you require within a private medical insurance policy – this will help determine which policy you will choose.

8. Check the qualifying period within a critical illness policy – many do not start to pay out until after an excess period of six weeks or three months. Could your business survive an absence of this length? If not, you will have to consider paying higher premiums.

# Appendices

# Appendix 1

# Useful Information

## SECTOR INFORMATION FOR LOW-INVESTMENT, PART-TIME AND FREELANCE OPPORTUNITIES

This is not an exhaustive list. However, it is an indicator of the range of opportunities available to people who want to work for themselves. Where possible details of trade associations and other sources of useful information are included. Information on training, qualifications and industry codes of conduct can generally be obtained from these sources. Further information can be obtained from *The A–Z of Careers and Jobs*, Kogan Page.

## ACUPUNCTURIST

The British Acupuncture Council, 63 Jeddo Road, London W12 9HQ; tel: 020 8735 0400; website: www.acupuncture.org.uk

British Medical Acupunture Society, 3 Winnington Court, Northwich, Cheshire CW8 1AQ; tel: 01606 786783; website www.medical-acupuncture.co.uk

*Working in Complementary and Alternative Medicine*, Kogan Page.

# AERIAL ERECTOR

Confederation of Aerial Industries Ltd (CAI), Fulton House, Fulton Road, Wembley, Middlesex HA9 0TF; tel: 020 8902 8998; website: www.cai.org.uk

# ANTIQUE DEALER

British Antique Dealers' Association, 20 Rutland Gate, London SW7 1BD; tel: 020 7589 4128; website: www.bada.org

# ART THERAPY

The British Association of Art Therapists, The Claremont Project, 24–27 White Lion Street, London N1 9PD; tel: 020 7745 7262; website: www.baat.org

*Careers in Art and Design*, Kogan Page.

# BEAUTICIAN

British Association of Beauty Therapy and Cosmetology, Meteor Court, Barnett Way, Barnwood, Gloucester GL4 3GG; tel: 0845 065 9000; website: www.babtac.com

International Health and Beauty Council, 46 Aldwick Road, Bognor Regis, West Sussex PO21 2PN; tel: 01243 842064

International Federation of Health and Beauty Therapists, 3rd Floor, Eastleigh House, Upper Market Street, Eastleigh, Hampshire SO50 9FD; tel: 0870 420 2022; website: www.fht.org.uk

*Careers in the Hairdressing, Beauty and Fitness Industries*, Kogan Page.

# BLACKSMITH

The Farriers Registration Council, Sefton House, Adam Court, Newark Road, Peterborough PE1 5PP; tel: 01733 319911; website: www.farrier-reg.gov.uk

# BOAT BUILDER

British Marine Federation, Marine House, Thorpe Lea Road, Egham, Surrey TW20 8BF; tel: 01784 473377; website: www.britishmarine.co.uk

# BOOKSELLER

Booksellers Association of the United Kingdom and Ireland, Minster House, 272–274 Vauxhall Bridge Road, London SW1V 1BA; tel: 020 7802 0802; website: www.booksellers.org.uk

# CARPENTER AND BENCH JOINER

Construction Industry Training Board, Bircham Newton, King's Lynn, Norfolk PE31 6RH; tel: 01485 577577; website: www.citb.org.uk

Institute of Carpenters, Central Office, 35 Hayworth Road, Sandiacre, Nottingham NG10 5LL; tel: 0115 949 0641; website: www.central-office.co.uk

_Practical Guide to Woodworking Careers and Educational Facilities_, Guild of Master Craftsmen.

# CARPET FITTER

National Institute of Carpet and Floorlayers, 4d St Mary's Place, The Lace Market, Nottingham NG1 1PH; tel: 0115 958 3077; website: www.nicfltd.org.uk

# COMPUTERS/IT CONSULTANT

Association of Computer Professionals, 204 Barnet Wood Lane, Ashtead, Surrey KT21 2DB; tel: 01372 273442; website: www.acpexamboard.com

British Computer Society, 1 Sanford Street, Swindon, Wiltshire SN1 1HJ; tel: 01793 417 424; website: www.bcs.org

*Freelance Informer*, Reed Publications, 01753 567567

## CONFERENCE ORGANIZING

The Association for Conferences and Events, ACE International, Riverside House, High Street, Huntingdon, Cambridgeshire PE18 6SG; tel: 01480 457595; website: www.martex.co.uk/ace

## CONSERVATION (HISTORICAL)

The British Association of Paintings Conservator-Restorers, PO Box 32, Hayling Island PO11 9WE; tel: 0239 246 5115; website: www.abpr.co.uk

Historic Scotland, Longmore House, Salisbury Place, Edinburgh EH9 1SH; tel: 0131 668 8600; website: www.historic-scotland.gov.uk

Institute of Paper Conservation, Bridge House, Waterside, Upton-upon-Severn WR8 0HG; tel: 01684 591150; website: http://palimpsest.stanford.edu/ipc

Museums Association, 24 Calvin Street, London E1 6NW; tel: 020 7426 6970; website: www.museumsassociation.org

Scottish Society for Conservation and Restoration, Chantstoun, Tartraven, Bathgate Hills, West Lothian EH48 4NP; tel: 0131 466 8512; website: www.sscr.demon.co.uk

Society of Archivists, Prioryfield House, 20 Canon Street, Taunton, Somerset TA1 1SW; tel: 01823 327030; website: www.archives.org.uk

United Kingdom Institute for Conservation, 702 The Chandlery, 50 Westminster Bridge Road, London SE1 7QY; tel: 020 7721 8721; website: www.ukic.org.uk

# COOKING

British Hospitality Association, Queens House, 55–56 Lincoln's Inn Fields, London WC2A 3BH; tel: 020 7404 7744; website: www. bha.org.uk

Careers Information Service, Hospitality Training Foundation, Third Floor, International House, High Street, London W5 5DB; tel: 020 8579 2400; website: www.htf.org.uk

_The Catering Management Handbook_, Kogan Page.

# DESIGNER

Chartered Society of Designers, 5 Bermondsey Exchange, 179–81 Bermondsey Street, London SE1 3UW; tel: 020 7357 8088; website: www.csd.org.uk

Design Council, 34 Bow Street, London WC2E 7DL; tel: 020 7420 5200; website: www.design-council.org.uk

_Careers in Art and Design_, Kogan Page.

# DETECTIVE/PRIVATE INVESTIGATOR

Association of British Investigators, 48 Queens Road, Basingstoke, Hampshire RG21 7RE; tel: 01256 816390; website: www. theabi. org.uk

The Institute of Professional Investigators, 83 Guildford Street, Chertsey, Surrey KT16 9AS; tel: 0870 330 8622; website: ww.ipi. org.uk

# DISC JOCKEY

Phonographic Performance Ltd, 1 Upper James Street, London W1F 9DE; tel: 020 7534 1000; website: www.ppluk.com

# DOG GROOMER

Pet Care Trust, Bedford Business Centre, 170 Mile Road, Bedford MK42 9TW; tel: 01234 273933; website: www.petcare.org.uk

# DRAMA THERAPIST

British Association of Dramatherapists, 41 Broomhouse Lane, London SW6 3DP; tel: 020 7731 0160; website: www.badth.org.uk

# DRIVING INSTRUCTOR

Driving Instructor's Association, Safety House, Beddington Farm Road, Croydon CR0 4XZ; tel: 0845 345 5151; website: www.driving.org

Register of Approved Driving Instructors, Driving Standards Agency, Stanley House, 56 Talbot Street, Nottingham NG1 5GU; tel: 0115 901 2500; website: www.dsa.gov.uk

*The Driving Instructor's Handbook*, Kogan Page.

# EDITING

The Society for Editors and Proofreaders, Riverbank House, 1 Putney Bridge Approach, Fulham, London SW6 3JD; tel: 020 7736 3278; website: www.sfep.org.uk

# ESTATE AGENT

The College of Estate Management, Whiteknights, Reading, Berkshire RG6 6AW; tel: 0118 986 1101; website: www.cem.ac.uk

The National Association of Estate Agents, Arbon House, 21 Jury Street, Warwick CV34 4EH; tel: 01926 496800; website: www.propertylive.co.uk and www.naea.co.uk

# FILM PRODUCTION

Broadcasting, Entertainment, Cinematograph and Theatre Union (BECTU), 373–377 Clapham Road, London SW9 9BT; tel: 020 7346 0900; website: www.bectu.org.uk

FT2 (Film and Television Freelance Training), Fourth Floor, Warwick House, 9 Warwick Street, London W1B 5LY; tel: 020 7734 5141; website: www.ft2.org.uk

Skillset – The Sector Skills Council for the Audio Visual Industries, Prospect House, 80–110 New Oxford Street, London WC1A 1HB; tel: 020 7520 5757; website: www.skillset.org

# FLORIST

Floristry Training Council, Roebuck House, Hampstead Norreys Road, Hermitage, Thatcham, Berkshire RG18 9RX; tel: 01635 200465

# GARDENER

Askham Bryan College, Askham Bryan, York YO23 3FR; tel: 01904 772277; website: www.askham-bryan.ac.uk

Institute of Horticulture, 14–15 Belgrave Square, London SW1X 8PS; tel: 020 7245 6943; website: www.horticulture.org.uk

_Careers Working Outdoors_, Kogan Page.

# GENEALOGIST

The Institute of Heraldic and Genealogical Studies, 79–82 Northgate, Canterbury, Kent CT1 1BA; tel: 01227 768664; website: www.ihgs.ac.uk

The Society of Genealogists, 14 Charterhouse Buildings, Goswell Road, London EC1M 7BA; tel: 020 7251 8799; website: www.sog.org.uk

# GLAZIER

Construction Industry Training Board, Bircham Newton, King's Lynn, Norfolk PE31 6RH; tel: 01485 577577; website: www. citb.org.uk

# HAIRDRESSER

Hairdressing and Beauty Industry Authority, Fraser House, Nether Hall Road, Doncaster DN1 2PH; tel: 01302 380000; website: www.habia.org

National Hairdressers' Federation, One Abbey Court, Fraser Road, Priory Business Park, Bedford MK44 3WH; tel: 0845 3456 500; website: www.the-nhf.org

*Careers in the Hairdressing, Beauty and Fitness Industries*, Kogan Page.

*Running Your Own Hairdressing Salon*, Kogan Page.

# HOMEOPATH

British School of Homeopathy, 98a Mill Street, Torrington, Devon EX38 8AW; tel: 01805 625494; website: www.homeopathy.co.uk

Society of Homeopaths, 11 Brookfield, Duncan Close, Moulton Park, Northampton NN3 6WL; tel: 0845 450 6611; website: www.homeopathy-soh.com

# HORTICULTURIST

See 'Gardener'.

# ILLUSTRATOR

The Association of Illustrators, 81 Leonard Street, London EC2A 4QS; tel: 020 7613 4328; website: www.theaoi.com

*Careers in Art and Design*, Kogan Page.

# INDEXER

Society of Indexers, Woodbourn Business Centre, 10 Jessell Street, Sheffield S9 3HY; tel: 0114 244 9561; website: www.indexers.org.uk

# INTERIOR DECORATOR/DESIGNER

British Interior Design Association, 3–18 Chelsea Harbour Design Centre, Chelsea Harbour, London SW10 0XE; tel: 020 7349 0800; website: www.bida.org

Chartered Society of Designers, 5 Bermondsey Exchange, 179–181 Bermondsey Street, London SE1 3UW; tel: 020 7357 8088; website: www.csd.org.uk

# INTERPRETER

Institute of Linguists, Saxon House, 48 Southwark Street, London SE1 1UN; tel: 020 7940 3100; website: www.iol.org.uk

Institute of Translation and Interpreting, Fortuna House, South Fifth Street, Milton Keynes MK9 2EU; 01908 325250; website: www.iti.org.uk

_Careers Using Languages_, Kogan Page.

# JEWELLERY

British Jewellers' Association, 10 Vyse Street, Birmingham B18 6LT; tel: 0121 237 1110; website: www.bja.org.uk

National Association of Goldsmiths, 78a Luke Street, London EC2A 4XG; tel: 020 7613 4445; website: www.jewellers-online.org

# JOURNALIST

Chartered Institute of Journalists, 2 Dock Offices, Surrey Quays Road, London SE16 2XU; tel: 020 7252 1187; website: www.cioj.co.uk

National Council for the Training of Journalists, Latton Bush Centre, Southern Way, Harlow, Essex CM18 7BL; tel: 01279 430009; website: www.nctj.com

# LANDSCAPE ARCHITECT

The Landscape Institute, 33 Great Portland Street, London W1W 8QG; tel: 020 7299 4500; website: www.l-i.org.uk

*Careers Working Outdoors*, Kogan Page.

# MANAGEMENT CONSULTANT

Institute of Management Consultancy, 3rd Floor, 17–18 Haywards Place, London EC1R 0EQ; tel: 020 7566 5220; website: www.imc.co.uk

Management Consultancies Association, 49 Whitehall, London SW1A 2BX; tel: 020 7231 3990; website: www.mca.org.uk

# MARKET RESEARCH

Market Research Society, 15 Northburgh Street, London EC1V 0JR; tel: 020 7490 4911; website: www.mrs.org.uk

# MASSEUR

The Northern Institute of Massage, 14–16 St Marys Place, Bury, Lancashire BL9 0DZ; tel: 0161 797 1800; website: www.nim56.co.uk

# MUSICIAN

Incorporated Society of Musicians, 10 Stratford Place, London W1C 1AA; tel: 020 7629 4413; website: www.ism.org

Musicians' Union, 60–62 Clapham Road, London SW9 0JJ; tel: 020 7582 5566; website: www.musiciansunion.org.uk

# MUSIC THERAPIST

Association of Professional Music Therapists, Administrator, 61 Church Hill Road, East Barnet, Hertfordshire EN4 8SY; tel: 020 8440 4153; website: www.apmt.org

British Society for Music Therapy, 61 Church Hill Road, East Barnet, Hertfordshire EN4 8SY; tel: 020 8441 6226; website: www.bsmt.org

# NATUROPATH

The British College of Osteopathic Medicine, Lief House, 120–122 Finchley Road, London NW3 5HR; tel: 020 7435 6464; website: www.bcom.ac.uk

# OSTEOPATH

See 'Naturopath'.

_Working in Complementary and Alternative Medicine_, Kogan Page.

# OFFICE SKILLS

Institute of Qualified Professional Secretaries, First Floor, 6 Bridge Avenue, Maidenhead SL6 1RR; tel: 01628 625007; website: www.iqps.org

# PHOTOGRAPHER

Association of Photographers Ltd, 81 Leonard Street, London EC2A 4QS; tel: 020 7739 6669; website: www.the-aop.org

British Institute of Professional Photography, Fox Talbot House, Amwell End, Ware, Hertfordshire SG12 9HN; tel: 01920 464011; website: www.bipp.com

The National Council for the Training of Journalists – see 'Journalist'

# PIANO TUNER

Pianoforte Tuners' Association, c/o 10 Reculver Road, Herne Bay, Kent CT6 6LD; tel: 01227 368808; website: www.pianotuner. org.uk

# PLAYGROUP LEADER

Council for Awards in Children's Care and Education, 8 Chequer Street, St Albans, Hertfordshire AL1 3XZ; tel: 01727 847636; website: www.cache.org.uk

Pre-School Learning Alliance, 69 Kings Cross Road, London WC1X 9LL; tel: 020 7833 0991; website: www.pre-school.org.uk

# PLUMBER

Institute of Plumbing, 64 Station Lane, Hornchurch, Essex RM12 6NB; tel: 01708 472791; website: www.plumbers.org.uk

# POTTER

Crafts Council, 44a Pentonville Road, London N1 9BY; tel: 020 7278 7700; website: www.craftscouncil.org.uk

Contemporary Ceramics, 7 Marshall Street, London W1F 7EH; tel: 020 7437 7605

# RIDING INSTRUCTOR

The British Horse Society, British Equestrian Centre, Stoneleigh Deer Park, Kenilworth, Warwickshire CV8 2XZ; tel: 0844 848 1666; website: www.bhs.org.uk

# SELLING

The Direct Selling Association, 29 Floral Street, London WC2E 9DP; tel: 020 7497 1234; website: www.dsa.org.uk

# SPORTS COACH/PERSONAL TRAINER

Sport England, 3rd Floor, Victoria House, Bloomsbury Square, London WC1B 4SE; tel: 0845 850 8508; website: www.sport england.org

SportScotland, Caledonia House, South Gyle, Edinburgh EH12 9DQ; tel: 0131 317 7200; website: www.sportscotland.org.uk

_Careers in Sport_, Kogan Page.

# STEEPLEJACK

National Federation of Master Steeplejacks and Lightning Conductor Engineers, 4d St Mary's Place, The Lace Market, Nottingham NG1 1PH; tel: 0115 955 8818; website: www.nfmslce.co.uk

# STONEMASON

Building Crafts College, Kennard Road, Stratford, London E15 1AH; tel: 020 8522 1705; website: www.thecarpenterscompany. co.uk

# TAXI DRIVER

Licensed Taxi Drivers Association, LTDA Taxi House, Woodfield Road, London W9 2BA; tel: 020 7286 1046; website: www.ltda.co.uk

# THATCHER

National Council of Master Thatchers Association, Foxhill, Hillside, South Brent, Devon TQ10 9AU; tel: 07000 781909.

# TOUR OPERATOR

Institute of Travel and Tourism, Studio 3, Mill Studio, Crane Mead, Ware, Hertfordshire SG12 9PY; tel: 0870 770 7960; website: www.itt.co.uk

The Tourism Society, 1–2 Queen Victoria Terrace, Sovereign Court, London E1W 3HA; tel: 020 7488 2789; website: www.tourismsociety.org

# TRANSLATOR

See 'Interpreter'.

# UPHOLSTERER

London Metropolitan University, 59–63 Whitechapel High Street, London E1 7PF; tel: 020 7320 1000; website: www.londonmet.ac.uk

Association of Master Upholsterers and Soft Furnishers, 102a Commercial Street, Newport, South Wales NP20 1LU; tel: 01633 215454; website: www.upholsterers.co.uk

# WINE TRADE

Wine and Spirit Education Trust, Five Kings House, 1 Queen Street Place, London EC4R 1QS; tel: 020 7236 3551; website: www.wset.co.uk

# WRITER

Institute of Scientific and Technical Communicators, PO Box 522, Peterborough PE2 5WX; tel: 01733 390141; website: www.istc. org.uk

Society of Authors, 84 Drayton Gardens, London SW10 9SB; tel: 020 7373 6642; website: www.societyofauthors.net

The Writers' Guild of Great Britain, 15 Britannia Street, London WC1X 9JN; tel: 020 7833 0777; website: www.writersguild.org.uk

See also 'Journalist'.

# Useful Contacts

## Government

**The Adjudicator's Office**
(For complaints against rulings by
Customs and Excise)
Haymarket House
28 Haymarket
London SW1Y 4SP
Tel: 020 7930 2292
Website: www.adjudicatorsoffice.
gov.uk

**Central Office of Information
Communications**
Hercules House
Hercules Road
London SE1 7DU
Tel: 020 7928 2345
Website: www.coi.gov.uk

**The Countryside Agency**
John Dower House
Crescent Place
Cheltenham GL50 3RA
Tel: 01242 521381
Website: www.countryside.gov.uk

**Department for Business, Enterprise
and Regulatory Reform**
BERR Enquiry Unit
1 Victoria Street
London SW1H 0ET
Tel: 020 7215 5000
Website: www.berr.gov.uk

**Department for Education and Skills**
Sanctuary Buildings
Great Smith Street
London SW1P 3BT
Tel: 0870 000 2288
Website: www.dfes.gov.uk

**Department for Environment, Food
and Rural Affairs (DEFRA)**
Nobel House
17 Smith Square
London SW1P 3JR
Tel: 020 7238 6000
Website: www.defra.gov.uk

**Department for Transport**
Great Minster House
76 Marsham Street
London SW1P 4DR
Tel: 020 7944 8300
Website: www.dft.gov.uk

**Export Credits Guarantee Department
(ECGD)**
PO Box 2200
2 Exchange Tower
Harbour Exchange Square
London E14 9GS
Tel: 020 7512 7000
Website: www.ecgd.gov.uk

**Her Majesty's Treasury**
The Correspondence & Enquiry Unit
2/52
1 Horse Guards Road
London SW1A 2HQ
Tel: 020 7270 4558
Website: www.hm-treasury.gov.uk

**HM Revenue & Customs (HMRC)**
New King's Beam House
22 Upper Ground
London SE1 9PJ
Tel: 020 7865 3000
Website: www.hmrc.gov.uk

**HM Revenue & Customs (HMRC)**
**National Advice Service**
Tel: 0845 010 9000
Website: hmrc.gov.uk

**The Information Commissioners'**
**Office**
Wycliffe House
Water Lane
Wilmslow
Cheshire SK9 5AF
Tel: 01625 545740
Website: www.informationcommission.
gov.uk

**Learning and Skills Council**
Cheylesmore House
Quinton Road
Coventry CV1 2WT
Tel: 0845 019 4170
Website: www.lsc.gov.uk

**Office of Fair Trading**
Fleetbank House
2–6 Salisbury Square
London EC4Y 8JX
Tel: 08457 22 44 99
Website: www.oft.gov.uk

**Office for National Statistics**
The Library
1 Drummond Gate
London SW1V 2QQ
Tel: 0845 601 3034
Website: www.statistics.gov.uk

**Small Business Service**
Kingsgate House
66–74 Victoria Street
London SW1E 6SW
Tel: 0845 001 0031
Website: www.sbs.gov.uk

**UK Online**
A gateway to all Government
Department websites:
www.direct.gov.uk

## Government Offices for the Regions

Four departments (Employment, Trade
and Industry, Environment and
Transport) have been organized into
integrated offices known as
Government Offices (GOs) for the
Regions.

**Government Office for the East of**
**England**
Eastbrook
Shaftesbury Road
Cambridge CB2 2DF
Tel: 01223 372500
Website: www.go-east.gov.uk

**Government Office for the East**
**Midlands**
The Belgrave Centre
Stanley Place
Talbot Street
Nottingham NG1 5GG
Tel: 0115 971 9971
Website: www.go-em.gov.uk

**Government Office for London**
Riverwalk House
157–161 Millbank
London SW1P 4RR
Tel: 020 7217 3328
Website: www.go-london.gov.uk

**Government Office for the North East**
Citygate
Gallowgate
Newcastle upon Tyne NE1 4WH
Tel: 0191 201 3300
Website: www.go-ne.gov.uk

**Government Office for the North West**
City Tower
Piccadilly Plaza
Manchester M1 4BE
Tel: 0161 952 4000
Website: www.go-nw.gov.uk

Cunard Building
Pier Head
Water Street
Liverpool L3 1QB
Tel: 0151 224 6300

**Government Office for the South East**
Bridge House
1 Walnut Tree Close
Guildford GU1 4GA
Tel: 01483 882255
Website: www.go-se.gov.uk

**Government Office for the South West**
2 Rivergate
Temple Quay
Bristol BS1 6ED
Tel: 0117 900 1700
Website: www.gosw.gov.uk

Mast House
Shepherds Wharf
24 Sutton Road
Plymouth PL4 0HJ
Tel: 01752 635000

Castle House
Pydar Street
Truro TR1 2UD
Tel: 01872 264500

**Government Office for the West Midlands**
5 St Philip's Place
Colmore Row
Birmingham B3 2PW
Tel: 0121 352 5050
Website: www.go-wm.gov.uk

**Government Office for Yorkshire and The Humber**
PO Box 213
City House
New Station Street
Leeds LS1 4US
Tel: 0113 280 0600
Website: www.goyh.gov.uk

## Government Office for Northern Ireland

**Department of Enterprise, Trade and Investment**
Netherleigh
Massey Avenue
Belfast BT4 2JP
Tel: 028 9052 9900
Website: www.detini.gov.uk

## Government Office for Scotland

**Scotland Office – Edinburgh**
Finance and Administration Division
1 Melville Crescent
Edinburgh EH3 7HW
Tel: 0131 244 9010
Website: www.scottishsecretary.gov.uk

**Scotland Office – Glasgow**
Economic and Industry Division
1st Floor Meridian Court
5 Cadogan Street
Glasgow G2 6AT
Tel: 0141 242 5958

**London Office**
Ministerial Offices
Parliamentary and Constitutional
Division
Dover House
Whitehall
London SW1A 2AU
Tel: 020 7270 6754

## Government Office for Wales

**The Wales Office**
Office of the Secretary of State for
Wales
Gwydyr House
Whitehall
London SW1A 2ER
Website: www.ossw.wales.gov.uk

# Start-up advice

## England and Wales

**Business in the Community**
137 Shepherdess Walk
London N1 7RQ
Tel: 0870 600 2482
Website: www.bitc.org.uk

**The National Assembly for Wales**
Industry and Training Department
Crown Buildings
Cathays Park
Cardiff CF10 3NQ
Tel: 029 2082 5111
Website: www.wales.gov.uk

**Welsh Development Agency**
Plas Glyndwr
Kingsway
Cardiff
South Glamorgan CF10 3AH
Tel: 01443 845500
Website: www.wda.co.uk

## Scotland

**Highlands and Islands Enterprise**
Cowan House
Inverness Retail and Business Park
Inverness IV2 7GF
Tel: 01463 234171
Website: www.hie.co.uk

**The Office of the Scottish Executive**
Enterprise and Lifelong Learning
Department
Meridian Court
5 Cadogan Street
Glasgow G2 6AT
Tel: 0141 248 2855
Website: www.scotland.gov.uk

Education Department
Victoria Quay
Edinburgh EH6 6QQ
Tel: 0131 566 8400

**Scottish Business in the Community**
PO Box 408
Bankhead Avenue
Edinburgh EH11 4HE
Tel: 0131 442 2020
Website: www.sbcscot.com

**Scottish Enterprise**
5 Atlantic Quay
150 Broomielaw
Glasgow G2 8LU
Tel: 0845 607 8787
Website: www.scottish-enterprise.com

**Small Business Gateway** (Scottish
Enterprise's small business
information service)
Tel: 0845 609 6611
Website: www.bgateway.com

## Northern Ireland

For a list of Local Enterprise Agencies
in Northern Ireland and information,
advice and resources for businesses
contact:

**Invest Northern Ireland**
44–58 May Street
Belfast BT1 4NN
Tel: 028 9023 9090
Website: www.investni.com

## Republic of Ireland

**Oak Tree Press**
19 Rutland Street
Cork
Ireland
Tel: +353 21 431 3855
Website:
www.startingabusinessinireland.com/
dirlea.htm

# National associations representing small firms

**British Chambers of Commerce**
65 Petty France
St James' Park
London SW1H 9EU
Website: www.chamberonline.co.uk

**British Franchise Association**
Thames View
Newtown Road
Henley on Thames
Oxfordshire RG9 1HG
Tel: 01491 578050
Website: www.british-franchise.org.uk

**Confederation of British Industry (CBI)**
Centre Point
103 New Oxford Street
London WC1A 1DU
Tel: 020 7395 8247
Website: www.cbi.org.uk

**Federation of Small Businesses Ltd**
Sir Frank Whittle Way
Blackpool Business Park
Blackpool
Lancashire FY4 2FE
Tel: 01253 336000
Website: www.fsb.org.uk

UK Press Office:
2 Catherine Place
London SW1E 6HT
Tel: 0207 233 7899

**The Forum of Private Business Ltd**
Ruskin Chambers
Drury Lane
Knutsford
Cheshire WA16 6HA
Tel: 01565 634467
Website: www.fpb.co.uk

**Smaller Firms Council (CBI)**
Centre Point
103 New Oxford Street
London WC1A 1DU
Tel: 020 7379 7400
Website: www.cbi.org.uk

**The Work Foundation**
Peter Runge House
3 Carlton House Terrace
London SW1Y 5DG
Tel: 0870 165 6700
Website: www.theworkfoundation.com

# Forming a company

**Companies Limited/Rapid Refunds**
376 Euston Road
London NW1 3BL
Tel: 020 7383 2323
Website: www.companies-ltd.co.uk
To buy an off-the-shelf company.

**Industrial Common Ownership Movement (ICOM)**
Holyoake House
Hanover Street
Manchester M60 0AS
Tel: 0161 246 2959
Website: www.icof.co.uk/icom
Advice on setting up worker co-operatives.

**The Institute of Business Advisers**
Response House
Queen Street North
Chesterfield S41 9AB
Tel: 01246 453322
Website: www.iba.org.uk

**The Institute of Directors**
116 Pall Mall
London SW1Y 5ED
Tel: 020 7766 8866
Website: www.iod.co.uk

**Lawyers for Your Business**
Law Society
113 Chancery Lane
London WC2A 1PL
Tel: 020 7405 9075
Website: www.lfyb.lawsociety.org.uk

**The Patent Office**
Concept House
Cardiff Road
Newport
Gwent NP10 8QQ
Tel: 0845 950 0505
Website: www.patent.gov.uk

**Registrar of Companies**
Companies Registration Office
Crown Way
Maindy
Cardiff CF14 3UZ
Tel: 0870 333 3636
Website: www.companieshouse.gov.uk

**Registrar of Companies – London**
Companies Registration Office
PO Box 29019
21 Bloomsbury Street
London WC1B 3XD
Tel: 0870 333 3636

**Registrar of Companies – Manchester**
75 Mosley Street
Manchester M2 3HR
Tel: 0870 333 3636

**Registrar of Companies – Scotland**
37 Castle Terrace
Edinburgh EH1 2EB
Tel: 0870 333 3636

# Banks

**Alliance and Leicester Commercial Bank**
Bridle Road
Bootle
Merseyside L30 4GB
Tel: 0800 056 5522
Website: www.alliance-leicestercommercialbank.co.uk

**Bank of Scotland and Halifax Business**
Business Banking eCommerce
1st Floor
Citywork
150 Fountainbridge
Edinburgh EH3 9PE
Tel: 0845 950 0505
Website: www.bankofscotland.co.uk/business

**Barclays Bank plc Small Business Banking**
PO Box 120
Longwood Close
Westwood Business Park
Coventry CV4 8JN
Tel: 024 76 694242
Website: www.barclays.co.uk

**HSBC Bank plc Business Unit**
Tel: 08457 43 44 45
For advice and business start-up pack
Website: www.banking.hsbc.co.uk

**Lloyds TSB Bank plc, Small Business Advice**
PO Box 112
Canons House
Canons Way
Bristol BS99 7LB
Tel: 08000 560 056
Website: www.smallbusiness.co.uk

**National Westminster Bank plc, Business Banking**
Level 20 Drapers Gardens
12 Throgmorton Avenue
London EC2N 2DL
Tel: 0800 028 2677
Website: www.natwest.com/business

**Royal Bank of Scotland Small Business**
Tel: Helpdesk 0131 523 4069
Website: www.royalbankscot.co.uk/Small_Business

# Raising capital

**Association of British Credit Unions Ltd**
Holyoake House
Hanover Street
Manchester M60 0AS
Tel: 0161 832 3694
Website: www.abcul.org

**British Insurance Brokers Association**
BIBA House
14 Bevis Marks
London EC3A 7NT
Tel: 020 7623 9043
Website: www.biba.org.uk

**British Venture Capital Association**
3 Clements Inn
London WC2A 2AZ
Tel: 020 7025 2950
Website: www.bvca.co.uk

**European Grants Ltd**
2 Gallands Close
Swanland
North Ferriby
East Yorkshire HU14 3GE
Tel: 01482 651695
Website: www.europeangrants.com

**Factors and Discounters Association**
Boston House
The Little Green
Richmond
Surrey TW9 1QE
Tel: 020 8332 9955
Website: www.factors.org.uk

**Finance and Leasing Association**
Imperial House
2nd Floor
15–19 Kingsway
London WC2B 6UN
Tel: 020 7836 6511
Website: www.fla.org.uk

**Institute of Patentees and Inventors**
PO Box 1301
Kingston-on-Thames
Surrey KT2 7WT
Tel: 020 8541 4197
Website: www.invent.org.uk

**Local Investment Networking Co (LINC)**
London Enterprise Agency
4 Snow Hill
London EC1A 2BS
Tel: 020 7403 0300

**The Prince's Trust**
18 Park Square East
London NW1 4LH
Tel: 020 7543 1234
Website: www.princes-trust.org.uk

**The Prince's Scottish Youth Business Trust**
Tel: 0141 248 4999
Website: www.psybt.gov.uk

**3i plc**
91 Waterloo Road
London SE1 8XP
Tel: 020 7928 3131
Website: www.3i.com

# Managing finance

**Association of Chartered Certified Accountants**
29 Lincoln's Inn Fields
London WC2A 3EE
Tel: 020 7396 7000
Website: www.acca.co.uk

**Chartered Accountants Directory**
Datacomp
4 Houldsworth Square
Reddish
Stockport
Cheshire SK5 7AF
Tel: 0161 442 5233
Website:
www.chartered-accountants.co.uk

**Chartered Institute of Taxation**
12 Upper Belgrave Street
London SW1X 8BB
Tel: 020 7235 9381
Website: www.tax.org.uk

**Institute of Chartered Accountants in England and Wales**
PO Box 433
Chartered Accountants Hall
Moorgate Place
London EC2P 2BJ
Tel: 020 7920 8100
Website: www.icaew.co.uk

**Institute of Chartered Accountants of Scotland**
CA House
21 Haymarket Yards
Edinburgh EH12 5BH
Tel: 0131 347 0100
Website: www.icas.org.uk

**The Institute of Financial Accountants**
44 Burford House
London Road
Sevenoaks
Kent TN13 1AS
Tel: 01732 467135
Websites: www.ifa.org.uk

**International Association of Book-keepers**
Suite 30, 40 Churchill Square
Kings Hill
West Malling
Kent ME19 4YU
Tel: 0844 330 3527
Website: www.iab.org.uk

# Marketing and sales

**The Advertising Association**
Abford House
15 Wilton Road
London SW1V 1NJ
Tel: 020 7828 2771
Website: www.adassoc.org.uk

**British Safety Council**
70 Chancellor's Road
London W6 9RS
Tel: 020 8741 1231
Website: www.britishsafetycouncil.org

**British Standards Institution**
389 Chiswick High Road
London W4 4AL
Tel: 020 8996 9000
Website: www.bsi-global.com

**Chartered Institute of Marketing**
Moor Hall
Cookham
Maidenhead
Berkshire SL6 9QH
Tel: 01628 427500
Website: www.cim.co.uk

**Chartered Institute of Public Relations**
The Old Trading House
15 Northburgh Street
London EC1V 0PR
Tel: 020 7253 5151
Website: www.cipr.co.uk

**Direct Marketing Association UK Ltd**
DMA House
70 Margaret Street
London W1W 8SS
Tel: 020 7291 3300
Website: www.dma.org.uk

**Institute of Direct Marketing**
1 Park Road
Teddington
Middlesex TW11 0AR
Tel: 020 8614 0277
Website: www.theidm.com

**Market Research Society**
15 Northburgh Street
London EC1V 0JR
Tel: 020 7490 0608
Website: www.mrs.org.uk

**Marketing Society**
1 Park Road
Teddington
Middlesex TW11 0AR
Tel: 020 8879 3464
Website: www.marketing-society.org.uk

# Export

**Association of British Chambers of Commerce**
International Division
4 Westwood House
Westwood Business Park
Coventry CV4 8HS
Tel: 024 7669 4484
Website: www.britishchambers.org.
uk/exportzone

**British Exporters Association**
Broadway House
Tothill Street
London SW1H 9NQ
Tel: 020 7222 5419
Website: www.bexa.co.uk

**British International Freight Association**
Redfem House
Browells Lane
Feltham
Middlesex TW13 7EP
Tel: 020 8844 2266
Website: www.bifa.org

**Department for Business Enterprise & Regulatory Reform (BERR)**
Export Control Organisation ECO
4th Floor
Abbey Orchard Street
London SW1P 2HT
Tel: 020 7215 4594
Website: www.berr.gov.uk/european
trade/strategic

**Euler Trade Indemnity plc**
1 Canada Square
Canary Wharf
London E14 5DX
Tel: 020 7512 9333
Website: www.eulerhermes.com/eti

**Euro Info Centre**
33 Queen Street
London EC4R 1AP
Tel: 020 7489 1992
Website: www.euro-info.org.uk

**European Commission Representation in the United Kingdom**
Jean Monet House
8 Storey's Gate
London SW1P 3AT
Tel: 020 7973 1992
Website: www.cec.org.uk
and http://europa.eu.int

**Export Credits Guarantee Department**
PO Box 2200
2 Exchange Tower
Harbour Exchange Square
London E14 9GS
Tel: 020 7512 7000
Website: www.ecgd.gov.uk

Lamborne House
Lamborne Crescent
Llanishen
Cardiff CF14 5GG
Tel: 029 2032 8500

**Institute of Export**
Export House
Minerva Business Park
Lynch Wood
Peterborough PE2 6FT
Tel: 01733 404400
Website: www.export.org.uk

**London Chamber of Commerce and Industry**
33 Queen Street
London EC4R 1AP
Tel: 020 7248 4444
Website: www.londonchamber.co.uk

**Simplifying International Trade Ltd**
Oxford House
8th Floor
76 Oxford Street
London W1D 1BS
Tel: 020 7467 7280
Website: www.sitpro.org.uk

**Technical Information Group**
British Standards Institution – Import and Export
389 Chiswick High Road
London W4 4AL
Tel: 020 8996 7474
Website: www.bsi-global.com/Import +Export+Advice

**UK Trade & Investment**
Kingsgate House
66–74 Victoria Street
London SW1E 6SW
Tel: 020 7215 5000
Website: www.uktradeinvest.go.uk

# Labour relations and personnel management

**Advisory, Conciliation and Arbitration Service (ACAS)**
Brandon House
180 Borough High Street
London SE1 1LW
Tel: 020 7210 3613
Website: www.acas.org.uk

**Chartered Institute of Personnel and Development**
151 The Broadway
London SW19 1JQ
Tel: 020 8971 9000
Website: www.cipd.co.uk

**The Chartered Management Institute**
Small Firms Information Service
Management House
Cottingham Road
Corby
Northants NN17 7IT
Tel: 01536 204222
Website: www.managers.org.uk

**Health and Safety Executive**
Public Enquiry Centre
Caerphilly Business Park
Caerphilly CF83 3GG
Tel: 08701 545500
Website: www.hse.gov.uk

**The Institute of Management Consultancy**
3rd Floor
17–18 Haywards Place
London EC1R 0EQ
Tel: 020 7566 5220
Website: www.imc.co.uk

**Recruitment and Employment Confederation**
33–38 Mortimer Street
London W1W 7RG
Tel: 020 7462 3260
Website: www.rec.uk.com

# Premises

**Country Land and Business Association**
16 Belgrave Square
London SW1X 8PQ
Tel: 020 7235 0511
Website: www.cla.org.uk

**English Partnerships**
St George's House
Kingsway
Team Valley
Gateshead
Tyne and Wear NE11 0NA
Tel: 0191 487 6565
Website: www.englishpartnerships.
co.uk.

**Estates Today**
84–86 Regent Street
London W1R 6AJ
Tel: 01483 855568
Website: www.estatestoday.co.uk
Online commercial estate agent.

**Royal Institution of Chartered Surveyors**
Contact Centre
Surveyor Court
Westwood Way
Coventry CV4 8JE
Tel: 0870 333 1600
Website: www.rics.org

# Information and communication technologies

**British Telecom**
Website: www.britishtelecom.co.uk
Advice on communications and information technologies for business.

**Central Small Business Solutions**
Website: www.bcentral.com
Exchange advertising banner with other sites.

**Digits.comWebCounter**
Website: www.digits.com
Adds visitor counter to your website.

**e.centre**
10 Maltravers Street
London WC2R 3BX
Tel: 020 7655 9000
Website: www.eca.org.uk

**Exploit**
Website: www.exploit.com

**List universe**
Website: www.list-universe.com
Provides details of mailing lists and joining details.

**Nominet**
To register internet domain names.
Website: www.nic.uk

**SubmitIt**
Website: www.submitit.com
This company will submit your website address to online search engines.

**Achieving Best Practice in Your Business**
Website: www.berr.gov.uk/european trade/best practice
Offers IT advice and support for businesses.

# FURTHER SOURCES OF INFORMATION

## Specialist libraries

**Business Information Service**
British Library
96 Euston Road
London NW1 2DB
Tel: 020 7412 7454
Website: www.bl.uk

**Chartered Institute of Marketing Library**
Moor Hall
Cookham
Maidenhead
Berkshire SL6 9QH
Tel: 01628 427333
Website: www.cim.co.uk

**Chartered Management Institute Library**
Management House
Cottingham Road
Corby
Northants NN17 1TT
Tel: 01536 204222
Website: www.managers.org.uk

**Competition Commission Information Centre**
New Court
48 Carey Street
London WC2A 2JT
Tel: 020 7271 0243
Website: www.competition-commission.org.uk

**Cyril Kleinwort Library**
The Cass Learning Resource Centre
106 Bunhill Row
London EC1Y 8TZ
Tel: 020 7040 8787
Website: www.city.ac.uk/library/ckl

**Department for Business Enterprise & Regulatory Reform (BERR)**
Information and Library Services
1 Victoria Street
London SW1H 0ET
Tel: 020 7215 5006

**London Business School Library**
25 Taunton Place
London NW1 4SA
Tel: 020 7262 5050
Website: www.lbs.lon.ac.uk/library

**Office of Fair Trading Library**
Fleetbank House
2–6 Salisbury Square
London EC4Y 8JX
Tel: 020 7211 8941
Website: www.oft.gov.uk

**Office for National Statistics**
The Library
1 Drummond Gate
London SW1V 2QQ
Tel: 08456 013 034
Website: www.statistics.gov.uk

# Websites of interest

**Better Business**
Website: www.better-business.co.uk
Offers independent and impartial advice to small businesses.

**BERR**
Website: www.berr.gov.uk
Good links to government-sponsored schemes.

**Electronic Telegraph**
Website: www.telegraph.co.uk
Access to full text of *Daily Telegraph* and directory listing of British business.

**Financial Times**
Website: www.ft.com
Business directory and up-to-date financial information.

**Keele University Management Web Resources Database**
Website: www.keele.ac.uk
Well-resourced database of business and management websites with good links.

**Kogan Page**
Website: www.koganpage.com
Extensive list of publications for start-ups and SMEs.

**Law Links**
Website: www.lawlinks.co.uk
Provides links to relevant government
legislation, TUC reports and BERR
guides.

**Strathclyde University Business
Information Sources on the Internet**
Website: www.dis.strath.ac.uk
Thoroughly recommended website with
extensive listings of sites and general
sources of business information.

**WhoWhere**
Website: www.whowhere.lycos.com
E-mail address, telephone number and
street address directory.

**Yahoo**
Website: www.yahoo.com
Search engine with extensive business
directory.

**Yell**
Website: www.yell.co.uk
Online version of the *Yellow Pages*.

# Appendix 3

# Further Reading from Kogan Page

*Accounting for Non-Accountants*, 7th edition, Graham Mott, 2008

*Bids, Tenders and Proposals*, 3rd edition, Harold Lewis, 2009

*The Business Plan Workbook*, 6th edition, Colin Barrow, Paul Barrow and Robert Brown, 2008

*The Complete Guide to Investing in Property*, 4th edition, Liz Hodgkinson, 2009

*Complete Guide to Selling Your Business*, 3rd edition, Paul S Sperry and Beatrice H Mitchell, 2005

*Consultants and Advisors*, Harold Lewis, 2004

*Dealing with the Customer from Hell*, Shaun Belding, 2005

*Dealing with Difficult People*, Roy Lilley, 2006

*Dealing with the Employee from Hell*, Shaun Belding, 2005

*Doing Business in the Countryside*, Jonathan Reuvid, 2005

*Essential Business Finance*, 2nd edition, Paul Barrow, 2008

*Essential Law for your Business*, 13th edition, Patricia Clayton, 2008

*The First-Time Manager*, 3rd edition, Michael Morris, 2005

*Forming a Limited Company*, 10th edition, Patricia Clayton, 2008

*The Growing Business Handbook*, 11th edition, Adam Jolly, 2009

*How I Made It*, Rachel Bridge, 2nd edition, 2009

*How People Tick*, Mike Leibling, 2nd edition, 2009

*How the City Really Works*, Alexander Davidson, 2008

*How to be a Successful Entrepreneur*, Helga Drummond, 2009

*How to Choose a Franchise*, 2nd edition, Iain Murray, 2004

*How to Prepare a Business Plan*, 5th edition, Edward Blackwell, 2008

*How to Understand the Financial Pages*, 2nd edition, Alexander Davidson, 2008

*How to Write a Business Plan*, 2nd edition, Brian Finch, 2006

*How to Write a Marketing Plan*, 3rd edition, John Westwood, 2006

*How to Write Reports and Proposals*, 2nd edition, Patrick Forsyth, 2006

*The Inspirational Leader*, John Adair, 2009

*Making Sense of Business*, Alison Branagan, 2009

*Marketing Plan Workbook*, John Westwood, 2005

*Not Bosses but Leaders*, 3rd edition, John Adair, 2009

*Practical Financial Management*, 7th edition, Colin Barrow, 2008

*Running Your Own Boarding Kennels*, revised 4th edition, David Cavill, 2008

*Running Your Own Driving School*, John Miller, 2009

*Starting a Successful Business*, 6th edition, Michael Morris, 2008

*Start and Run a Profitable Consulting Business*, 2nd edition, Douglas Gray, 2004

*Start Up and Run Your Own Business*, 7th edition, Jonathan Reuvid, 2008

*Successful Presentation Skills*, 3rd edition, Andrew Bradbury, 2006

*Successful Project Management*, 2nd edition, Trevor Young, 2006

*The Top Consultant*, 4th edition, Calvert Markham, 2004

*Ultimate Business Presentations Book*, Martin Yander and Peter Sander, 2003

*Working Abroad*, 30th edition, Jonathan Reuvid, 2009

*You Can Do It Too*, Rachel Bridge, 2008

The above titles are available from all good bookshops or direct from the publishers. To obtain more information, please contact the publisher at the address below:

Kogan Page
120 Pentonville Road
London N1 9JN
Tel: 020 7278 0433
Fax: 020 7837 6348
www.koganpage.com

# Index

# Index of advertisers

# The sharpest minds need the finest advice. **Kogan Page** creates success.

## www.koganpage.com